Mary Sawell

Life and letters of Mrs. Sewell

Mary Sawell

Life and letters of Mrs. Sewell

ISBN/EAN: 9783337818517

Printed in Europe, USA, Canada, Australia, Japan

Cover: Foto ©ninafisch / pixelio.de

More available books at **www.hansebooks.com**

THE LIFE AND LETTERS

OF

MRS. SEWELL.

Yours in true affection
Franz Liszt

THE LIFE AND LETTERS

OF

MRS. SEWELL.

BY

MRS. BAYLY,

AUTHOR OF "RAGGED HOMES AND HOW TO MEND THEM,"
"THE STORY OF THE ENGLISH BIBLE," ETC.

"Thou hast dealt well with Thy servant, O Lord, according unto Thy Word."—PSA. cxix. 65.

LONDON:
JAMES NISBET & CO., 21 BERNERS STREET.
MDCCCLXXXIX.

TO

PHILIP SEWELL

AND HIS CHILDREN

This Book

IS AFFECTIONATELY

DEDICATED.

INTRODUCTORY.

When requested by the relatives of my dear friend Mrs. Sewell to write a short memoir of her life, I at first hesitated, not from any unwillingness to undertake so pleasant a task, but because I questioned if a life so quiet and uneventful could furnish sufficient material to ground the hope of obtaining for it general interest. The materials at hand for use were by no means abundant. The bulk of her family correspondence had been destroyed, and she had not escaped the sorrow—the lot of most who live to an advanced age—of seeing her earlier friends drop one by one by the way. There are now few living who remember anything of her earlier life.

My own acquaintance with her did not begin until she was upwards of sixty years of age, but the friendship which existed between us for more than a quarter of a century, secured to me the privilege of a very near and intimate acquaintance.

From her own lips I have heard many passages

of her life, and she was in the habit of speaking unreservedly to me of past and present, also of her thoughts and opinions on a great variety of subjects. Still, with all these advantages, I really knew so little, connectedly, of the first sixty years of her life, that had it not been for the existence of her autobiographical letter, addressed to her grandchildren, it would have been impossible to have ventured on the task. The desire to make this simple and beautiful story of home life in a farmhouse ninety years ago known, in her own words, to the present generation, has formed one of my strongest inducements to carry out the wishes of those whose object in making the request has been well expressed by a modern writer :—"The usefulness and influence of many excellent people have been extended far beyond their natural lives by the faithfulness with which their thoughts and deeds have been recorded."

Still another motive which has much influenced me, is this. Does not the quiet, unobtrusive life of my dear friend largely represent, in its outward aspect, the kind of life lived by far the majority of our fellow-creatures? How few—how very few of us are born to any kind of distinction (I mean, in the eyes of the world), either in the way of surpassing talent, wonderful performances, or position! With most of us the main duties of our lives are very simple and oft repeated. May it not, after all, be a helpful thing to endeavour to show that this apparently monotonous mode of existence can be invested with a charm and a dignity all its own?

It is said there is much in every life which will not set to music. As a member of the Society of Friends, Mrs. Sewell was not educated as a musician, but I know no one who, to the extent she did, possessed the capacity of investing common things with a charm equivalent to music. That there were times in her life when she must have bent under her heavy burdens, no one can doubt; but even then she could rejoice that she was learning lessons which would teach her how to comfort those who are in any trouble, by the comfort wherewith she herself was comforted of God.

We are living in times of much difficulty. No thoughtful person can regard the condition of our working classes especially, without grief for the present, and apprehension for the future.

An historian of the French Revolution tells us that during the years before its outbreak, when the peasantry were driven mad with starvation and taxation, the French aristocracy appeared to be almost universally without sympathy in the sufferings of the people.

Very different from this is our present position. Although many deeply needed workers are still withholding their aid, we have a large army in the field, enlisted from all classes, who are fighting for better times for the poor and needy. This army would probably be greatly augmented if it could be made more clear how the object in view can be attained without either pauperising the poor, or, in increasing their wealth, also increasing the consumption of intoxicating drink. At such a time, when the public ear is not only open, but anxious to learn from any who can teach, we have thought that the experience of a very successful worker might be regarded with some interest. Perhaps Mrs. Sewell's greatest success in life was in her personal work among the poor. She was doubtless inspired for the work: she had few rules to guide her: every fresh case was a subject for individual thought, care, and effort—something between herself and God.

A friend, in writing of her, says:—" The thought in my mind about our dear Mrs. Sewell is, 'Blessed is she that *considereth* the poor.' There have been many who have done more notable things for the poor, but I know of no one who has *considered* them as she has done. The Spirit of God has given us this word 'considered'—it fits her life exactly."

Description or comment on her plans would fail to convey a true idea of the *spirit* in which her kind deeds were accomplished, and which made her influence among the poor almost unique. My hope is that by simple, truthful narrative, given as far as possible in her own written or spoken words, the fire of love which burned so brightly in her own heart may kindle a like flame in the hearts of many others. It has been well said, "Commentaries may teach, but it is the text that inspires."

If inaccuracies in reference to either time or place are found in these pages, I must beg to be judged leniently. The packets of letters and papers sent me were, with few exceptions, without date, and without any order as to subject. I felt at first more at a loss than Amos, who had to date his Vision "two years before the earthquake." I do most sincerely thank the kind friends who, at considerable trouble to themselves, have supplied me with many missing dates.

I have throughout received the most valuable assistance from my dear daughter, who also contributes the chapter on Mrs. Sewell's literary work.

Some portion of this book was written nearly three years ago. The delay has been occasioned by prolonged illness.

STREATHAM COMMON,
Nov. 5th, 1888.

CONTENTS.

	PAGE
INTRODUCTORY	vii
AUTOBIOGRAPHY	1

CHAPTER I.
LIFE AT BRIGHTON 77

CHAPTER II.
THOUGHTS ON EDUCATION . . 98

CHAPTER III.
LITERARY WORK . . 130

CHAPTER IV.
BLUE LODGE—LIFE AT WICK . . . 164

CHAPTER V.
MRS. WILLIAMSON AND OTHER FRIENDS . . 190

CHAPTER VI.
LIFE AT OLD CATTON 214

CHAPTER VII.

"MY NANNIE" . . 244

CHAPTER VIII.

CLOSING YEARS . . . 287

CHAPTER IX.

THE LAST STEP 313

LIFE AND LETTERS OF MRS. SEWELL.

AUTOBIOGRAPHY.

This letter was written by Mrs. Sewell at intervals, during the last five years of her widowhood.

MY DEAR GRANDCHILDREN,—I entirely sympathise with your wish to know all I can tell you of your ancestors on the Wright side; and as the day of my life is now very near the horizon, and will soon sink below it, and memory does not become more retentive as days decline, it behoves me to make speed and no longer linger or delay.

I am now eighty-two, and the night may come before I have completed my task.

It will be a very meagre little memoriam—mere scraps that have had sufficient vitality to keep from being submerged in the flow of the years.

In looking back it seems to me that the lightest things keep at the top, whilst the more important sink and are lost. This may be in mercy—the heaviest might sink us.

The years through which I have lived have been some of the most interesting in our country's history. I came into the world in the year 1797 —about the time of the great French Revolution —and from that time to this includes the grand march of commerce, science, and invention, including the lives of some of the first historical characters. I attempt nothing but family scraps —odds and ends—to set them down as they link together in my memory, without any attempt at painting character. Many a little family has for itself its hero or heroine. I want to try to immortalise my father in the memory of his descendants. This would not be easy, as he was a quiet, rather reserved character, always living in comparative privacy, and never called to take any conspicuous place in life's stirring battle. Besides this, he was always cramped by the narrow limits of external circumstances, so that it can only be by miniature touches here and there that I shall be able to give you a likeness of him. He lives in my heart and memory as a hero who, if education and circumstances had favoured him, would have been a leading man in almost any place. He had excellent talents and wide views; he was far-sighted and clear-sighted, with considerable inventive and scientific talent, very accurate and quick perceptions; full of enterprise and quiet enthusiasm; a most humane, tender, and compassionate heart; indignant at wrong and oppression, and prompt to right the injured. He was refined in every thought, word, and action: vulgarity and meanness could not approach him; he was an ardent patriot, and as a husband, father, master, and neighbour he could not be surpassed. From my childhood to old age I can never remember anything that in the slightest degree impairs my admiration, veneration, and deep love. I always feel that my words cannot represent the full glow in which I ever see him stand. There was an elasticity, buoyancy, and promptness peculiar alike to his physical, mental, and moral nature; shrewd without an atom of guile, and true to the very core of his being.

I have often wished it had been possible to obtain a clear description of his father and mother, so as to judge what he might have inherited from them, but they died when he was very young, and he could give but few particulars; but these few were sufficient to show that his father was a man of good education, and remarkable for good commonsense. He was counsel and arbitrator for all difficulties and differences that arose in the village.

The ancestors both of my father and mother joined the Friends in the time of the Commonwealth, when George Fox was a preacher. There is evidence in two of the churches near Lammas that members of the Wright family had there been clergymen; but my father and mother continued Friends till they died, and now lie in the little Lammas burying-ground, with their nearest relatives around them. The Meeting-house was shut up when my mother died, she being the last member of the Society belonging to it. She was most punctual and conscientious in attending the meeting, both on the First day and week-day, at which last she not unfrequently sat alone. At one time the number of Friends in the neighbourhood must have been large, as a half-yearly meeting was held there. The stable still remains where the horses were tied up during the time of meeting, and only recently the steps were removed from which the lady Friends mounted their horses.

. . . When my grandfather died, which he did whilst his children were quite young, his widow removed with her six children to a house in Norwich which had no garden. The change from the liberty of the country to a cramped house in the city was distasteful to my father. I have often heard him describe how he pulled up a boulder in the street close by his mother's door, and planted a grain of wheat that he might have the pleasure of seeing it grow. His mother was then very delicate, and he was her mainstay in the house, rendering all the little service that he could. How long this continued I do not know—I expect not long, as he and his brother Richard, two years younger than himself, were sent by Cousin Wright (a near relative who, on the death of the father, had become guardian to the family) to a school in Yorkshire, at Gildersham, kept by a Friend of the name of Ellis. There he evidently recovered his spirits.

John Ellis's school must have been a boy's romance. In after-life I often noticed if my father met with any one who had been educated there, they both became boys again. It had the true

freemasonic touch in it; everything was earnest
—hard work, hard play, liberty unrestrained; no
promenade of two and two with gymnastic pre-
cision; it was up the trees, over hedges and
ditches,—anywhere their spirits and limbs could
carry them. Work was work, and play was play,
and I have no doubt, from the enthusiasm with
which my father spoke of his life there, that it was
a healthy discipline both for mind and body, giving
courage, energy, and the dauntless spirit of adventure. I do not suppose that either my father or
uncle ever had the experience of physical fear.
The halcyon days passed at this school came to
an end, and they left Gildersham and liberty for
Ackworth, where the Society of Friends had established a school, supported by annual subscription,
with the view of providing for the education of
orphans, or for the children of members whose
parents were not able to provide for their education. It owed its institution to Dr. Fothergill, and
has remained one of the most valuable aids in the
Society, ensuring to the poorest of its members a
solid education, as well as the rudimental branches
of learning. It remains flourishing to the present
time, but has greatly enlarged its scope of instruction, and abolished many of the regulations which
then made Ackworth school a sort of prison discipline to the two young Wrights. It doubtless was
considered a place in advance of Gildersham, at
least in manners. The discipline was exceedingly
strict, not to say severe. The law and the word

of command ignored all the little peccant places and infirmities of the flesh to which the young as well as the old are subject. Little shrinking things unused to the water had no time given to stand and plead at the water's edge, but were heroically seized and plunged in, and sent off to make way for others. Stone stairs, stone floors—nothing to comfort the desires of the flesh in dress, food, or affection. I have no doubt that all this hardness endured for many years had a tendency to strengthen the self-denying characters of many who were educated there. They went forth to battle with the world, unspoiled by indulgence. The Honourable John Bright was an Ackworth scholar.

Children were taken into this school very young, as early, I think, as seven or eight, and did not leave till they could be apprenticed, at fourteen or fifteen. There was no regular holiday all this time, so that unless the parents or friends could afford to visit the children, they might almost forget even their appearance. Here poor John and Richard found themselves in chains. Richard, especially, was always in disgrace, from his unbounded spirits, his exuberant fun, wit, and ingenuity—always a leader of malcontents and adventurers. The boys at Ackworth had to mend their own stockings—to my uncle, a most repulsive occupation. In order to extract a little fun out of it, he on one occasion quilted a ball into the calf of the leg, and wore it, attracting attention to it, as if it were a part of his leg.

The awful superior of the school was named Don Bavon, and when any grave misdemeanour had been committed, the delinquent was summoned before the green cloth on a long table, at the head of which sat Don Bavon. I never heard in what the awe of his presence consisted, but there must have been something either in his bearing or his judgments, which caused the green cloth to be mentioned with very solemn countenance. One day my father was summoned into his presence for a very heinous offence; he had caught a fly, and had daintily attached a piece of down to its wing, and sent it off on its rambles during school-time, which of course excited much amusement. The offence was noted with all solemnity in the note-book of the school, as having caused considerable disorder. On another occasion my father was summoned before Don Bavon, and was informed that his mother was dead, and that he should communicate the information to his brother Richard. My father, wishing to do this gently, probably used the master's words, and said, "Richard, we have lost our mother." "Well," said my uncle, "I suppose they will find her again." Nothing more passed; probably he had no explanation to give, and my uncle did not, till a long time afterwards, realise what had really happened. There were two brothers in the school at that time who in the same night dreamed the same dream—each had a vision of his father coming to his bedside and looking at him. A letter afterwards informed them that their father was drowned that night at sea. I have always thought it a very affecting story, that the spirit of the father should immediately seek out his two little boys at their school.

How long they remained at Ackworth I do not know, but my father from Ackworth went to a school near London, considered a Friends' finishing school.

Cousin Wright (their guardian) at this time lived at Esher, in Surrey; he was one of the partners in the banking house of Smith, Wright, & Gray— a considerable bank at that time. On one occasion there was a general run upon the banks in the City. The head clerk of their bank had a hogshead rolled into the Exchange, and mounting it, proclaimed that any one who wished to settle his account with Smith, Wright, & Gray could be immediately paid. This restored confidence, and their bank was not affected.

When the boys left school, it was into the banking establishment that their guardian proposed to introduce them, with a view to their future advancement; but Mr. Gray, one of the partners, having sons of his own, did not approve of this scheme; and as, after a little while, the two lads were much disgusted with their position in the bank, they having to sleep under the counter at night, with monotonous work and uncourteous treatment from some of the younger clerks, they were not displeased when it was decided that Richard should be apprenticed to a buckle-maker in Birmingham. Buckle-making was a great business at that time, and very many workmen were employed in it.

The infidel works of Voltaire and Tom Paine were then being greedily read among the artisans of Birmingham, and my Uncle Richard, who was never second in anything, swallowed this poison with zest, and it unhappily influenced his fine nature till near the end of his life. But I must not stay to sketch his erratic life. I return to my dear father, whom Cousin Wright now proposed to bring up as a farmer. To this end he sent him to learn farming with John Holmes of Tivetshall, in Norfolk, who had the reputation of being a good farmer. He was the father of my dear mother. As Cousin Wright had considerable landed property in different places, I have no doubt it was his intention, then, ultimately to place my father on one of his farms. My father's character suited him well—they were both by nature gentlemen, intelligent and self-reliant, with clear sight and prompt action.

I must here give a slight sketch of Tivetshall Hall in the olden time. The gentleman-farming of the present day was then little known among the middle-class farmers. Art and science, books and leisure, were not at home in the old farmhouse. Pictures on the walls were considered dangerous, as possibly leading to idolatry. Music was a vain amusement, and hymns as well as songs were prohibited. The voice was not cultivated, and a musical instrument was never seen in any Quaker's house. It was so when I was a child. There remained much of the Puritan strictness in the families of Friends at that time, some hundred years ago.

My grandfather Holmes, as I remember him, was a tall, gaunt man, with what would have been a handsome countenance had the expression been more genial. He was very tall and strong-built, with black eyes, strong eyebrows, and good features; his complexion was dark, and his hair was all combed back from his forehead. He wore a very broad-brimmed black beaver hat, looped up with three silk loops—not sharply cocked,—no hat of the present day can compare with it in dignity and costliness; it gave a reverent aspect, well suited to those who took their place in the preaching gallery. His coat, waistcoat with deep pockets, and breeches buckled at the knees with silver buckles, were all of one colour—a very dark brown. His shoes had large buckles, and he wore a white cravat.

I have drawn my grandfather Holmes's picture for you, as the like has passed away from this generation. He was a minister among the Friends, and not unfrequently preached, but I believe he had rather a limited gift. He was of a nervous temperament, and had rather an irritable temper, but a good man. My grandmother Holmes, on the contrary, possessed a most sweet and amiable nature, always on the side of peace, ruling her large household with as much gentleness and skill as such a family could be ruled. She was a fine woman, with a sweet countenance, a fair complexion, a set colour, and blue eyes. Under her large white linen apron was a place of refuge for her little grandchildren when there were storms outside. My mother always spoke of her with intense affection. Though not more than four years old at the time of her death, I can well remember my mother's grief when her brother Charles rode over to Felthorpe one Sunday morning, to tell us she was dead. Her mother was a great loss to her; she never spoke of her without adding in a tenderly affectionate tone, "Dear creature." My father also admired and loved her, and spoke of her with much sympathy, as of a good woman, oppressed, but standing tender and firm in the midst of the battle of life, persevering to the utmost.

When my father was introduced into this family, I suppose he would be about seventeen. He found there six stalwart sons and two daughters, some older and some younger than himself. He was two years older than my mother. They were all, according to their capacity, hard at work on the farm. Their names were Robert, John, Benjamin, William, George, and Charles, Ann and Mary. These, with my father and an apprentice and two men servants, composed the family, with the addition of my grandfather, grandmother, and two female servants. In the farm-house all the washing, brewing, baking, cooking, and needlework were performed by the women of the family, and the dairy work also—an important part. The produce of the dairy was carried to the Norwich market, and I have heard my father say that my grandmother would sometimes ride there on a pillion, behind a man on horseback, and "sit the market," as it was called. Other farmers' wives did the same. It was an industrious and honourable calling; the women did their full share in making the farm prosperous, and the house a place of plenty and liberal hospitality.

I just remember my grandmother, and being allowed to go with her into the dairy and dip my fingers into the cream. She was very indulgent to her grandchildren, but few of them can remember much of her, as she died more than twenty years before my grandfather.

My father, when speaking of the time when he was an inmate at the farm, would say, "That was a rough house." My grandfather's irritable temper provoked a spirit of obstinacy in the sons, which often made rather stormy weather.

You may well suppose, from what I have said of my father, that this was not congenial society for him, and you may also well suppose that to the women of the family, used to the rough, uncourteous ways of the young men, his refinement and kind feeling, which led him to pity and help whenever he could, made him in their eyes a gentle squire; and no wonder poor Ann lost her heart, and found love lighten labour. My grandmother very fully appreciated the difference between him and her lion-hearted sons; she was always very fond of my father. They say that pity is akin to love, and out of that soil I believe my father's love first grew, and by the time he left Tivetshall it was firmly rooted.

Cousin Wright had found a much better position for him. This was with Maurice Birkbeck, who lived at Blandford, in Dorsetshire. He was a gentleman farmer of the first order, in every respect a contrast to the family my father had left. He was a man in advance of his age—I mean the farming age. He was of good family and well educated, a gentleman in his manners, and full of enthusiasm and enterprise. This led him eventually, in about 1813, to emigrate to America, with a view to form a settlement in the far West; but, like the generality of pioneers in difficult enterprises, he fell a sacrifice to it, being drowned one night in attempting to ford a river on horseback. When I was a girl at Tottenham school, I saw two of his daughters; they had come to London to take leave of their friends preparatory to their departure. They were two lovely, elegant creatures, looking little like denizens of the backwoods. My father always spoke of Maurice Birkbeck as of a man he entirely admired and esteemed. On the map of England out of which we learned the geography of our country, he had marked the position of Blandford by writing in very small characters, "I lived here."

When my father was twenty-two years old,

and my mother twenty, they were married. Cousin Wright and a goodly company of Gurneys and others were at the wedding. My father was considered a young man of good expectations. Their first home was at Buxton, where my sister Anna and my brother John were born—Anna in 1793, John in 1794. My mother never told us anything about her courting days, but I knew she always considered my father a very handsome man, and superior to other men. She always upheld his authority and influence, and the same may be said of him. He always showed a marked attention and respect to my mother; her children never saw any cross purposes between them, and I should say through rough and smooth they were a very happy and entirely united couple. My mother was remarkable for sound judgment, kind feeling, and common-sense; she did not damp my father's greater enthusiasm, but probably she moderated it; and if he did not find in her a strictly intellectual companion, he found an excellent helpmeet, a good manager, industrious, neat, and very orderly; she was thrifty and economical, but with a truly hospitable heart and liberal hand, and she was a pleasant, sociable neighbour. Her moral qualities were admirable, and she had sufficient self-respect never to pretend to understand things she did not. Sensible of her own want of education, she was very ambitious that her children should not labour under the same disadvantage. We have all to thank her for the untiring efforts she made to secure for us every advantage that lay in her power. My dear mother had a good countenance; she was an average height, and square built; her face was square, her eyes brown, and her hair black. She had rather a dark complexion, with a set colour. She was a comely woman, and pleasant to look upon. My father and mother, in most ways, were physically and mentally a contrast, and I have no doubt beneficially supplemented each other. I will not describe my mother's dress till I come to the time when I first recollect it.

I was born in 1797, at Sutton in Suffolk, where my father was occupying one of Cousin Wright's farms. Before I was two years old, my father removed to another of Cousin Wright's farms, at Felthorpe, six miles from Norwich. Of course I can personally remember nothing of Sutton, but many little stories told by my father and Anna and John invested it with some romance. There was a pit, called the "Crag pit," in which were found many antediluvian fossils. My father found a remarkable knife, and until the day of his death my uncle Richard persisted that he had found a musical instrument of mechanical construction, and of course the artificer was Tubal Cain. My uncle lent it to a great antiquarian who never returned it, which, you may suppose, rendered its worth inestimable. I have often heard him describe it with the minutest exactness.

Vancouver, the celebrated navigator, visited my father at Sutton. Sutton was not far from the sea, and after the battle of Camperdown he saw the victorious fleet under Admiral Duncan sail past with the captured vessels, the sails hanging in rags, and riddled through with cannon shot.

The farm at Sutton was very poor land, with a great deal of common covered with fern and furze bushes. It served as pasture for sheep, of which my father had a large flock. It happened one winter that a deep snow lay for many weeks upon the ground, and thus the sheep's food was unattainable. All their resources were exhausted, and the sheep were perishing of hunger, when my father's inventive genius constructed an implement which I cannot describe. To this he fastened several horses abreast, who by dragging this implement removed the snow from the vegetation. The sheep, following after, were thus saved. My father often told us how the horses went plunging through bush and brake.

There is another little incident which shows the home life of the young couple. When my father went to the common to look at the sheep, he would sometimes carry my sister Anna in his arms, no doubt to relieve his busy wife. His intelligent dog, Briton, accompanied him. One day when he reached home he found one of the little girl's feet bare—the shoe had probably fallen somewhere on the common. He called Briton and showed him the shoeless foot, and then the other, touching the shoe; then exclaimed, "Hie off, Briton!" The dog started, and after some time returned with the shoe in his mouth.

On the remove journey to Felthorpe we stopped at Tivetshall Hall, where my sister Elizabeth was born in 1798. I, at the mature age of one and three-quarters, proceeded with my father to take possession of the new home, where I lived till I was twelve. Shall I say it was the happiest part of my life? No, I will not do that, although my memory can recall very few shadows that rested upon it. Very heavy clouds were passing at that time over the country at large. It was the time after the terrible French Revolution, when the wars of Bonaparte threatened to overturn all Europe. But events of that kind reach children very softly. The newspapers came to Felthorpe only once in the week. No railway train speeded evil tidings, and no telegrams startled people out of the steady joy of life. My father went to Norwich market every Saturday and brought the news home with him. As we increased in years, my father's zealous patriotism infused itself more or less into each of us. I have a sense now of the thrill which used to pass through my whole frame when any great event had happened, when my father's animated words, kindling eyes, and the manner in which he turned over the newspaper whilst giving my mother details, sent the blood through my veins with quickened speed. My father's spirit had a potent influence on his children. I was a still child, and did not break out, but I felt. You may imagine how I was stirred one Saturday when he came home from Norwich, and coming to me, unrolled a paper parcel and displayed a long piece of scarlet bunting to make a flag which was to be hoisted on the church tower at the moment when the notice came that Bonaparte and his conquering army had landed on our coast. "Here, Mary, my dear," he said, "thee must make this flag to put on the steeple to let the people know that the Frenchmen have come." An officer appointed Admiral to the fleet, or Commander-in-chief to the army, could hardly have felt himself of more importance than I then did, and indeed it seems difficult now to believe that I did not do something for the relief of our country at that time. It was a time to be remembered, for the country was stirred from one end to the other with the expectation of immediate invasion. In the southern counties by the sea the Martello-towers were built, and on part of the coast of Kent preparations were made for letting in the sea to flood the portions of the coast likely to be chosen as landing-places. There was a great enlistment of soldiers all over the country. I think it was compulsory—the expression used was, "He is drawn for a soldier."

I well remember the day when the intelligence came to our house that my father was "drawn." You know that it is one of the strongest principles among Friends not to bear arms. To this day Friends never become soldiers, and many have become prisoners for refusing to do so. My father did not think it was a convenient time for him to leave his family and go to prison, and his principle was not too strong for him to obtain a substitute. This was allowed. I think my father paid £40 for his substitute, and he was appointed to a much more suitable office. Being a farmer, he had horses and waggons at his disposal, and he undertook, should it be necessary, to convey the women and children to a place of safety when the landing-place of the enemy was known. As this was uncertain, he was obliged always to keep in readiness. My sister Elizabeth and I entered very energetically into this preparation for removing. We had a fine baby-house, with which Elizabeth and I spent many happy hours, enacting many little plays in the drama of life. Now all had to be packed up, for the general remove was daily expected. On the highest land in the county, telegraphs were erected, and a system of signals prepared to communicate intelligence speedily from one village to another. Bonfires were also arranged for the same purpose. The whole country was in anxious suspense, especially on the south and east coasts, but the French ships withdrew, and that panic passed away. There was always a subject of interest in the atmosphere when the men met together. Definitely we of course knew nothing of politics, but we took a kind of infection from my father which was very definite. The agony of his mind was so great when he heard of the death of Nelson at the battle of Trafalgar, that he paced the room the whole evening unable to sit down. Some of his dreams at this time were very extraordinary, anticipating events which afterwards really occurred. I remember the exultation with which his light, rapid step entered the room where we were sitting, bringing with him the joyful tidings of victory. Yarmouth was illuminated from one end to the other, and everybody was feasted on the quay.

But I must return to the early days when we lived at Felthorpe, and the family consisted of my father and mother, Anna, John, Elizabeth, and myself. About this time John, five or six years old, was considered fit to begin his education. In a village about a mile from our home there was a school kept by a man of the name of Bligh, and thither John was sent, escorted by my sister Anna, not two years older. She was a brave little woman, and undertook the responsibilities of the eldest in the family with much prudence and authority. I always remember her then as a ruler; she was specially John's patron and caretaker. No doubt they both pursued their education under Mr. Bligh, but I think it did not continue long. It was my earnest desire to go with them, and one day my mother trusted me to their care. It was a first and last time. A boy had displeased the master, and was called up to undergo punishment. This infliction was administered on the palm of the hand, on which the master struck several times with a wooden implement which the boys called a "cussis." The boy roared vehemently, and I joined in the outcry, and never desired to visit this seat of learning again.

After this they went to a school at Norwich kept by a Miss Coe. John could not then pronounce all his letters distinctly, and Anna was his protector, doing battle with any boy who molested him. She had, as a child, a great deal of character. I think they lodged with Friends, returned home on the Saturday, and were sent back on the Monday.

My father and mother were very fond of their children, but we were never indulged so as to be spoiled. On one holiday, when John had been pleading for something his mother did not choose to grant, he, thinking to alarm her, threatened he would run quite away, and started off on the road leading to Norwich, repeating as he ran, "I will run quite away," when my mother's cheerful voice followed him, saying, "Run, John, run." After a time he quietly returned by himself.

The next school John went to was at Hitchin, in Hertfordshire. After this he went to Isaac Payne's school at Epping, and then to Josiah Foster's at Southgate. This was the best school amongst the Friends at that time. He finally finished his school education at my uncle John Reynolds's at Enfield. John Reynolds was a scholar and a gentleman, the husband of my father's sister Mary.

My sister Anna went to a Friends' school at

Plaistow, in Essex, and Elizabeth and I were left at home; but our education was not to be neglected. My dear mother necessarily had little time to spare. Cousin Wright's words to her when he first saw my brother John lying in his cradle, " Nancy, that boy is my heir, and thee will ride in thy carriage," were not fulfilled. Farmers' wives, as I have before said of my grandmother, held no sinecure position. The farm servants were hired by the year, at what were called Statute Fairs, where they stood together to be looked at and questioned. Women servants were often hired in the same way. The men slept and were boarded in the house. No baker or brewer ever came to the door; bread and beer were always home-made; all the bacon for the family was pickled, the cows were milked by the maids, and the butter and cheese made by the mistress. The washing was all done at home, and the needle-work for the family. Besides this, a large poultry-yard had to be attended to, so that it will be no matter of surprise to you that my mother looked about for a school for Elizabeth and me. We were such united playmates and workfellows that I do not remember the time when I felt older than she was, though there was a year and three-quarters between us. She was a spirited little thing, and never would be left behind. We were driven in our little chaise by the boy to Mrs. Outlaw's, at the farther end of the village. Hers was one of the old dame schools, and she was quite primitive.

My brother Richard was born when I was about

six years old; he was a charming little boy, and very pretty. He was always my special charge. It was my business to dress him in the morning and give him his basin of bread and milk before I had my breakfast, and I used to put him into bed at night. I was very proud of his appearance. On a Sunday, when his best frock was put on, his brown ribbon sash, and his beautiful drab beaver hat, I would walk with him up Bilney Lane to meet my father and mother coming from Meeting, and they would stop and take him into the chaise to ride home with them.

I keep lingering over the remembrance of our early years at Felthorpe; they were happy years. No doubt there were cloudy days, but I do not remember them; and there was all the joy and freshness of a young, natural development, with no checks from my mother, and great animation and encouragement from my father. To the last day of his life he delighted in his children; and he knew they loved him, and this cheered him when all beside was sad and stormy.

I must tell you a little about his farm, and Felthorpe itself. The quality of the land then, and ever since, has been some of the poorest to be found in Norfolk, all reclaimed from heath land, by which it was surrounded. The farm contained eight hundred acres, four hundred of which were heath and wood; it was a poor sand in most of the cultivated parts, and there was some meadow land for the cows—a discouraging tract for a farmer.

The trees were mostly oak and Scotch fir. My Cousin Wright was the first man in Norfolk who planted these firs with a view to timber, but he said if they would grow in the poor bleak soil of Scotland, they would not find themselves much out of their element in the poor, scant soil of Norfolk. He planted a considerable breadth of the soil with firs. At first this was called by the gentry "Wright's Folly." But the folly in a few years was accounted wisdom, and the Royal Society presented him with a handsome gold medal, which your dear father now has. From the success of the experiment, the planting of heath land with the Scotch fir rapidly increased. When I was a little girl there was not much fir wood; now the heath lands, then so bare, are thickly covered, and it has added a very picturesque feature to that dreary, thinly peopled district.

When I say "dreary" you must not suppose we children thought it so; to us it was a delightful pleasure-ground. On the common, and in the swamp, where we made our first acquaintance with flowers, there was the sundew, the maiden's hair, the bog pimpernel, the grass of Parnassus, three varieties of heath, and a number I cannot now call by name; and there were the lapwings calling "peewit." Besides this there was a sandpit, which had in it a mixture of clay, and here we gave ourselves our first lessons in modelling. I am sure ours was a more entire enjoyment than Palissy's; we had no need to burn chairs and tables to dry our articles.

The high-woods were close by, where the first primroses and violets were found, and here my delighted eyes first saw the wood-sorrel, which I did not meet with again for forty years. We needed no one to provide amusement for us; we had free access to all those places, and many more of varied interest. In the field just before our house there was a wide dry ditch on the farther side, with a white thorn hedge on one side and the grass road on the other. This ditch was a very delightful place for making bowers to sit in; we used to arch them over, and then make our roof of ivy, which we would strip from the pollard-oaks. My father would sometimes go to an osier-ground which he had planted, and bring us a few long wands, which he would help us to drive into the banks on both sides, and tie them at the top with a piece of cord which he usually had in his pocket, and he seemed to enjoy it all as much as we did.

There were four lanes which started very near our house, each running to the village in a different direction—the Common Lane, the Church Lane, the Bilney Lane, and Brick Lane. We did not very much like the last, from a sort of mystery which hung about it. The report current was, that a man of the name of Brand had killed himself in that lane, and if any one drove down it after nightfall, they would see a man without a head running along by the side of the cart. I always felt a degree of solemnity in walking down it, as we did sometimes when sent to fetch our letters, which were left at "The Bull," the only public-house in the village. You may be sure I never saw Brand.

On one side of our house was a fruit garden and orchard. The orchard was a notable place, as there grew the summer apple-tree, which we might pelt with stones and brickbats when the main crop was gathered. We might also eat those that had fallen in the night, which made a visit to the summer apple-tree our first morning exercise. Whatever was granted us was freely granted; we had no perplexing laws to provoke us to break them. We might pelt the damson-trees, but not touch the plum and greengage trees; we understood, and obeyed. In this orchard Elizabeth and I performed our first charity which meant giving something from our own small store of money. A very poor family had removed into the village, and my father did all he could to find the man and his family employment. He ordered one of the boys, about twelve, to come and dig a deep hole in the orchard. Our sympathies were much stirred for these poor people, especially for this boy, and we consulted together how we could give him a little of our money. Our income was a penny a week. We were too delicate of his feelings to offer it as charity, so we went and stood by the hole he was digging, and as it were accidentally dropped our pence into it; and when he picked them up to return to us, we said, "Oh no, it was of no consequence."

I am sure my sister Elizabeth and I shall never forget our secretly getting into debt. We were taken to Norwich with our father and mother. Not far from the inn where my father put up was a small shop where children's toys were sold. These were the high times of our baby-house, and in the shop-window we saw some little tin and lead plates, the very things for our baby-house kitchen. We ventured into the shop to inquire the price; they came to more than we had by a penny or half-penny, I forget which. Temptation was very strong, and we asked if the man could trust us till we came again and paid him. He evidently saw that we were not thieves, and consented, and we went off with our prize. We very seldom went to Norwich, and we were unwilling to trust any one with our disgraceful secret, and this penny hung about our necks for weeks, attended with the most anxious fear lest the man should see my father and tell him of it. I forget the particulars of the repayment, but I know in some way our consciences obtained peace. I tell you these two instances to show the influence of our parents on our morals. They taught us not so much by talking or preaching; they walked before us in the uprightness and integrity of their hearts, and we followed. I will give you another little instance of this silent influence. Some sparrows had made their nests in the thatched roof of our wood-house, and my father had ordered one of the men to mount a ladder and destroy them. He went himself to see it done, and I walked with him. We returned to the house together quite silently. As I paced along by his side without speaking a word, I have no doubt he thought I was sorry for the birds, and he laid his hand on my head and stroked it tenderly. I immediately divined his thoughts, and felt ashamed, for I was not thinking of the birds at all; but my thoughts were not explainable. I have often thought since how wise it is to give people credit for thinking and feeling rightly; it really helps them to do so.

Among the events of those years of which I have the keenest remembrance were sheep-shearing and harvesting. My father had a very large flock of sheep. The nightly folding them in field after field was profitable for the poor, dry land. My father had imported from Spain some Merino sheep, and had parted with his long-legged, blackfaced Norfolk sheep, with wide standing horns, for the Southdown, thus improving his wool, which was at that time a profitable article of trade. Many farmers came to see my father's Merino rams, for in this, as well as in other things, he was a man in advance of his day. As far as I can remember, he had four of these Spanish rams, and gave £10 each for them. The sheep-washing took place in a long meadow, a considerable distance from the house, through which ran a very small stream. At a certain place this stream was dammed up, so as to form a pond, and the sheep were penned up close by it. I vividly recall this rough, active, and noisy scene. There were washers, slightly dressed, standing in the pond, ready to seize the unfortunate animals from the catchers in the fold, who flung them unceremoniously into the water, where they were ducked and towzled about, and then, bewildered, and bleating most piteously, were driven off into the meadow to dry their dripping fleece as best they could. The sheep-shearing day was of the most momentous interest to us. My father had given a sheep to each of us, and when it was shorn, the fleece was weighed and we each received the market price of the wool. Of course we were anxious that our fleece should be heavy. To assist this, on the morning of the sheep-shearing day my father called us early, directing us to the fields and lanes through which the sheep had passed, leaving a good many locks of wool upon the bushes. Oh, kings' daughters! what have they to equal the delight of getting locks of wool from the bushes in the early morning, and then fresh home to breakfast on our bread and milk, sweetened by our father's exhilarating pleasure in our success? It was a very sensational time with us when our fleece was weighed, with our little gathered accumulations. He always gave us the exact weight.

One cold spring morning, in the lambing-time, my father came into the kitchen with a newly-born lamb in his arms, as near dead as it well could be. He was just going off with my mother to the monthly meeting at Norwich. He called me quickly, saying, "Here, Mary; if thee can make this lamb live, thee shall have it for thy own." By the time they returned, a joyful resurrection had taken place. I had been sitting all the morning with the lamb laid on flannel before a good fire. I kept rubbing it and giving it a little milk, as it could take it, and before they came home it could stagger about the kitchen. My father was as good as his word—it was *my* lamb.

I must not omit a little description of harvest-time, for that—to us children at least—was a season of joy. The harvest-men were all boarded in the house, and the coppers full of dumpling, the boilers full of beef, were a sight to see. If the men were working near the house, a horn was blown, and they came trooping home, washed at the pump, and then took their seats at the long table. There was always a leader chosen among them, called a captain, who sat at the top and kept order. When they were working farther from the house, which we preferred, a horse was put into a light cart, and the eatables were placed in tins, the meat in one, puddings in another, and vegetables in a third, with baskets full of bread, and kegs and stone bottles of beer, with pewter plates and tin mugs, so that there was not much to break. When the cart appeared in the field, the scythes and sickles were laid down, and a place was chosen for the repast under a tree or hedge as might be. We children were often allowed to go with the cart. The fine rounds of beef and long puddings make me almost hungry now to think how good they looked. Everything was well cooked in my mother's house, and the harvest-cakes, of which every man had one in the afternoon, with a horn of beer, were better than I have ever been able to make since. Of course, they had the dew of youth upon them.

When all the fields were cleared, the harvest supper was the crowning achievement. The last waggon full of corn was adorned with branches of trees and drawn into the yard ; then all the labourers went home and dressed themselves in their best, to come, with their wives, to the harvest supper. There were two long tables in the kitchen, which were plentifully covered with roast and boiled meat, plum - puddings, and home - brewed beer. After this was all finished, the captain would come to the parlour-door to ask my father's presence in the kitchen, where my father's and Madam Wright's health was drunk, and I do not know what more. Any one who had a voice was called upon for a song, and the evening ended with taking the tables and boards off the tressels and having a dance, of which I remember the comic effect, as we children peeped behind the blinds of the glass door which separated the kitchen from the keeping-room.

Perhaps no one was more glad than the farmer's wife when the harvest was gathered in, and her labours ended. I do not wonder at her being glad when the change was made when the men boarded themselves and all their wage was paid in money, but it snapped some of the ties which bound the servant and master together as fellow-creatures.

But the first real loosening which I can remember was the introduction of the threshing-machine, instead of the everlasting flail with which hitherto all the corn had been beaten out on the barn-floor. Dear me! I can hear it now, the first sound in the early winter morning, the regular monotonous bang, bang. Of course it made work when it was scanty on the farm, and the men looked on the new contrivance with no favour, prognosticating, of course, no good—as they do now at any change. But the day came when, in my father's absence, a man's hand was so much injured that he had to lose his arm. Worse was to come. On another Saturday, when my father was in Norwich, a woman who had no business to be there was caught in the wheel, and died that evening from her injuries. This was the warrant for the threshing-machine to stop, and my father yielded to it.

My mother and our governess, with Elizabeth and me, walked through the village on the Sunday evening. Instead of the greetings and curtseyings common on such occasions, there was a dead silence, and even as a child I felt the weight of the solemnity painfully oppressive.

My mother was the lady of the village; there was no other; all the little kindnesses proceeded from "Madam Wright." There was a great stir about vaccination at this time, and my mother had Maria and Richard vaccinated. The village people were of course opposed to the change; they preferred the veritable thing and have done with it. There was a family where the small-pox was raging, and at the worst my mother took Maria and Richard to the house to show that she had full confidence in the cow-pox as a substitute for the small-pox.

Most of the labouring people at that time brewed a little beer for themselves, which was called "small beer." Those a little above them brewed a larger store. In my father's house a good deal was brewed. The dairymaid was also the brewer. When the yeast had risen, my mother bottled what she needed in stone bottles, and kept it in the cellar; the remainder was put into jugs, and Elizabeth and I carried it to those who brewed their own beer; and when they brewed, they returned the compliment. This was one of the convenient and pleasant little ways through which a neighbourly feeling was kept up. At that time people who did not make their own bread were considered very bad managers; it was a kind of test of the quality of management.

In Felthorpe there was no society; the only neighbour with whom we visited lived in the next parish. He was a farmer. His name was Harsant, a fine man with a fine spirit. His wife was as good a soul as ever lived. I am sure we children thought so, for her heart was full of love, and her cupboard full of cakes and mince-pies and all sorts of good things. We could not eat too much to please her. They had the old genuine hospitality that would fearlessly run the risk of making you ill, so that you did justice to their provisions. Our friendship with them continued through their lives. The rest of our society was amongst the Friends at Norwich and my mother's relatives. Mr. and Mrs. Harsant not unfrequently took a cup of tea with us. On these occasions my father and Mr. Harsant would play quoits; they were both good players, and it was a delight to us children to watch them. I have never seen quoits played since. My father used to play trap-and-ball with us. If he came in a few minutes before dinner, he would catch up the bat and say, "Come, girls, where is the ball?" And then he would send us such "nice catchers;" and if we missed catching, he would say, "Ah, butter-fingers!" Whatever he did was full of life; he never sent us bad, erratic balls. Dear man! there was no chafe or worry about him, but, strong, hopeful, and kind, he delighted in development and any exercise of ingenuity.

I remember once a complaint being urged against me by my sisters. I was, like my father, very fond of speculation. I cannot remember what feat I had thought I could perform, but one of my sisters said, "Mary always thinks she can do everything." I felt a little abashed, which I suppose my father saw, for he laid his hand lovingly on my head and said, "That's right, my dear, always hope."

I believe we were as happy as children could be. But now there came a change. Our education, begun at the dame school, was now to go on under a bright young governess. She was a fine creature, all life and intelligence. I think she was the only daughter of an officer who was with our army in America, she and her mother remaining in England. I suppose their means were not very abundant. At that time, if girls went out for governesses, it was always supposed they were poor. She had been educated at Mr. Thurgar's school at Norwich, which was a first-rate school for the day. He inspired the girls with a delight in learning, and this pupil certainly infused the same into her scholars, and our school became a pleasure. She was specially clever in teaching history, and giving it the charm of reality. She would read Roman and Grecian history to us, and then talk about it; then she would make an abstract of what we had read, which we learned by heart and repeated, not like parrots, for I know I had a living appreciation of both characters and events. The coldest day in winter I would sit muffled up in a quiet place to learn the history-lesson. She introduced us to a much more stirring kind of poetry than we had known before. In the afternoon whilst we worked she would draw from her own store of imagination, and as she went on, produce little romances. These were the little Quaker girls' novels. My sister Anna, who slept with her, and sat up later than the rest of us, had the benefit of a story told in bed. After school she was as ready to play as we were. She would fly over the ditches, inciting us to follow her, and dig up primroses and violets to plant at the sides of our long house. Once in the half year we had examinations. The room was decked with flowers. My father and mother were present; rewards were on the table, and no ambitious student at college could be more anxious to distinguish himself than we were. Once in the week a French master came from Norwich to teach us French; also a drawing-master, who taught many families in the county; and he sometimes took us out to sketch. He was a pleasant, friendly man. He would bait his horse in my father's stable, take tea with us, and then go on to some one else.

There is no knowing what we might have turned out had this governess remained to carry us along the way of knowledge in such high heart. Our afternoon reading with her was in Plutarch's Lives. I must have been nearly ten years old when she left us. Her father wished her and her mother to join him in America, so there was no help for it. Our hearts were filled with sorrow and our eyes with tears for the loss of one who had given us so much joy. She entirely fulfilled my father's idea of a teacher for children, and great was his sorrow, in watching her successor, to see that, instead of climbing, we slid down the hill. All that Nancy Wardell could boast of was good temper, and that was inexhaustible. Fortunately for Anna, she was sent to a Friends' school at Tottenham, kept by Abigail Firth. Her education was completed by one year's finishing at this school; she, with two other girls (the Clarks of Downham) were parlour boarders, with whatever privileges that might confer. Her friendship with these girls was a great pleasure to her through her life. Anna was a girl of good abilities, not quick but thorough; she was silent and abstracted. I, being four years younger, was not a companion for her, nor was she for me. Elizabeth and I were inseparable. Anna was thus a good deal thrown upon herself, when, at the end of the year, she returned home to be *our* teacher. To Elizabeth and me the year had been a lost one in the way of intellectual progress; verbal accuracy was all that was required of us, so we learnt our tasks and repeated them. From the time Anna went to school at Tottenham our drawing-master was discontinued; our governess was supposed to teach us drawing and French. She knew a good many songs, which she would sing and teach to Elizabeth and me. We none of us ever learned music, therefore we had not the torment of learning to disgust us; but we delighted in music, as I believe all Quaker girls do to whom it is forbidden. Mr. Harsant's organ (a barrel-organ) was enchantment to us, also a musical snuff-box he had; and he played on the violin; so you may suppose that the house of our neighbour was charming to us.

Personally, Elizabeth and I liked Annie Wardell. She amused us, for she was very good at chat and gossip, and we got acquainted with all her little world of interest. My mother liked her for her willingness to help, but my father almost despised her. My father and mother were very kind to all our governesses; they were never made to feel themselves in the way.

On Anna's return from Tottenham, our governess left us. We did not like Anna's reign, nor did we learn happily; saying lessons was a dull business, and perhaps it was natural not to like the rule of a sister, especially as there was no animation in it. She was now growing into a pretty young woman, at the age when ambition to be something springs up in girls' minds. I think she and the Clarks were working themselves out of the pupa state, and emerging into something into which we were not permitted to look, much less intermeddle with. In her bedroom she had some Latin words written on a card, of which we did not know the meaning, although we learnt the words by heart. She was, I believe, teaching herself Latin. She was so reserved that my mother often wondered what Anna could be thinking about. Elizabeth and I used to say, "Anna has got away to her old thoughts."

I must not forget to say during this year we had an addition to our family. A distant relative of my mother's died; she was the wife of a farmer living not many miles from us. She left a large family of little children. The eldest girl, not more than fifteen, was expected by her father to take the management of the farm-house. Our parents felt so deeply for this young girl and her father, that my mother offered to take her for a year, and to teach her all she could to fit her for her responsible position. This offer was most thankfully accepted, and Betsy Parkham became my mother's willing and most obedient pupil, and afterwards discharged the duties of her life most creditably. She taught us the steps of the Highland Reel. I think this was all.

But the time drew on when we must leave our happy childhood life at Felthorpe—leave our common; the high wood; the four-acre meadow; the oak grove; the fields of which we knew the names as familiarly as our own. During the early part of this century, when the price of corn was exceedingly high, a farmer could live even upon poor Felthorpe land, and comparatively prosper, especially where a large flock of sheep were kept, making it unnecessary to bring manure in waggons from Norwich. The cultivation of land was at that time much stimulated by the encouragement and example of Thos. Wm. Coke (now Lord Leicester) of Halkham, in the north part of Norfolk. There were annual gatherings at his house at the time of sheep-shearing, and all the farmers of any mark were invited to be present and partake of his hospitality. On these occasions all new inventions and improvements were exhibited, and many a farmer returned home with his head full of new ideas. I remember the time when lucerne was introduced as food for cattle. Mr. Burrows was the first cultivator in Norfolk. He wished my father to come over and look at his crops, and my father drove over with my mother, Elizabeth, and me to see them, and he soon adopted the plan for himself.

As soon as the cessation of war removed the obstruction to commerce, and the price of corn became as low as it had been high, the gentlemen farmers who had grown up found a sad reverse, especially on poor land like Felthorpe; and I have no doubt it was this which induced my father to give up the farm and join a shipowner at Yarmouth, who appeared to be very prosperous, and had several vessels engaged in profitable commerce. He came several times to see my father, and it was at last decided that all the farming stock should be sold by auction, and whatever else would not be needed at the new home. It was on the day of the auction I first saw my dear father's face look anxious, almost agonized. I remember now how that look struck to my heart when he saw his beautiful farm horses and other stock selling far below their value. The old perennial sunshine ceased that day, for though he was never moody, and mostly cheerful, he became more silent, and his face more thoughtful. Worldly prosperity never visited him again, but he was speculative, enthusiastic, and hopeful; depression was foreign to him, and he never damped the family by recounting his own anxieties. We spent our last night at our dear friends the Harsants', who were as sorry to lose us as we were to leave them.

I believe my dear mother was very anxious about this remove. She often talked to my sister Anna about it. My father was *at home* on the farm. But of shipping he knew nothing. He had gathered together about £10,000. My mother never opposed my father, nor doubted that he understood better than she did what he was doing; still, while packing her movables, she was anxious and thoughtful, having had no experience of any but the farm life, and being well content where she was. As for myself, when I had taken a heart-aching look round on the dear old place where all my life had hitherto been spent, I set off full of hope and curiosity to enter on the experience of the new home. Maria and Richard were left behind with our good friends the Harsants, till we should be settled. Elizabeth and I went with my father and mother in the family chaise, drawn by Sportsman, our father's favourite driving-horse. It was a cold day at Michaelmas. We overtook the waggon with our furniture. We had to pack into a small house at first, as the house my father was building for us was not completed. He had bought a piece of land, on which he built a good comfortable dwelling-house, a laundry, wash-house, and dairy detached, also stable and chaise-house. There was a good-sized meadow, which ran down to the marshes, and a large kitchen-garden—everything planned for comfort, and nicely furnished.

Here we began a residence of six or seven years. I was not thirteen, Elizabeth eleven, Maria nine, Richard about seven. John was at school, Anna was a young woman of seventeen, and it is curious how soon Elizabeth and I, from children, were raised to considerable importance.

There were several Friends' families in Yarmouth. They were all in trade, and thoroughly respectable. There were a large number of young people, with whom we soon became acquainted. They were a pleasant, sociable community of Friends. William Sewell and his good wife were the leading Friends in the Meeting. He had a large grocer's shop in the market-place, where his sons and daughters were trained in business habits, without at all becoming what is commonly called mere shop men and women. William Sewell held a high place in the town. The opinion of Quaker Sewell had great weight. He was very watchful over the young men, promoting in every way their intellectual studies, and by his open-house hospitality encouraged them to meet together and exercise their powers in composition, discussion, &c., &c. An annual Essay meeting was held at his house, at which the young men read their essays, &c., to the young ladies and other friends of the meeting. They called their society the Demosthenian Society. The young women afterwards founded another called the Agenoria. Societies like these are common enough now, but they were rare in those days. The meeting for worship was rather large. There was no minister, only the same quiet sitting for two hours, morning and afternoon, on the first day of the week. There were no kind of religious advantages, only a steady moral training, and a watchful guard against any deviation into worldly amusements or fashions. William Sewell's wife was an Elder, and kept her eye jealously upon *us*, lest we should lead the other young Friends out of the way of plainness of speech, behaviour, and apparel. My dear mother had herself rather a taste for dress, though she kept strictly within the letter of the law; but her children she liked to see prettily dressed, and with this unfortunate proclivity, she ordered for our winter dresses, at a fashionable dressmaker's in Norwich, cloth pelisses of a very pretty sage green colour, with capes. These capes, with the collars and wrists, were trimmed with swansdown, which made them not only very pretty, but very striking, when worn by *four* girls. When we took our seats at the top of the Meeting-house, all eyes were upon us, especially the eyes of the dear Elder, whose silent cogitations were very painful and perplexed. When we went again in the afternoon, she passed us without speaking. This was very eloquent; but more soon followed. On the next morning she came to our house and asked for an opportunity of speaking alone with my mother, when she so seriously set forth the danger of leading other young girls into the temptation of dress, that my dear mother was overcome with the fear of our becoming a stumbling-block in the way of others, and much to our disgust and disappointment, she sent back the pretty pelisses to have the swansdown taken off and a trifling little cord put round them, thus depriving them of all their glory. We were very angry, but to wound the conscience of a good Friend, and set a dangerous example, were sins not lightly committed at that time. There was great deference shown and respect paid to the Elders who bore rule in the church; they were not tyrannical, only firm to their convictions of duty—especially this dear woman who despoiled us.

When I was fourteen, my father and mother thought that I should have a year at a boarding-school, as Anna had done. I was sent to the same school at Tottenham. The method of teaching was the same as at most other schools at that time —just learning lessons and repeating them word for word. We had a few lessons to learn out of school hours. All this, lodged in the memory, was considered as volumes of knowledge for future use. I believe a great deal of it was dead seed. We had a French master and a drawing-master. I made a small proficiency in copying flowers, of which I was very fond. I was a parlour boarder, which gave me the advantage of dining in the parlour when there were visitors—always having tea there with the governesses, and sitting up to supper. The only thing I have to show for this year is the piece of embroidery in wool, which, when I came home, was duly framed and hung up. This kind of work was then in fashion.

My education being now considered finished (we should now consider not begun), I set myself to carry it on after my own taste. We each of us took some little part in household matters, and Anna and I took it in turn, a week at a time, to teach Elizabeth and Maria as we had been taught ourselves. I am sure they gained little enough from me. My great delight was in poetry, and the works of Moore, Southey, Byron, Scott, and others, continually coming out, gave me a perpetual feast. For two years I think I read little besides, learning whole books, and repeating them to myself in the silent meetings. I do not think I derived any harm from this almost exclusive attention to poetry. Quaker girls have little excitement in their quiet lives, and these works afforded to the craving imagination all the excitement and variety it needed. There were other books that Elizabeth and I read and half-studied together, and with drawing, and attending the various meetings of the Agenorian Society, our time passed pleasantly enough. We every now and then got a novel from the circulating library, but this being forbidden fruit, we devoured it in our bedroom. Our little room, being far away from the others, admitted of secret practices; but it was not often that we so trespassed. We lived very open lives, with little concealment amongst us, and in perfect harmony with each other. Through life it has been our blessed experience never to quarrel or misunderstand each other. In the midst of my precious father's secret trials, the unbroken love of his children was his sweetest solace—the deep, true, and warm love we bore him never failed.

From our settlement at Yarmouth I come upon eight eventful years—eventful in many ways. I have not the courage to recall the saddest portions very minutely, but will just touch upon them sufficiently to carry the history forward.

In the year 1815 the battle of Waterloo gave peace to our long-troubled land. We had a grand illumination in the town, and a great dinner feasted the people, the tables being placed all along the quay. It might well be a time of rejoicing; the price of food had become exorbitant — I think flour was five shillings a stone. When my brother Richard was ten years old, my sister Ellen was born. An event of equal importance was my brother John's marriage to Anne Harford, by which our family became enriched by the possession of one of the most charming of women — superior in intellect, in sweetness, and amiability; simple and unselfish in the greatest degree. If she had enjoyed the education given to women at the present day, and had her unusual amount of natural talent been developed, she would have been distinguished in more than one field of art or science. Her manners were charming; she was the central attraction in every little company, though altogether unconscious of it herself; her aim was always to interest and bring out the talents of others. She enchanted children, instructing them with the utmost simplicity. She could address a company of children anywhere; her interest and affection flowed out to them so intensely that she never felt the burden of self-consciousness, and the plentiful store of her imagination always seemed within reach. She wrote several works for young people, the names of which you will remember. "The Observing Eye," which after many years still retains its place; two works on geology, the title of one (I think), "The World prepared for Man;" and another work much valued, "What is a Bird?" I give you this sketch of dear Aunt Wright as at the time I mention she became a member of our family; and my brother John, having become of age, he settled at Dudwick House, according to the intention of Cousin Wright, and began the management of his own property, which had been somewhat neglected by the executors.

The next important event of this period was the starting of the first river steam-packet in England. My uncle, Richard Wright, had brought his steamboat to perfection, and proposed to have it placed on the Yarmouth river to run between Yarmouth and Norwich, and as his schemes always emptied his pocket, he proposed to my father to join him and take the management of it. My father did so, and my uncle went off to something else.

[Here follows an account of the draining of Mr. Wright's resources through the dishonesty of another. At last he determined to have the matter sifted by competent arbiters. "This went on for some time—a time never to be forgotten by those who heard my father's step come into the house after those meetings," his daughter writes; and during the arbitration the offender died, and the wrong was never righted.]

My sister Anna and I had often very grave consultations at this time as to our own duty. We could not bear to increase the burdens of our dear father, and yet we could not see any way before us. Situations as governesses were not so easy to be obtained then as they are now, and to be a governess involved a great descent in the social scale—much more than at present. When I was between seventeen and eighteen your dear grandfather proposed to be taken into my good books, but I was not so minded, and he went to a Manchester warehouse in London for two or three years.

[It was probably two or three years after this, though the date is not given, that an explosion took place on one of the two river steam-packets, and a number of persons were killed. Mr. Wright came up to Norwich by the other boat, and saw thirteen dead bodies laid side by side close to the river. Mrs. Wright was then at Tivetshall, and a friend went to tell her of the calamity and bring her to Norwich, where her daughter Mary was staying. They remained together till the following evening, when the parents returned to Yarmouth in the other packet.]

It steamed slowly off, drawing the wrecked packet behind it. Each side of the river was lined with a speechless crowd; the air was perfectly still; there was the solemnity of death, and silence that might indeed be felt. I longed to go with them, but I could not leave the friendly duty I had undertaken, and Henry Aggs, quietly drawing my arm within his, took me back to the Friends' house.

[Life had to begin again. Mr. Wright had lost all, and the daughters looked out in good earnest for situations as governesses. Mary obtained one in a school in Essex.] —

I had undertaken to teach writing and ciphering to all the school, as well as reading, besides hearing all the usual lessons, and a quantity of mending of stockings, &c. I was not afraid of anything but the ciphering—that was my weak point. My dear father engaged one of the tutors in a school in Yarmouth to come and initiate me before breakfast, but I was as much afraid of the man as I was of the figures, so it did not pay. But I got on, and nobody found me out; and I was a very pretty writer *then*, and could make good quill pens, and as I had to make and mend about forty every writing-day, I had some practice. The mistress and her sister both liked me, and were very kind, and after a while I felt pretty much at home— as much as you can when the servants call you familiarly by your name as if you were one of them. I had always been used to be called "Miss" from the time when our governess first asserted our dignity as young ladies. Dear Elizabeth went as teacher to a family at Yarmouth, and dear Anna to a Friends' family not far from me, and when we met or wrote, we made ourselves merry over little things—whilst at home the way was very clouded.

My father's property was entirely lost, and my dear brother John proposed that he should occupy the small farm at Buxton—about ninety or a hundred acres. This offer was accepted, and there the dear people came, with Maria and Ellen, and returned to old farm life, but oh, how different! I can never sufficiently admire the patient submission with which my mother again took to the irksome drudgery of a small farm-house, after the ease and comfort she had enjoyed at Southtown, with her two competent servants; now she had only one, very inefficient. The many and various trials of the first few years can only be realised by those upon whom they especially fell. My father turned to the management of his little farm with the earnest, quiet energy of his character, and never complained. We were scattered about, each of us with our own difficulties, every one doing their best, no one adding to the other's burdens. My brother John did all that the kindest son and brother could do, alleviating the burdens and adding to the pleasures of the little crushed company; and as time went on, more sunshine came into the atmosphere, and continued to increase till the end, when the home had long been the happy meeting-place of sons and daughters, children and grandchildren.

I well remember the first Christmas holidays when the scattered sisters met together again in their new home. It was such a delight to us to meet, and escape from our duties,—except for the feeling that my dear mother—indeed all of them—were making a great effort to make us this holiday, and not to let us feel the straitened resources of the house, with our youthful spirits, we enjoyed our home again.

The great trial, to me, of this epoch, was that your dear grandfather came forward again with his proposition. . . . My heart had never been entangled, and was not at all ready to put on chains; . . . but when I returned to my teaching, a correspondence was decided on.

The holidays came again, but the way did not seem to clear up; there was no spark upon the tinder. I was enthusiastic and sentimental—

[Here follows an amusing account of the way in which the poetical maiden gradually became inclined towards her business-like lover.]

So I wrought myself up to saying, "Yes," and I did not repent while I kept my castles in view. When there came a fog, the wheels dragged heavily, but they did drag on till they came to the wedding-day. I was then twenty-two years old: I am now eighty-four, and looking back through the years, I am sure I made no mistake—a kinder husband or better father could rarely be found. Our dissimilarity has probably introduced much more variety and interest into our lives, which have been anything but dull.

The wedding took place in the little Meeting-house at Lammas, and the wedding-dinner was at my brother John's house. We went at once to Cromer for a week, accompanied by my sister Elizabeth. Wedding-trips were not so long and adventurous then as they now often are. This was many years prior to the opening of the first railway in England, and travelling made easy. We had a good horse and a chaise which held us three, and before we turned ourselves to the little home prepared for us at Yarmouth, we visited Tivetshall Hall, for many years the home of my mother's brother, John Holmes, and his large family of sons and daughters, with whom we were very intimate. None of them are now remaining.

Our little house in the church trees close to the large church was very diminutive, but large enough to be happy in; able to take in a friend, and to enter on my first experience in housekeeping. Isaac's father and mother, and his brother Abraham, with his sweet and lovely wife Dorothy, at this time lived in Yarmouth, and my sister Elizabeth was still teaching Joseph Hunter's children (his wife, Fulleretta, was sister to Isaac), so that we were very happily placed among our relatives. Before many months had passed, I found plenty of needlework to do in preparing baby linen. There were then no sewing-machines, and the *Friends*, at any rate, did not go to ready-made linen shops. All the preparations for baby garments were made by loving fingers at home, or by friends and relatives ever ready to "welcome a little stranger." On the 30th of March the little stranger came—an unclouded blessing—for fifty-eight years the perennial joy of my life.

A few days after her birth, it was discovered that Issac and his partner had been overreached in taking the business—that it would not support two families, and that my husband, as the younger partner, must look out for another business, and that speedily. The world was all before us, it is true, but it was very difficult to choose a place of rest. We would much rather have remained in Norfolk near our friends. I abhorred the idea of London; but William Sewell, Isaac's brother, led by some unlucky genius—if we own such agents at all in our affairs—found out a little street leading out of Bishopsgate Street, having neither shops nor traffic in it. There he spied a small private house, opposite a public-house where hackney-coaches, as cabs were then called, stood waiting when unemployed. The house consisted of an underground kitchen, a room upon a level with the street, and four stories above, each with one room. William Sewell was considered by his brothers a man of business, and when he was called upon for counsel, his ideas were generally adopted, as they unfortunately were in this case. He recommended turning the ground floor into a shop, chiefly with a view to Quaker custom, as it was not far from the Meeting-house. He left out of the calculation that within a very short distance there was a long-established and well-supplied Quaker shop, which would naturally engross the custom of the Friends.

At considerable expense, the requisite alterations were made. Whilst Isaac was staying in London to superintend, I and my baby went to stay with my dear father and mother. At Michaelmas, when my little darling was six months old, we started for London. My father and mother Sewell accompanied us, as they had decided to leave Yarmouth and live in the neighbourhood of London. I have always had good courage and plenty of hope, and I was young. All these advantages were needed for this enterprise, which very soon manifested its character. As might have been divined, the place was not known, and very few customers came. It was a small new shop, with no ability to look attractive. I made some little fancy things to put in the window: I forget if they were sold. Whatever we might do, however, things daily grew worse and worse. The want of fresh air, the high stairs, the noise, and incessant work began to tell upon me, though I kept up my spirits. At last *nobody* came to the shop, and a council had again to be called. This resulted in Isaac's going into partnership in a much larger concern with a man who brought in most of the money, and was very reckless and unsound in his trading principles. We removed to a large house with a number of assistants, and as it was a long-established business it was expected to answer well; but before two years it was broken up, and so was I. It was a miserable failure; Isaac lost everything he had. At this juncture my Philip was born, a blessing to me every day of his life to this self-same day. The doctor said I must leave London, and lodgings were secured at Hackney, where I went with the two children. Whilst I was there, our furniture was sold by auction. This we both gave up freely to pay our debts. I must say I grieved a little over some of my wedding-presents, especially the tea-urn which my dear mother had given me. My dear brother John and another friend bought in a small quantity of our furniture, sufficient for a small house which we took at Dalston. Here we lived, I think, nine or ten years, and here the dear children's happy childhood was passed. Isaac had to begin life again without capital. He engaged himself as traveller to a large lace manufactory at Nottingham. He continued in this some years, and then became assistant to his brother, William Sewell.

It will be easily supposed that strict economy had to be practised at Dalston, but there is no hardship in plain, simple food and clothing. Trouble often comes when these are superabundant, but as long as there is *enough* without carking care, there is freedom; and I believe this is the best atmosphere for a child's mind and body. I had only one little servant, and we washed at home. As the children grew up, they shared with me in little household occupations. They were always with me; we were workfellows and playfellows, and wished no greater happiness. I think we were exceedingly happy. Isaac saw very little of his home; he had to leave at eight o'clock in the morning, and seldom returned till eight in the evening. Sunday was a very happy time, when we were all together.

About this time I wrote my first little book in words of one syllable.[1] I wanted to earn money, if I could, for the purchase of books to help me in the children's education. I sold it for £3, which was a little fortune to me then, when all my wants were in subjection to our circumstances, and small gifts and possessions were much prized. A happy state! the most enduringly healthy. The children had very happy dispositions and fine tempers; we knew nothing about punishments—to have a kiss withheld was too severe for either of them. How beautiful their young lives seem to me now, as I look back upon those promising young plants! Even if I had not loved them so dearly, I should naturally have been proud of them, for they were fine, attractive children, and very intelligent. Anna very early manifested her talent for drawing, and they both delighted in natural history. It would be almost ridiculous to mention the number of sciences into which they took the first steps. Sometimes their father would bring them home a shell; by

[1] "Walks with Mamma."

degrees they had a nice little collection, and would occasionally visit the British Museum to learn their names. Whilst on a visit at Folkestone they saw the Blue Clay full of fossils; this was a great interest to them. Gerard Edward Smith, a great botanist, was staying there at the time, and helped much to foster their love of flowers, which ever went on increasing.

Entomology was delightful to us all, but we never compassed death to make a collection; we made one trial—that was sufficient. I have always been glad that we gave it up. I believe the habits of the insects were observed much more accurately than if the ambition of possessing them had been gratified. I often used to paint moths and butterflies that had been captured and kept under a glass for a short period. We went on to many little chemical experiments, and increasingly found the world a very beautiful and interesting place to live in. Their fellow-creatures with whom they were particularly disgusted were men who shot birds for amusement—they always designated them Boobies. One day one of these shot a blackbird, which fell into our front garden. The man came to the gate to get possession of it. Anna rushed to the door. With an obsequious smile, the man said, "If you please, Miss, will you let me take my bird?" "No," she said, "thee cruel man, thee shan't have it at all." Cruelty or oppression of any kind roused all their indignation. They were very unselfish. At the time we lived at Dalston the potato famine occurred in

Ireland. We had been planning for some time for a visit to the seaside, and I had been carefully economising so as to have sufficient money to meet the expense. Our plans and conversation centred on this trip. With rather a fainting heart I pictured to them the sufferings of the Irish, and how much money was wanted to buy food for them. I told them I had no money to spare except the money I had laid by for our trip. Would they be willing to give that up and send the money to the Irish people? They both at once said they would. I told them to think about it during the day, and if at night they were of the same mind, the money should be sent. At night they were quite determined that the money should be appropriated to the starving Irish. Eventually they gained more than they had given up. Without knowing anything of this act of self-denial, my husband's kind brother William proposed to send us all to the sea at Sandgate for some weeks, at his own expense. This was a most delightful treat, giving us great increase of knowledge, as I have said before. Philip was about seven years old, Anna nine—old enough for us together to explore and enjoy in all directions. Lucy Sewell joined us, and we were very happy.

The first school that Philip went to was the Hackney Grammar School, where he won a very good character from Mr. Ellis, the master. My Anna did not go to school. She had a great deal of courage and independence of character, never burdened with any kind of fear. As very little children I accustomed them to playing in the dark. Many a game of hide-and-seek have I had with them in a room bordered by a dressing-room and two closets, and admitting of all kinds of surprises. They were never afraid of any kind of insect, would handle beetles, spiders, earwigs, &c., with pleasure, and were much amused if any one was afraid of them. One of the great delights of their early days, and many later ones, was a visit to Buxton. Buxton was the Paradise of children— there they found the joy of unfettered freedom in the country; and, besides aunts and grandmother, there was the grandfather, the central attraction to all the grandchildren. When he was sitting, they were sure to be round him; when he walked, they were by his side. There was never any noise or boisterous play, but any one who watched could see that the conversation was full of deep interest. My father knew the heart of a child; his own nature was full of hope and experiment—that high temperature in which intelligent children delight to dwell. My father was, as I have said before, an enthusiast held in the fetters of circumstances; but it always remained latent, and he could kindle it in the spirits of children. Swimming, shooting and riding were all learned at Buxton: the shooting was, I think, confined to garden thieves—the sparrows and blackbirds. Their Aunt Wright had also a perfect fascination for children, with her never-failing power of interesting them in natural history. These were halcyon days, to be held in remembrance through life. A free, active, happy childhood is the best foundation for a happy life, and if they have as much responsibility as they can carry without anxiety, they enjoy it, and it strengthens the character.

Whilst living at Dalston we made the acquaintance of Mrs. Wright, a very charming and superior woman. She was fond of natural history, and much encouraged the children's taste for it. John Coppen's family also became our friends, also the George Brightmans and a few others. Whilst living here my precious Anna dislocated her elbow, which was some time in recovering its strength and usefulness. In speaking to her aunt of this painful accident she said, "I bored it well;" and so she might have said of the many painful accidents and sufferings of her life; she always had a cheerful, patient courage. They were both early accustomed to the care of animals, and kept an accurate account of expenses—money was very precious in those days.

I must not leave Dalston without speaking of the Christmas hamper from Buxton, when every gift *was* a *gift*. Children were not overwhelmed with presents at that time, as they now often are. The unpacking as well as the packing was all heartfelt. The children stood round, and as every labelled article came out, it was received with joyful acclamations. Grandmother sent ducks and sausages and mince-pies, and grandfather, apples, pears, and walnuts, and things on which were written, "For my dear boy," or "For my little maid;" something from each aunt then at Buxton, and letters—not very much in money cost, but oh, how much in deep love!

Whilst we were living at Dalston my dear sister Anna was married to that excellent man Joseph Crewdson of Manchester, a widower with six chilren.

As I linger on the life at Dalston, I recall many occupations and interests. I was associated with Sarah Brightman in the Anti-Slavery Association and in penitentiary work at Shoreditch. At that time there was much attention called to the sufferings of little chimney-sweepers, and I found courage to go round the neighbourhood to beg money to purchase one of the brooms now in use. I succeeded in getting £10, the needed sum, and the broom was successfully introduced in Dalston. There was also a good deal of visiting the poor.

But our house began to feel too small, and Isaac, who delighted in places which afforded scope for alteration and improvement, spied an empty building which had been coach-house and stable to a gentleman's house close by. The present tenant needed only a house and a strip of garden behind it, leaving four acres of meadow land, a large fruit and vegetable garden, and some outhouses. This square empty building—I shall never forget the morning when your grandfather first took us to see it. The traces were there of what had been beautiful when cared for; it was now quite ruinous. A broad, straight piece of water, in which gold-fish were swimming, divided the garden from the meadow; the old damask rose was growing wild; there was a fine acacia and tulip tree, besides walnut, apple, pear, and plum trees. I and the children were almost beside ourselves with delight. Of course the house-walls had to be filled with rooms, and a great deal besides to be done before we could live in it. Uncle Philip Sewell lent the money, and in about half a year it was finished, and we left Park Road and entered upon our new life. Philip left the Hackney Grammar School and went to a Friends' school at Stoke Newington, where we now resided. A private carriage-road led from the main road to our house, which was quite secluded, and after the garden was laid out and all made complete, it was a very pretty and pleasant home.

The great change to me was keeping cows. Your grandfather's idea was, that our small income might be increased by selling milk in the neighbourhood. This involved keeping a man and his wife to attend to them and carry out the milk. Beside the cows, there were pigs, ducks, hens, and rabbits. The dear children here were very busy and very useful. Philip used to see the milk measured out in the morning, and often milked a cow; he would sharpen the knives or clean the shoes, or anything to help on the general comfort of the family. There was no idea of degradation belonging to work, but a great deal of animation, and time passed most pleasantly as we worked together. At this time my brother Richard, who had taken some land at Enfield, came to live with us. With this addition to the family, I could not find time to help on dear Anna's education. There was a good day-school within a mile of our house, and we decided that she should be a day-boarder there. Your grandfather's salary did not increase, and the cows were not very remunerative. The strain on our income became too great, and I decided to dismiss my servant and do the work myself, with a little assistance in the morning, and all that the dear children could give me when they were at home. As I was alone all the day, there was plenty of time to do the work, and the churning and making the butter was a pleasure rather than otherwise. I had no sense of hardship, and our domestic interests and employments were many and various. Natural history (practical) was still a great pleasure, and there was some time for reading. Wherever my children were, I was happy, although prosperity never came.

When we had been at Palatine Cottage about a year, your Uncle and Aunt Wright, who had been staying at Sidmouth and Jersey, came to see us on their way home. Aunt Wright was taken ill, and in consequence their visit lasted seven weeks. Uncle Wright was returning home full of joy and peace, in the blessed realisation of salvation through Christ's atonement; he was always full of praise and persuasion, and from that time he began that earnest, Christian, and beneficent life which he consistently maintained till the end. His simple, uncompromising, courageous faith helped to develop all his fine qualities—his high-principled morality, his generosity and kindness of heart, and his admirable common-sense. He had little imagination, and sometimes failed to see all the bearings that a subject might properly admit of; but his thoughts and plans always stood four-square, with justice and truth at the foundation. He was always the friend of the poor, a most kind son and brother; liberal in all directions, at the same time most conscientious and self-denying in all his own expenses. I often wish something could be written which would do justice to his fine character and that of his excellent wife. You none of you knew Aunt Wright, but I am sure you have never heard her mentioned without love and admiration. She was a woman of unusual endowments. Without ever having any regular school education, she and her sisters, with the help of their widowed mother, so diligently availed themselves of every opportunity and circumstance of advantage, that they were always considered women of cultivated minds, especially Aunt Wright. Having no children of her own, she had more leisure to devote to study, especially of natural sciences; and being an enthusiast herself, she communicated her animation and delight to groups of children who would gather round her, attracted and entranced by her charming manner. She was one of the least self-conscious, the least self-seeking, most artless and charming of women I have ever met with. Guileless herself to a degree, she never suspected guile in others. This very guilelessness, however, prevented her having a quick perception and understanding of humankind at large; she always intended what was kind and amiable herself, and gave others credit for the same disposition. She was a great favourite in society. In the near neighbourhood of Buxton, a party was scarcely complete without her; she always went out with the thought of giving pleasure—only to gain herself by giving. She was not at all handsome, but she had a very animated and intelligent countenance. She had fine grey eyes, with black eyelashes, eyebrows, and hair. She was tall, and when becomingly dressed had a picturesque appearance; she had a full voice, and a very pleasant one. She could always chain the attention of the rough boys at the Reformatory when she addressed them, as she often did—no speaker was listened to by them with so much attention and affection. She had a beaming, pleasant smile for every child and young person; her delight was with the young; she was so young herself, in her unaffected, cheerful sympathy. I wish you could have seen her and known her; you would have loved her. My father and mother were very fond of her; the difference of their position, which in many cases would have had a contrary effect, only served to show out the intrinsic excellence of the characters on both sides—the parents in the cottage

E

in comparative poverty, and the son and daughter in the large house, with all its fitting appointments—no jars or jealousy ever arose. John was proud of his father; he loved him, and he loved his mother, and the sound of his step was always music to their ears. There was much that was very touching in this position, better known to those who lived there than to me, who was only an occasional visitor; it brought out beautiful traits of character all the way round.

I must now go back to the time when your uncle and aunt stopped seven weeks at Palatine Cottage. It was a time of deep interest to me personally. I had for a long time been very unsettled in my religious views. The Friends' preaching at this time rarely entered upon doctrine, and was for the most part *silent* on Justification by Faith. I had not at all apprehended this doctrine; on the contrary, I had almost entirely adopted Unitarian views, through reading the works of Channing, the admirable American preacher and writer. It was this doctrine of Justification through Christ which had now become Uncle Wright's stronghold—the one on which he daily expatiated, rather to my annoyance; but I saw it had given him a happiness which I was very conscious I did not possess—he had rest, peace, and joy overflowing. After they left us, I set myself to read the New Testament more critically than I had ever done before, with earnest prayer that I might know the exact truth which it was God's mind to impart through His

Word. I laid aside Channing, and read day after day and month after month, and I saw verbally the truth of Christ's full atonement; but it was long before I believed it to the salvation of my soul. The very reasonable and attractive views of the Unitarians were difficult to escape from; but through God's exceeding mercy I did make a clean escape.

At this time many Friends were feeling that this doctrine of Justification by Faith was not held with sufficient clearness by the Society generally, and certainly was not preached. A little book of Isaac Crewdson's, of Manchester, called "The Beacon," brought the subject prominently forward, and very many members left the Society. The number in Manchester was considerable. For a short time they formed a little company and met together for worship; but the larger number united in worship with other Christians, and some kept unattached, feeling that the true bond was in Christ the Head. The subject of sound doctrine was thus brought prominently before the Society at large, the views of many who remained were much changed, and the ministry also, as well as their published works. In a Society so peaceful and exemplary as the Friends, this division was exceedingly painful. It was at this time I left the Society. It appeared to me then that the confession of Christ by Baptism, and of His death for us and His coming again as expressed in the Communion service, was binding upon Christians, and

I feared to neglect what I saw to be a duty laid upon me. This involved (at that time) dismissal or withdrawal from the Society of Friends. Your dear grandfather preferred my withdrawing to being dismissed. I sent in my resignation to the monthly meeting at Gracechurch Street, of which Stoke Newington was a part, and then I ceased being a Friend in *name*. It would be difficult to express to you the exceeding pain which this severance cost me. Thinking and feeling as I did then, I could not conscientiously have done otherwise, but it was distressing in so very many ways, that if the Lord had not given me abundance of peace, I could not have gone through with it. It was heart-breaking work not going with dear grandfather to Meeting. I wished to have gone to the Friends' Meeting one part of the day, and to church or chapel on the other, but he did not approve of this. Philip continued to go with his father, and dear Anna, being lame, could seldom go anywhere. Oh, I was very lonely—almost all my friends and acquaintances were Friends, and there was, as might be supposed, much misjudging. Some thought I wanted more liberty, and that I was impatient of the little distinctive peculiarities of Friends, and I wished to get rid of the Quaker bonnet. So far from this, it was quite a trial for me to give it up; for I thought then, and think still, that the Friends' dress is the prettiest a woman can wear.

Several families of Friends with whom we were

acquainted left the Society of Friends about the same time; so did your Uncle and Aunt Wright and your aunts; but we were far apart, and each had to be led in a way and by a Wisdom higher than their own. Your dear grandfather was exceedingly kind and patient. He was not led to take the same views which I had had pressed upon me, and he remained a Friend to the end of his days. Never bigoted or pronouncing harsh judgment on others, his spirit was truly catholic and charitable. But with all this, my experience leads me to say that not to be fully united in external practical religion is a matter, if possible, to be avoided in domestic life. I made many mistakes through ignorance, which I remember with much pain.

But I must return to Palatine Cottage and its busy interests. Darling Aunt Anna and I papered the house throughout, and did a good deal of the painting. We never thought we could not do things that wanted to be done. I now often wonder at the difficult things I trusted and encouraged my children to attempt.

There came a great discouragement to our hope of swelling our income through the cows. The milkwoman turned out to be a thief; she gathered in the money and used it herself, saying that the regular customers had put off the payment of their bills. As they were all thoroughly respectable persons, and many of them Friends, I was not troubled about it; but at last the delay seemed so strange to me, I mentioned it to one of the Friends, and found that her account had always been kept close paid up. This led me to inquire of others, and I found the same story. A large sum I had been reckoning upon to make ends meet was gone. The woman in some way caught a hint of the discovery, and before we could call them to account, both husband and wife had decamped, leaving no trace behind them. Then we tried lodgers, but this proved neither pleasant nor profitable.

We were now in troubled waters; but the worst had to come. Returning from school one afternoon, a heavy shower of rain came on, and my Nannie, having no umbrella, ran home very fast. The carriage-road sloped rather steeply to the garden gate, and just as she reached the gate she fell and sprained her ankle. It was a very bad sprain. She called out, and I helped her indoors, little thinking that henceforth her dear life was to be coloured by this event—*not dis*coloured. I conclude *now* that the Blessed Lord saw that He could make a more exquisite character out of that noble, independent, courageous, capable creature by imprisoning it within the strictest limitations than by giving it the play of a full development. But oh, how often did my heart yearn over those apparently wasted faculties! how it bled to see the cramp of those crippling fetters sometimes upon one faculty, sometimes upon another, leaving her powerless to execute what she could see so clearly and do so well! Recurring again and again to the treatment of this first injury, in which many mistakes were made, how often have I unavailingly said, "Oh, if I had done *this!*" "Oh, if she had not done that!" "Oh, if the doctors had been wiser!" or, "Perhaps if we try this or that, she may be cured." And we tried everything, as far as our circumstances would allow, for I always kept alive the hope that the healing-time would come. And so the years passed on, neither of us yielding to despair—she always doing the most she could do, and doing all cheerfully. Though she is now safe in heaven, with all her work done, I can scarcely bear, even now, to recall the beginning of this life of constant frustration. But God has given her the victory. All who knew her loved her; and she has left them an example of the most persevering industry and cheerful patience. Her sufferings never made gloom or a cloud in the house. She never brooded over her loss of power, or the loss of the changes or amusements which others enjoy. Her own mind was always a storehouse of refreshment to herself; it was a rich garden, which circumstances never allowed to be fully cultivated, but it was full of thought and ready appreciation of the genius and talents of others. She was my sunshine always; there never came the slightest cloud between us. Thank God.

I must go back to our circumstances. We could not make both ends meet. The only plan we could devise was to let the home we had made so pretty and pleasant, and take a less expensive one. We could let it to an advantage of £20 a year—not much, but something. A dear friend about to be married offered to take the house; this was a great consolation, that our loss would be the gain of some one we loved, and I experienced great pleasure in fitting it up for him. We found a house at Shacklewell, a very short distance off, where we did not remain quite a year. This was to us an eventful year. I left the Society of Friends, and your grandfather decided to take the management of the London and County Joint-Stock Bank, which was to be opened at Brighton. He was considered a thorough man of business. He had seen a variety of business, was scrupulously upright and exact in everything, exceedingly industrious and persevering, and never saved himself trouble by throwing it upon others. He was most considerate to all he employed, and never made an enemy. He was so skilful in training young men in the conduct of bank business, that clerks intended for other banks were often sent to him first.

On this year I attended for the last time the yearly Meeting of Friends, which I have always considered the most unique and interesting assembly held in the country. From all the counties of England, from Scotland, Ireland, and America, came representatives bringing reports of the state of the Society from all these parts, and competent to speak upon the report if needful. All the ministers who could leave their homes attended this gathering. Those who had friends in or near London visited them. Many of the rich Friends kept open house, and invited large companies to dinner between the meetings. Mildred Court, where Elizabeth Fry presided, was very popular. A number of the ministers went there, and often spoke after dinner.

I never expect to see so pretty a sight again as the Women's Meeting at Devonshire House— perfectly unique. No colour was to be seen in it except the varying shades from white, silver grey, every gradation of dove-colour, drab, fawn, and brown, up to black, which usually was confined to the bonnet. The Friends' bonnet was almost universal; here and there might be seen a straw cottage, but it was not considered genteel. The young Friends were far from being indifferent to their dress, and as they sat in quiet rows on the forms, with their sweet, pure faces and modest demeanour, it was a lovely sight to see. The friendly, unimpassioned countenances of the elder members gave a comfortable consciousness of being safe amongst those who were and would be your friends. The yearly Meeting was a grand time for meeting acquaintances from far and near; it was quite a gala-time for the young men and women, and many parties were made up for visiting exhibitions of painting, and other London sights. The experiences of the yearly Meeting were something to talk about when they returned to their quiet homes. Friends are so generally known to each other, at least by name, that, more than any other religious assembly, it had the feeling of a great family meeting—and parting.

In the course of this particular yearly Meeting occurred the discussion to which I have before alluded, and which resulted in my leaving the Society. I felt it my duty to be baptized, and that was contrary to the principles of Friends, and I was no longer eligible as a member. To find myself suddenly cut adrift from so much that had been precious to me all my life was more painful than I can express. I was still one with Friends in almost all my views. Almost all my relatives as well as acquaintances were Friends, in whose opinion, for the most part, I had now sadly fallen. The heaviest part of the trial was changing the place of worship. I had not thought how difficult this would be. Spiritual worship was the leading idea in Friends' Meetings, and the solemn silence, broken only occasionally by solemn ministry or prayer, favoured the idea of its general reality—they were solemn assemblies. I left Friends so suddenly, I may say unexpectedly, that I had never given myself the time or trouble to search into the opinion or opinions held by other religious bodies, such a complete separation had existed in our modes of worship.

I went first to church, and did not feel at all at home. The Prayer-book was quite a puzzle, and the continual up and down was a great disturbance; the rapid transition from prayer to praise and confession was quite beyond the facility of my mind, and whilst following hard to catch the words of the service, I quite missed the spirit of the worship. One thing struck me as painfully irreverent. The children in the choir, a large number of them, were placed in full view of the congregation. These children had to go through the whole of the service in an audible voice, whilst a man with a long stick kept touching them up to their duty. This struck me as nothing better than mockery and hypocrisy, and I was greatly shocked; and I cannot say I have ever become reconciled to it, or could think it likely to promote a spiritual mind. The preaching at this church was very good, but I could not get at home with the form of worship. I longed for silence, and to *mean* what I said.

I thought I would try whether an Independent chapel would suit me better. Robert Philip, the minister, had written several useful little books, which your Uncle Wright very much approved. Here I had much more peace than at the church, and the extempore prayer and teaching seemed like bringing me back somewhat to the old times again; but the rest there did not continue long. I was seeking spiritual food, and I found high Calvinistic doctrine, stern dogmatism, and, it seemed to me, little spirituality. By degrees I felt a good deal discouraged by my want of success, still fully believing that what I wanted would certainly be found. Philip went to Meeting with his father. Anna sometimes, when she was able, went with me. She never liked silent meetings; she chafed against them as purposeless.

The time was getting near for going to Brighton. The winter of [   ] was extremely cold.

Here the pen was laid down, and not again taken up, and the dear grandmother's letter to her beloved grandchildren remains unfinished.

CHAPTER I.

LIFE AT BRIGHTON.

> "Little else is so worthy of study as the incidents in the development of a soul."—BROWNING.

IN the foregoing "little Memoriam" we see how

> "Close comprest
> The Present holds the Future."

The spirit of the child was in the father who pulled up a boulder to plant a seed, that he might see one cornstalk growing among the lifeless walls and paving-stones. Not less clearly may be traced, in Mrs. Sewell's life and writings, the stern, uncompromising morality of "Grandfather Holmes." The same hand which could draw such pretty pictures of the happiness of goodness in all creatures,—boys and girls and birds,—drew, without flinching, "sorrow dogging sin." It is rather striking that one so full of intense sympathy with the erring and fallen could be so merciless, not only on cruelty and oppression, but on easy, slippery faults—laziness, bad work, wastefulness, and every sort of giddy way that tends to break the hedge of modesty and reverence. As child, wife, and mother, the writer had drunk so deep herself of pure home joys, there were no words strong enough to express her indignation against whatever tainted and destroyed them. In these days, when the voice of sympathy is sometimes too apt to drown the voice of warning, a good many of her verses give us cause to say, "Thank God for Grandfather Holmes."

A young friend writes :—

"I remember Mrs. Sewell's pulling me up sharply for advocating forgiveness of a personal injury which involved cruelty to an animal. '*Forgive* him!' she said. 'I'd have roused the town against him.' She was very conscious of her own tendency to speak sometimes more strongly than she intended, whether in criticism or rebuke, and had a kind of despairing admiration for those who could keep the iron hand in a velvet glove,—'So different from me,' she would say; but her strong words reminded one of what Miss —— says of her father: 'His open, hasty rebukes did not put me out nearly as much as some of dear mother's attempts to restore us in the spirit of meekness.' She has been very plain-spoken in her criticism both of me and of my work, but I cannot remember a word that rankled; one felt so entirely that she only cared to make both work and character as perfect as could be. She would not allow that any of my faults were necessary infirmities; they were to be stamped out. When those firm lips were closed for ever, my deepest sense of personal loss came with the thought that no one else would ever be as willing to hurt me for my good."

Her own narrative leaves nothing more to be said of her inheritance from her father. The tones of her voice come back to us again as she would say, "I never see anything very good and beautiful without thinking of my dear father; he lives in my mind with everything of the highest and the best." Once she said, "I have kept all my life the feeling in my mind that his love for me has outlived death. In times of spiritual darkness, or in great calamities, there have been moments when I have felt his hand placed tenderly on my head again—not so much in any way of deliverance, but as if to say, 'I am walking with thee through this valley.' Oh, how all this has helped me to understand the Fatherhood of God! He is 'very pitiful and of tender mercy,' and so was my dear father."

Perhaps no period of Mrs. Sewell's life was more trying to her than the two years spent in London. She little dreamed what was to result from this residence

> "Amongst the narrow courts and lanes
> Where toiling people poorly dwell."

In "Thy Poor Brother" she writes:—"I was a young married woman then, and had come to live in London—in the very heart of the great city. I was taking my first lessons in fog, dirt, noise, and distraction. Till then I had lived in the country, and loved it with the ardent love of childhood and youth. I was a most rebellious scholar. I loathed and hated the place, and I was nearly a stranger in it. I thought it would be impossible for me to bring up my little girl among black houses and dirty streets, with never a flower for her little hand to gather, nor a bird's song for her to hear. I used to sit and look over the roofs of the opposite houses at the floating clouds and bits of blue sky, and cry like a child. Great London was to me like a huge cage with iron bars—so did I torment myself, and was almost wickedly discontented with my lot."

Only a very few years before her death, when speaking of this period, she said, " There is nothing in my life which I look back upon with so much regret as the time I have wasted in wishing things different from what they were."

We had been speaking on the previous evening of the epitaph Theodore Monod said he would choose for his tombstone : " Here endeth the first lesson." Mrs. Sewell said, " I have been thinking of this almost ever since. The lessons of life come to an end, whether we have learnt them or not, and I can't help thinking it may be a lasting loss to us to have grumbled over our lessons instead of learning them. I *was* rebellious at having to live in that dingy place in London. I only existed on the hope of its coming to an end, and yet I am sure I should never have understood the poor and been able to help them as I have done, if I had not had that experience. The depths I was taken down to during these two years taught me more than any number of years of looking on. And yet how I hated it! I blotted my lesson-book with my tears."

" I wonder," she added, "if the love which puts

away our sins also does away with their evil consequences, or must our second lesson suffer loss, because the first was so imperfectly learnt?"

I have always thought that one of the sweetest lessons to be learned from my dear friend was her indifference to wealth as an adjunct of refinement; it was not necessary to it in her eyes. She could exceedingly enjoy the sight of things superb and rich, and there was no period of her life when she would not have liked to have had more money to give; but had it been her lot to have no more than a hundred a year to spend, she would have managed, with the most simple and inexpensive materials, to have given to her surroundings as true an air of refinement as if she had been living on ten times that income. I have heard her say, "In my days of poverty, one of my great pleasures was that I had to do the waiting on friends who came myself; it seemed a sweet addition to the welcome of words, to add the deeds. 'By love *serve* one another,' is like other things the Bible tells us to do, just something to add to our happiness."

And again, "I shrink more than I can express from the thought of abject poverty; it seems to me like having to live in a vault instead of under the sky; but to be deprived of the power of surrounding ourselves with luxury need be no calamity at all; indeed I often think whether our well-paid working friends (and there are still many of this class) who know how to make a right use of their means, might not really be reckoned among the happiest of people—wealth brings with it so many cares which they are exempt from." Or again, "That good and perfect life once lived on earth, always healing, always blessing, had *no* luxury in it. . . . How well our earthly life must have been understood by whoever it was who offered that prayer, 'Give me neither poverty nor riches'! My unspeakable hatred to our liquor laws, and all that pertains to strong drink, is, that drink has done so much to fill our country with these two extremes—on one hand, the vulgar pride of wealth, and on the other, the most abject, degrading, soul-destroying poverty."

To each, perhaps, Jane Taylor's lines may apply :—

> "Such is his household, such, perchance, that he
> Would blush to ask the Apostle Paul to tea."

A young friend who visited Mrs. Sewell in her latest years has sent me a few interesting reminiscences of conversations with her, taken partly from notes made at the time. The following refer to parts of her life included in the Autobiography :—

"We were talking one day of conversion, and of those blessed children who seem never to require it, and Mrs. Sewell told me of her own first conscious sense of the touch of the Almighty. It was on a calm, still summer evening: she was a little child, standing on a broad, flat stone which made the step to her father's front door. The sky above was full of the sunset glow, and a great tree on the grass plat stood out solemnly against it. 'And it seemed as if all the beauty and the stillness flowed into my little heart and filled it,' she said, 'and I felt God there.'

"From that time she knew Him as her Father in creation, though many years passed before she learned to take the place of a child redeemed. The great joy of this later lesson carried her through the heavy trial which followed soon afterwards, when she felt it her duty to leave the Friends. I cannot remember the little series of circumstances—rather striking ones, I think—which gave her an opportunity of speaking in confidence to Benjamin Wills Newton, whom she had heard preach: he was then taking the place of a pastor in the neighbourhood who was absent. She told him her convictions, and he felt no doubt that it was her duty to act upon them.

"'But I do not know where to go,' she said, 'and I have no one to be with me.'

"She felt it right to be baptized by immersion. There was a baptistery, I think at the chapel where Mr. Newton was then preaching, and he said, 'I would baptize you, and my wife could be with you, if you liked.'

"All that remained now was to ask her husband's consent. He was often late home: he was very late that night. Mrs. Sewell would not begin the subject till he had had his supper, and she felt it would be impossible to sit by him with this upon her mind unuttered; she left all ready, and went up to her room, where she sat in the dark, listening for him. Ten o'clock passed; at last he came. She heard him go into the room where his supper was laid: presently he came upstairs. It was dark, but he knew by the first sound of her voice that something had happened, and asked, 'What's the matter?'

"She said, 'Let us kneel down together beside the bed, and I will tell thee.'

"They knelt down side by side. In telling of it she said, with streaming tears, 'His kindness to me I shall *never* forget.'

"The step was taken, and thenceforward Mrs. Sewell had no outward home on earth, in spiritual things: she never gave her heart to any other denomination. 'If I ever joined any religious body again,' she said, in her old age, 'it would be the Friends—though I've left them.' She thought no other system of government comparable to theirs. I was so ignorant as to ask whether that of the best type of Plymouth Brethren resembled it. She was indignant, and eagerly described the balance of liberty and control, the elastic, self-acting machinery, simple and yet so complete, which regulates the life of the Society. She believed that she owed much to individual Brethren, but their system was not to her mind."

Many years afterwards, in speaking of the time of her baptism, Mrs. Sewell said, "I never read those verses in Matthew about the baptism of Christ without remembering the great happiness I had then. I think I may truly say that I was influenced, as He was, by the wish to 'fulfil all righteousness.' I dreaded lest by any disobedience I should miss the *fulness* of the blessing. And when it was done, I shall never forget the peace that followed. The heavens were opened to me as never before, and the Spirit of God filled my heart with indescribable joy."

Among the letters of her old age is the following:—

"More than forty years since, when my chains were all broken, and I became enamoured of Christ's beauty, desiring above all things to retain the joy of His presence, this text was impressed on my mind, and the impression has continually grown deeper, 'If ye keep my commandments ye shall abide in my love, even as I have kept my Father's commandments and abide in His love.' I immediately took the Testament and began to write down all the commandments and precepts I could find. But I quickly saw that these were not so much to be learnt by heart— they must be *in* the heart, shewn by daily obedient practice, whilst living among my fellow-creatures and amidst all the various surroundings of my life—not drawing me away from life and duty into selfish isolation—not seeking crosses for myself, but taking up those that came in the way.

"I have often felt it a great advantage to have been brought up as a Friend or Quaker. I believe practically in the quickening, teaching, guiding power of the abiding Spirit. When, added to this, the Word of God has been diligently hidden in the heart and memory, He will act both upon the will and the understanding, making them alike quick in the fear of the Lord."

Before passing on to the next period of Mrs. Sewell's life, I will copy extracts from old faded papers, looking as if they had not seen the light for many a long day, which form an amusing comment on the eulogistic account of her children written for her grandchildren's benefit. The papers are headed either "Anna Sewell's Birthday" (with date), or "Philip Sewell's Birthday." Two passages will serve as specimens of the rest.

"12 PARK ROAD, 30*th of* 3*rd month*, 1829.

"Anna Sewell has this day completed her ninth year, and is in many respects a delight and comfort to her mother, who, that she may be able to test her progress from year to year, wishes now to write a short account of her attainments in her learning, and of the qualities of her mind, &c." [Then follow entire approbation of her truth and candour, and her progress in some branches of learning. But the mother, with her intense love, has withal a high standard of perfection, not easily satisfied. She goes on to speak of Anna's want of persevering industry.] "Much disposed to idle over lessons and work. She needs to get the habit of a cheerful surrender of her own will—to give up entirely telling tales of her brother. She begins to be useful to her mother, but is not tidy. In *everything* her mother hopes she will be improved by another year."

Of Philip, she says :—

"More persevering in play than in work: he has an awkward habit of repeating what other people say; can neither sit nor stand still; takes no pains to speak distinctly. Altogether he is a nice little boy, and his mother hopes by this day twelvemonths he will have lost all his bad habits, and increased his good ones."

I looked on to the next year's papers with some curiosity, to see if the mother's wishes were realised. Instead of improvement, the faults and failings recorded are more numerous than before. Far from being blind to her children's faults, she was keenly alive to them. Her desires for her children were such that nothing short of the highest and the best could satisfy her motherly ambition.

Removal to Brighton in 1835 brought new and varied interests. Anna's lameness continued, and one of the remedies tried proved worse than the disease : while on a visit away from home, she fell into the hands of a doctor who bled her severely. To this draining-away of life, her mother attributed the many disablements which afflicted her—fluctuating while youth was strong, with intervals of "better" as well as "worse," but as time went on, gradually multiplying and increasing till, one after another, her loved employments had to be laid aside. In the Brighton days, however, she must have had, at times, some considerable amount of walking power, as in a journal written there in 1844 she speaks of pleasant walks with her friends, visits to London to see picture-galleries, and other things which imply a measure of activity. The brother and sister grew from childhood into youth, and the mother felt her own interest in life continually expand with theirs. One source of profit and enjoyment to them all, which Mrs. Sewell would often gratefully refer to, was the ministry of the Rev. C. Maitland, a clergyman of the Church of England. He was truly a pastor as well as a preacher, and watched over these members of his flock, although they never definitely entered its fold, Philip continuing his father's faithful companion at Meeting on First-day.

As the young people developed, they made friends of their own, and each one of these had an individual place in the mother's mind or heart, and opened new vistas of interest. She would often speak of the delight brought into her life by her son's long friendship with Henry S. King (connected with the firm of Smith, Elder, & Co.), who eventually married the lady known to the world as the author of "The Disciples." He was a very intimate friend of Robertson, and inspired Mrs. Sewell with his own ardent admiration for his friend's character, but I do not think she ever attended Robertson's church.

The restless, beautiful sea never made up to Mrs. Sewell for the loss of fields and flowers. "It was all dead in Brighton, houses and stones," she said, and her husband would sometimes make time to go with her by rail to some country place where they could feast their eyes on copse and stream. In the sketch prefixed to the collected poems, my daughter mentions one of these little excursions when they lost their way in a wood. They had passed a woodman some time before, and Mr. Sewell went to try and find him, to inquire the way. While he was gone, his wife came upon a bank of wood-sorrel, the slender flowers trembling in the soft air. "It was *so beautiful*," she said, "I stood before it, and could scarcely help praying that Isaac mightn't find the man, that we might be lost, and have to stay there all day long and look at it."

All through her long life it was her custom to be out before breakfast, listening to those "morning hymns"

"Which people might hear, if they would but arise
When little birds first tune their notes to the skies."

The cry of the sea-gull was a poor exchange, she thought, but the following passage from "Thy Poor Brother" shows that she kept up the practice:—

"Many years ago, when we lived in B——, it was my habit to take an early morning walk upon the end of the chain-pier, and at that time I was commonly the only occupant, and had the lessons of the winds and the waves all to myself. One morning, I especially remember, I had risen earlier than usual, for I had many troubles on my mind, and I wanted to be alone. A thick gloom was spread over the whole face of nature ; the wind was wild and cold, the sky a leaden grey, and the sea rolled its heavy, discoloured waves with an angry growl upon the shore; the jarring creak of the chains beneath the pier, and the cold dash of waves round the buttresses, were all in harmony with each other, and in harmony with my oppressed spirit. Nothing spoke of hope; all spoke of discouragement, and my thoughts grew heavier, and my heart sank lower; but whilst I turned and returned upon my path, I observed a large flock of wild ducks leaving the land; and regardless of frowning sky, stormy wind, and surging sea, without chart or compass to direct them on their untrodden way, with the wind directly ahead, they boldly steered off for the land to which faith or instinct drew them. I watched them with intense interest, as, in a compact squadron, their wings cleft the air; presently, I observed one of them lagging behind—further and further behind—it must have been a feeble one—further and further—and then I saw it suddenly fall to the surface of the waters. 'Oh!' I exclaimed, 'it will be left behind, it will never overtake those strong flyers.' Presently, however, I observed it, flying along, just above the crest of the billows, and there, out of the force of the wind, it made rapid progress. Again I lost it. Had it given up the journey? No! I discerned it again far ahead, and soon, it rose into the air, and, as if invigorated by its lowly solitary travel, it darted forward with increased speed, and gained rapidly upon its disappearing companions; and though I did not see it overtake them, I felt sure that it would do so. I turned my steps homeward my faith confirmed, that He who guided these trustful voyagers across the billows to their haven of rest, would assuredly guide His children across the rough billows of their life's journey, and not suffer the feeblest amongst them to fail, or be overwhelmed."

We have no clue to the nature of the troubles which made the writer feel the need of that lesson just then—whether they belonged to the natural course of chequered life, or were part of the cross she bore for others, or arose in the inner life; but she has left some record of sorrows there, belonging to this period.

"We came into a world of very varied interest at Brighton," she once said, "and I was not as quick as I might have been, to see that all is not gold that glitters. I am afraid I wasted a good deal of my time on people and theories that gave me nothing worth having in return."

I told her a story which I had heard from a lady addressing a Mothers' Meeting. In a certain town, some placards appeared on the walls, announcing a Socialist lecture, which, it was said, would explain the absurdities of religion, and so enable people to live much happier lives. Admission, Threepence.

There was a large attendance. Among the audience was an elderly woman with a large cotton umbrella — she sat at the end of the room, and patiently heard the lecture through. Directly it was over she rose and made her way up to the platform, and without waiting for permission to speak, said (emphasising each sentence with a knock on the floor with her umbrella), "I have come up here to say I'll have my threepence back again, for I haven't got nothing in the world for it. Talk about teaching us a better way indeed, and that we can get on without God—I never heard

such nonsense talked in all my life! Why, years
agone, when I was left a widdy with four children,
it wasn't these people as come and helped me—it
was the Lord Jesus, and He have come along with
me all the way, and provided for us wonderful.
I ain't agoing to stand by and hear anything said
again' Him. No! I'll stick to my dear Lord Jesus,
and have my threepence back again."

Mrs. Sewell was much amused with this story.
"I have a great sympathy with the audience who
went to hear that lecture," she said, "I am so
ready to believe there must be something to learn
from those who profess to teach. I have been
rather given to listen to 'Lo heres' and 'Lo theres'
in my time, and pay my threepence, or whatever
it might be. And *I* have been bitterly disappointed, many times; but it never occurred
to me to have my threepence back again. I took
the loss as a punishment for my folly."

A valued friend of Mrs. Sewell's writes:—

"One of her chief characteristics was the power of
growth; she must have grown all her life. Certainly, in
the years I knew her, she was always growing. She never
lived in a groove, which saintly old ladies are apt to do,
and this power gave her a wonderful sympathy. It did
not matter to her that people were not like herself. I
think a difference was rather an attraction—she could at
once throw herself into the minds of others, ready and
eager to absorb whatever her heart and mind recognised
as admirable."

Every virtue has its attendant fault—every
power its danger, as surely as light casts a

shadow, and before this eager readiness to learn was chastened by experience, it led its possessor into some thorny paths. There came to Brighton one who professed to have received direct teaching from Heaven, and to have fresh light to impart, especially concerning the work of the Holy Spirit. Always thirsting for more light, Mrs. Sewell and Anna attended his services for a short time, expecting much, and were proportionately disappointed when the disenchantment came.

"Oh," she said, " I *have*

> 'Made idols, and have found them clay,
> And have bewailed that worship.'

Nothing makes me more sure that the good hand of my God has been upon me, than the way He has guarded me from receiving errors, just as He did that good woman with the cotton umbrella. I have come out of all these 'advanced theories,' or whatever they may be called, more heart-satisfied than ever with 'my dear Lord Jesus.' Our souls crave for living, loving sympathy, and theories *don't* give it."

In one of Carlyle's letters, he writes :—" Yesterday there came a pamphlet by some moral philosopher named Julian, which, in looking into, I find to be a hallelujah on the advent and discovery of atheism. . . . The real joy of Julian was what surprised me—sincere joy, you would have said— like the shout of a hyæna at finding that the whole universe was carrion."

For a moment we may look at the great philosopher and the tender-hearted woman as standing side by side; the first thought with each was the intense degradation to humanity involved in such a theory. If star after star must go out, till all is night, then what is there left but the profoundest sadness?

"Oh, I am so sorry for people who will shut God out," Mrs. Sewell would say, "for there is no other 'exceeding joy' left for them. It used to trouble me so, in walking the streets of London, to see so few happy-looking faces. So many people seemed to be carrying burdens too heavy for them: they looked crushed, and I wanted them to be comforted."

The following extract from a letter addressed to the editor of the *Labourer's Chronicle* probably belongs to a later period, but is inserted here as bearing on this subject. It bears no date, nor any mark to say whether it was ever printed:—

"It is a serious thing to endeavour to shake the faith of our fellow-creatures in God when we have nothing to give them in its place. I would entreat you, dear Sir, whatever your opinion may be, that you do not carelessly take away from the suffering, ignorant, perplexed people their instinctive confidence in the protecting providence and guiding hand of the great and good Father. At present we are blind, and cannot see afar off—our comfort and strength is to believe that God our Father knows all; that He is with the right and not with the wrong—with the oppressed and not with the oppressor, and that He who came to break every yoke has said, 'For the crying of the poor and the sighing of the needy, I will arise, and set him in safety from him that puffeth at him.' Let, then, our poor labourers, while using every lawful means to improve their condition and lessen their hardships, earnestly cry to God and heartily put their trust in Him. Unfair charges, bitter invectives, sweeping accusations, are dangerous two-edged weapons to use. A house divided against itself cannot stand, and whichever part falls will wreck the other in so doing."

Very often was it our dear friend's privilege to comfort those who were crushed, and perhaps at no time in her life more frequently than during her residence at Brighton. In working among the poor and sorrowful, she had the great advantage of being able immediately to secure the confidence of those she visited. She speaks in "Thy Poor Brother" of the folly of setting young lady visitors to ask questions "which only an angel or a government officer could ask without giving offence." For herself, she was seldom tempted to err in this way. No time had to be spent in soliciting confidence; it was at once poured out, freely, joyfully, gratefully, the sufferer only too thankful to get the ear of one in whom it was so pleasant to confide. Many instances of this might be given, did time and space permit. We must content ourselves with giving the narrative, told in her own simple way, of her visit to a ward in the Brighton Workhouse.

"Many years since, a young girl came to me, begging I would get her into a penitentiary. On conversing with her, I learned that she had just come out of the Workhouse, and that several other young persons of the same character were now there, who, when their health was restored, would probably return to their former sinful course of life.

"I learned from her that the ward they were in was the general receptacle for the miscellaneous cases of sin and poverty, which could not readily be classified and admitted into the other wards. It was looked upon as an ignominious place of punishment. The chaplain did not often visit it, and there were frequent cases of insubordination, which terminated in the correction of the black-hole —a little bare cell underground, not entirely dark.

"Upon hearing this relation, I applied to the chaplain for permission to visit this ward. He dissuaded me from it; he did not think it would be safe for me to do so; he hardly thought it safe for himself; he would be glad to have my help in any other part of the house where there would be some hope of doing good and being gratefully received. He gave me alarming accounts of window-smashing, of fighting and swearing in this ward, and the governor and matron fully corroborated his statements, and advised me not to adventure myself into it. But I was not discouraged; I had faith in the help of God, and believed that love would make its way all but everywhere; and I at last obtained the chaplain's consent and an offer to introduce me, which I declined.

"I went quietly up the stairs, and walked into the middle of the room. It was a large, bare, barn-like looking place, with no furniture but two rows of beds. 'Dear friends,' I said, 'I have heard that many of you are in trouble and difficulty. I have come to see if I can help or comfort any of you. I have been advised not to come; it was thought you would not receive me well; but I did not believe that.' An old woman instantly interrupted me—'Oh dear! my lady, we would not mislist you upon no account; we are very glad to see you.' 'Come, then,' I said, 'let us sit down and talk together; tell me your troubles, and let me see if I can help you.' They made a cluster round me in the centre of the room, sitting on the beds, and many a perplexed and sorrowful story did I learn from them, requiring indeed a friendly helper. After a long conversation, I read to them a portion of the Scriptures, and then they knelt down with me, whilst we prayed God to help us all, and at their earnest solicitation I promised to come again.

"I visited this place regularly once a week for a long time, and by degrees became acquainted with the individual cases of trouble. Some poor girls were assisted to go to a penitentiary. Others were prevailed on to return to their parents, or their parents to receive them. Some required to have letters written to their friends. Some wanted to have explanations made for them to the overseers in distant parishes; all wanted something, and many could be effectually helped. There was one Irish-woman who long withheld her confidence from me—her tale was too sad to be told in public. I noticed her listening always with earnest attention to what I said, and especially when I read and explained the Scriptures—then she would sit and rock herself to and fro. At last she drew me away into a corner of the room, and told me she was a Roman Catholic; that she had been a widow some months; that her poor husband's soul was in purgatory, and she had no money to give to the priest to get it out—this evidently preyed upon her mind. Her only child, a boy, was now in prison, having been led into crime by a band of young thieves. Her intense love and commiseration for this poor entrapped boy were most touching—she was truly a widow and desolate. She had no parish from which she could claim relief, and she would not return to Ireland till her boy was dismissed from prison. She had been a servant, and thought she could take a cook's place with a little more instruction. Perhaps you will think me rash, but this poor destitute mother threw herself upon my sympathy, and I could not leave her there. I knew there was help stored away for the widow, which some one might be privileged to render; and as I was changing my cook, I gained permission to take her home with me, and not being a bad cook myself, I determined to instruct her; and never was a more apt or grateful scholar. When her boy came out of prison, some kind friends obtained a service for him on board a ship, as he wished to go to sea; and I found a place for her as cook in a clergyman's family. I had every reason to believe that she became a sincere Christian.

"I visited all the wards in the Workhouse afterwards, but my deepest interest lay in the bad one. More than once have I sat upon the floor with a culprit in the black-hole, and found penitence more apt to follow upon kindness than upon correction."

CHAPTER II.

THOUGHTS ON EDUCATION.

"Often have sensitive natures been withered, often have fine intellects been stunted, because a well-meaning and ambitious teacher has never tried to understand how much a child's heart can feel, and how little a child's brain can bear."—MRS. PENNEFATHER.

IN 1845 the Sewell family left Brighton, but Mr. Sewell continued to go there daily from the new home at Lancing, about ten miles off. A pony-chaise was now a necessary part of the household stuff, and Anna unconsciously studied for "Black Beauty" in driving her father to and from the Shoreham station. Brighton was still the centre of interest outside the home, although distance made it impossible to keep up the work formerly done there. In looking back, Mrs. Sewell used to include what happened at Lancing in her recollections of "Brighton days."

In 1846 she went to Germany with her son and daughter, accompanied by her youngest sister. Anna remained behind for a time. On their return Miss Wright had a very severe illness at Brussels, so that the pleasure-trip ended sadly.

The reminiscences before quoted say :—

"The times which Mrs. Sewell seemed to look back on as the very brightest in her whole life, were the evenings when her son and daughter, and her future daughter-in-law, sang together. I believe it was the only time in her life when she had her fill of music, and she used to speak of the happiness of those evenings as something so heavenly, the like of it could never come again. The only descriptive word I remember her using of her son's wife, in looks or mind or voice, was 'lovely.' 'Sarah was *very* lovely.' After Mr. Philip's marriage, Mrs. Sewell and her daughter were more than ever all the world to each other as companions. Mr. Sewell was away all day, and though he sympathised in all their works of kindness, I do not think he cared much for the books they read. I have sometimes wondered how much his downright, matter-of-fact view of things had to do with the intensely practical turn of some of Mrs. Sewell's poetry. But he must have been an example of acting on Sir Arthur Helps' maxim that 'a domestic ruler should not attempt to regulate the pleasures of others by his own tastes.' I once quoted some observation about the selfishness of *mankind*, and said it did not agree with my experience. 'Nor with mine,' Mrs. Sewell said. 'I have known great unselfishness in men;' and after a pause, she added, 'Isaac was very unselfish,' and told me touching little instances of his self-denial."

Mr. Philip Sewell's marriage took place in 1849, and in the same year his father removed from Lancing to Hayward's Heath. The next move was to Grayling Wells, near Chichester, in 1853. Very little record remains of this time. In 1850 Mr. P. Sewell undertook important engineering work in Spain, and went to live there with his family. The following year brought a sorer parting—Mrs. Sewell lost her beloved and honoured father. She has told us what he was to her. One cannot but think she had him in her mind when she wrote "The Funeral Bell—A Lament for Adam Hope."

"Alas for the village! alas for the day!
  The church bell is tolling a funeral knell,
Adam Hope from the parish is taken away,
  And a sorrowful sound has the funeral bell.

"Oh! toll for him—toll for him, funeral bell!
  Fall sad on the heart, as you fall on the ear;
Good neighbour, good master, good Christian—farewell!
  Good husband, good father—in glory appear!

"Oh! what will become of the destitute poor?
  He was eyes to the blind, he was feet to the lame!
To the fatherless orphans he open'd his door,
  And the widow's heart sang at the sound of his name.

"He put down oppression, he righted the wrong,
  The cause of the helpless he made it his own;
He wrested the weak from the grasp of the strong;
  His conduct was led by his conscience alone.

. . . . . .

"Good measure pressed down to his bosom return'd,
  Well shaken, o'erflowing, till room there was none;
Whilst brighter and brighter his light ever burn'd,
  Then sank like the glow of the evening sun,

"To rise where the faithful, apparell'd in white,
  Stand round by the throne of their Saviour and King,
To work in His service with growing delight,
  Whilst the waves of eternity circle and sing.

"But toll for him—toll for him, funeral bell!
  Fall sad on the heart, as you fall on the ear;
Good neighbour, good master, good Christian—farewell!
  Good husband, good father, in glory appear!"

Mrs. Sewell was conscious that, next to the

work of the Spirit in her heart, her father's influence over her was the strongest motive-power of her life. "Oh, what a thing it is," she said, "to have looked back, all one's life, on parents whose walk was *perfect!*" To have the Invisible reflected in the visible is just what the mind of a child needs, and can grasp. As time goes on, and the growing spirit demands to "see greater things than these," the transition from the earthly parent to the Heavenly is easy and natural—it is the expansion incident to steady growth.

In one of her letters to District Visitors, Mrs. Sewell says:—

"The metal of a child's character must be formed early. The soul must be trained to govern the body, and not to be its slave. A noble life of truth, humanity, and reverence should be lived before him, and its influence will fall upon the ductile nature that is gathering in its character, and moulding itself after the pattern of its surroundings."

After commenting upon the fact that gardeners expend much more judicious care upon their plants that many parents do upon their young children, she goes on to say:—

"I think I hear you say, 'But our little human plants are not like those in the conservatory; they have the taint and root of sin in them.' They have, dear friend; therefore the more need of care to check its development, and to nourish the heavenly affinities of the soul by keeping them constantly under the influence of the waiting Spirit, ever, I believe, watching to draw little ones into the ways of love and peace."

The following letter from a clergyman in Devonshire is a specimen of many which have come to hand, addressed to Mrs. Sewell by persons in various positions of life, entreating her to put her thoughts on education into some form fitted for general circulation :—

"... I am glad that poetry has not had your undivided attention, and now that you have engaged in prose writing, I do trust you will seriously think of a work I have mentioned to you before, as being one in which you would do much good. If you will only tell us how to bring up our little ones, you would benefit both rich and poor, and I know one household where your advice would be followed very strictly. I am sure it is a most important question, and one which the present age does not work out very satisfactorily. Some suggestions that have come from you are carried out in my own household, and I for one shall feel truly grateful if you will give the world the benefit of your thought and experience."

This letter, and the others referred to, of course belong to the period when Mrs. Sewell had become known as a writer, but it is quoted here because it was while at Chichester that she seems first to have expressed her thoughts on education connectedly, in a series of letters written at the earnest request of a friend who visited her there, and was herself the mother of a little boy and girl. One of these children has still a vivid recollection of the old-fashioned country house at Grayling Wells, standing in its large garden, where bulrushes grew in the pond, and there was a crab-apple tree laden with bright-cheeked fruit. Besides these letters, kindly placed at my disposal, I find an undated manuscript, written apparently with some idea of publication, but unfinished, and evidently unrevised.

I have thought it might best meet the wishes of those who desire to be made acquainted with the plans of this successful teacher, if I copy as I find them portions from this paper and the letters mentioned above, as well as recollections of different conversations on the same subject. The effect produced in this way must unavoidably be somewhat desultory, and may perhaps remind us of a string of beads, threaded by a child without reference to size, colour, or shape. Still they will be all *beads*—the genuine thing.

I fear it may be impossible entirely to avoid repetition. Some of her favourite thoughts on education were often repeated, but illustrated and enforced in different ways. Always to attempt to separate the new from the old would require an amount of editorial interference prejudicial to the individuality of the writer.

"All who have had to do with little children know how wearing it is to the temper of mother or nurse to have to listen to children's drawling exclamations and questions—'What shall I do?' 'I don't know what to play at.' 'Give me this or that,' &c. It is a great point of wisdom so to arrange the periods of the day that this weary time never comes: for this purpose, habitual regularity is invaluable. At stated times the child should be set up at the table to amuse itself quietly, without any assistance except being furnished with its amusements for the time, and these should generally be the same. Children should not be accustomed to too much variety; they do not need it, and it is a waste of our resources. A child will amuse itself for a very long time in stringing beads, putting different kinds of seeds or beads into different divisions of a box, drawing, cutting, &c., &c. There should be a degree of perfectness, and even something approaching to business habits, encouraged and expected, even in these little amusements, to give a worth and interest to them. Perfect play is the anticipation of perfect work. Habitual restraint and self-dependence for an hour once or twice in the day will be invaluable as habits for the child, and a great relief for the parent.

"It is surprising how soon a little child will accommodate itself to, and expect a routine, if it be invincibly regular. When the clock strikes, let the child be laid down in his bed, or set up at the table; when it strikes again, let him get up. It is irregularity and uncertainty that fret a child and put his obedience to the test, and bring the will of the parent and child into collision. It is more humane to make obedience a virtue through habit than through trial. Let every good thing that admits of it be easily and pleasantly acquired. A child will inevitably have its little trials, springing out of its conditions and suited to its strength; no need for parents to devise plans for exercising self-denial. Obedience that flows as it were naturally out of regularity and habit should satisfy them.[1]

"In the faith that evident spiritual conversion of heart belongs only to God, we are apt to give up human nature

---

[1] "When the colt has been taught to let you mount him, take a few turns round the yard or shed, and then get off his back and lead him, or drive him with the reins, a mile away from home, and then get on him and ride him home at a walking pace. Be sure that you do not at first attempt to ride him away from his home, his stable, his company, or any strong attraction, as it may lead to a fight in which you may not be master. If such a fight is carefully avoided at first, it will not take place after he has learned thoroughly to understand all your signals, and acquired, as he soon will, the impression that he must obey them."—"Our Horses," by Alfred Saunders: Sampson Low & Co.

altogether, and because the direct power of conversion is not in our own hands, to neglect and despise the great work with which we are entrusted—the building of a beautiful natural temple which the Blessed Master may irradiate with His own light, and invest with His own life, at whatever time He may please to enter and appropriate to Himself that which has been dedicated with faith and prayer."

This subject is continued best in the following letter :—

"The first thing to teach a little child is that he has a Father in heaven who loves him and wishes him to be as happy as he can be—as happy as the little birds that sing and fly about; as merry as the lambs that frolic with one another, and eat the grass that has grown for them, and lie down in safety by their mother's side.

"Do not too early impress upon the mind of a little child that he is a sinner; let him discover this by his own experience. When he has done wrong, let the natural consequences of wrong-doing fall upon him. Do not shield him from the consequences of ignorance or disobedience; let them fall with their full weight, but let them be the only penalties. Let him distinctly feel in himself the difference between obedience and disobedience. Cultivate a quick and tender conscience. Require prompt obedience. Refer constantly to the happiness and obedience of the insect and animal world.

"Do not let the atonement for sin through the sacrifice of our adorable Saviour be presented early to a child—he is not at first able to conceive of the malignity of sin, which made the extremity of sacrifice needful. Presenting it to him when it is impossible for him to feel it properly, can hardly act otherwise than to make both sin and sacrifice appear light matters. God begins in His first teaching to the human race with the law. By the law is the knowledge of sin. We must begin as He begins. Never think to lower the standard of the law by way of bringing it nearer the capacity of the child. The law is God's appointed schoolmaster to bring us to Christ. It is through

'The broken vow, the frequent fall,'

we learn our need of the righteousness of Another.

"Self-denial, the milder form of sacrifice, may be touchingly and effectively taught, by various examples from the animal world, by facts and anecdotes, and whenever possible, from living human example. Let the Bible be always at hand, also books of natural history with good pictures. Both from God's Word and His works let the truth be ever impressing itself on the mind of the child, that every living thing around him belongs to the great family of God, and that He watches over all. Gradually let him understand his responsibility for the power he possesses, in God's creation, for making happiness or misery, and that all cruelty or injury inflicted is displeasing to Him who made His creatures to be happy, and who has provided for their being so.

"Let punishment as much as possible be felt to be the natural consequence of misconduct. If a child soils himself unnecessarily, let him be excluded from the clean party.

"Chastisement should aim at the same end at which our Heavenly Father aims—to make His children humble and grateful."

To return to the MS.—the part which follows relates chiefly to the cultivation of the mind in the earliest years.

"I should be very glad to see the art of drawing from nature more systematically and thoroughly carried out in the education of young girls. I have often thought if half the time were given to that which is now all but exclusively devoted to music, it would prove, if not a more valuable acquisition, at any rate to the full as valuable—I think far more valuable to those who are

THOUGHTS ON EDUCATION.

likely to have the care of children, which all may expect in some way. A lady who has a free use of her pencil, and able to make a ready sketch of any living thing she sees, is sure to attract a group of delighted children round her. Scarcely anything pleases children so much as to see graphic sketches of men and animals growing under the pencil of a lively artist. I admire pictures that are painted and framed and hung on walls, but far, far before these the constant lively succession of dogs, cats, horses, birds, beetles, frogs, &c., &c., that follow one another on a slate with a company of animated, rejoicing little artists round it. A mother who has this facility would have her slate with pencil and sponge attached to it as constantly on the table as her workbox. I will just give a little practical sketch of its use. A little boy—we will say about four years old, runs from the garden to his mother.

"'Oh! mother, do come and look at this beautiful thing on the rose-tree. I want to know what it is.'

"'I am busy now, Charles. Tell me what it is like. What colour is it?'

"'Oh I think it is red.'

"'Oh I suppose it is a ladybird.'

"'Oh no, it is a great deal bigger than a ladybird.'

"'Well, perhaps it is a tiger-moth, that has two red wings. Look—like this,' and the mother slightly sketches the tiger-moth on the slate.

"'Oh no, it is not at all like that.'

"'Is it this colour?'

"'No, it is not so red as that.'

"'Perhaps it is the colour of this mahogany chair?'

"'No, not just like that.'

"'Perhaps like this nut?'

"'Yes, it is very much like that.'

"'Well, this is light brown, not red. But what shape is this beautiful creature?'

"'Oh, I think it is round.'

"The mother draws a round figure on the slate. 'Is it like this?'

"'No, not so round.'

"The mother makes a long thing in the form of a long caterpillar.

"'No, it is not so long.'

"The mother then draws an oval.

"'Yes, it is very much like that.'

"'And has it no feet?'

"'I think it has some feet.'

"'How many? I suppose two feet like the birds. Are they like these?'

"'Oh no, I am sure they are not like those.'

"'You had better go and look at it again, and come and tell me.'

"'Mother, it has six legs.'

"The mother draws two on one side and four on the other. 'Is that right?'

"'No, it has three on each side.'

"The mother corrects it. 'Is that right?'

"'Yes, that is really right.'

"'And what sort of a head has this wonderful creature?'

"'Oh mother! its head is like the branches of a tree.'

"The mother immediately attaches a small branch of a tree to the body, with several twigs, not forgetting a few leaves. 'Is it like this?'

"'Oh no, it has no leaves.'

"She rubs out the leaves. 'Like this, then?'

"The child looks at it intently. 'It has not so many little twigs.'

"'Perhaps you had better go again and see how many twigs there are on the branch.'

"'It has two branches, and one little twig on each.'

"The mother then carefully sketches the stag-beetle, and a rapturous burst of applause follows; and the mother turns to her 'natural history,' shows the delineation, and ends its history.

"You will see by this example how much of accurate observation this lesson will have taught the child. Children will never weary of this sort of instruction, and it is impossible to calculate how much the child will gain: very soon he will endeavour to guide his mother's fingers to the correct form, and next endeavour to form the figure himself. The value of the habit of accurate observation is not to be told, nor the unceasing occupation and interest it has given to children. In this way a child obtains the power of using his own mind, and he learns the value of correct language and description. There would be no end to lessons of this kind, including all natural and artificial objects, and each one bringing fresh knowledge and, if the teacher be skilful and cheerful, both moral and spiritual instruction. Had the mother simply complied with the child's request, and gone into the garden, and said 'That is a stag-beetle,' the subject would have been closed and the child's interest quenched. Had a servant been with the child, she probably would leave the question thus—' Oh, that's a nasty beetle; don't touch it or it will kill you with those great nippers: come away from it:' then the child would not only have its interest quenched, but fear created, and the creature would become an object of disgust.

"Children led on after this manner will daily become less troublesome and more interesting: they will find their own amusements, and the more they learn, the more independent will they become of toys and nursemaids. Do not help too much. If they are utterly at a loss, suggest and hint, or furnish a clue which, through their previous knowledge, you believe they will be able to follow; but let them come to the end of their capacity before you give direct information: this will teach them their own ignorance, and increase their sense of your superiority, and their confiding trust in your wisdom. What little things will make fairy days of enjoyment for children! Take two intelligent little children who have been accustomed to prove all things as far as they can, and give them a chaffinch's nest and a summer afternoon to collect materials similar to those of which it is composed, and then try their skill in making one. I would say again and again, foster in bringing up children a courageous, independent spirit: make them free of woods and fields as early as the little cottager—and then imagine the delight of that search for wool, moss, hair, grass, &c., &c.; fancy the many thoughts that will occur to them as to where these things are to be found; fancy the eager eyes questioning every nook, collecting enough to make twenty nests if it could but be matted together; fancy the joy over a hair or feather, a tuft of wool gathered from a thorn bush, and the little sprigs of velvet moss. Life may have many joys afterwards, but that long summer afternoon will stand out radiant amongst them. And then the nest-making—the ineffectual attempts, the bungling performance, and then a lesson upon the exquisite faculty of instinct preparing the way for a hundred thousand more. Natural history may always be made to lead happily and gracefully and tenderly to God the Creator and Father, not through sermons, but through the things that He has made. The happiness of birds and insects, and all creatures living a natural life, should be often brought before children. Their hearts are always in sympathy with happiness—that is, if they have not been roughly thrown out. I believe some persons would immediately say that children are naturally cruel. To this I would answer, it is when the education in this particular has been neglected.

"Bring your little children into harmony and friendship with all God's works; and keeping this tender relationship in view, never suffer them to make collections of insects. I say never, for directly the greedy spirit of acquisition finds place in a child's mind, the whole range of their feelings is changed towards the creatures which they had before admired with sympathy and something approaching to love. Now, it is only to possess: directly any lovely creature meets their eyes in sun or shade, to capture, to destroy, to appropriate, is the sole object; all desire to know or observe them is gone, all sympathy with their innocent enjoyments is fled. When persons grow older, these collections may be made with less damage to character; but the effect is baleful to the character of little children, in whom one should endeavour to form an open heart of love towards all God's creatures. The accounts of naturalists' murderous tours have been often very revolting to my mind; but the plea of scientific discovery turns black to white.

"Again, give them a piece of quicklime and a little water, a handful of sand and the same, a lump of clay, and so on. Draw their attention to effervescence, absorption, moulding, &c. Show them then the effect of an acid on an alkali; give different simple experiments in dyeing, extraction of colour, going on step by step (for you can scarcely set one intelligent step in natural history but another must follow it), and before you are aware, your little ones are on the borders of science—yes, they have got their little feet within the charmed line before they can even read.

"Weighing and measuring are quite within the compass of a child under eight years old, and with scales and weights and a marked measuring line, and a little, a very little, calm distinct help, they will learn the rudiments of long measure and avoirdupois weight much more delightfully and intelligently than in the visionary tables of weights and measures submitted to the jaded memory. The relative weights connected with the bulk of different materials would amuse children for many an hour.

"I would earnestly say, Do not be in haste; do not crowd one thing upon another: let the first steps be true, and then, by continued repetition, be trodden in till they become a practical fact to the child's eyes and hands—what he has seen, handled, and experienced, and can describe: on this I would lay great stress. Do not be content with confused description. Let the child do his very best first, then supply him with the words he needs to make his detail accurate and complete. Children are delighted to use their minds if you do not push them on too fast or too far, or miss the steps or links by which the mind travels with a comfortable firm foothold. There is no need to hasten: one foundation-stone well laid will bear a great weight laid upon it in the general building."

In the training of children in town, Mrs. Sewell acknowledges there is more difficulty. Wherever possible, she recommends that a good-sized, airy, uncarpeted room be given up to the children, where they can try their experiments without fear of injury to furniture or annoying any one with the sound of hammers and nails; can grow seeds in saucers, plants in pots, and keep a few pets. She goes on to say :—

"If expense is an object, instead of buying feathers for the children's hats, take railway tickets to the nearest country station. This would bring bloom to the cheeks of the little ones, and sunshine to their spirits; you would find it as 'bread cast on the waters, to be found after many days.' These would be the days which the children would look back upon in after life. They would remember them as festivals when they sat upon the green grass under the spreading trees, eating their buns and making all kinds of discoveries among things whose beauty never wears out. It was through the beauty of nature that God first spoke to my own heart when I was a child of not more than four years old, and I believe if parents can reverently and lovingly turn over the pages of God's book before the charmed eyes of their little ones, they will find a natural and happy response."

Extracts from Letters to various Friends.

"There is one thing in which I think parents of the present day err so frequently—it is in making children so very *dependent*. My idea is, that children should be made as independent as possible, consistent with their personal safety. In this way they gain so much more real experience, and they learn the natural effects of temper and principle. If children are continually with servants when not with their mother, every little thing is done for them, all their little quarrels are set right for them, and they are never, as it were, acting on their own foundation and receiving the natural rewards of their conduct. There are appeals and interferences which prevent a child from seeing cause and effect simply, and also from gaining an independent mastery in many little matters suited to their abilities. For instance, if you wish to be alone or to go out, I would not give over the children to others, but leave them together, with what ought to be sufficient amusement. It is their interest then to make themselves agreeable to each other, and also to call forth all their ingenuity for their own amusement. 'Don't do this,' and 'Give your brother that,' and 'I'll tell your ma,'—all these ill-working speeches are done away with. However excellent a servant may be, she can never stand to a child in the place of unquestioned rule and authority, and that invaluable virtue of simple, unquestioning obedience in a child's mind is necessarily impaired."

I am afraid this passage requires the comment of the following extract from the published sketch :—

"Mrs. Sewell was speaking of the idea that every human being (not only motherless crossing-sweepers) receives the whole care of one angel. She said, 'I don't think I could believe it. We are so untoward. Think what a wearisome job they would have with us!'

"'But when you were entirely devoted to the care of two human beings, you did not find it wearisome,' I replied.

"'Ah! but I had nice little toward children,' she said, as if unconscious that her own management had anything to do with this 'towardness.'"

It sometimes happens that nervous, delicate children, by no means singularly "untoward," will come to stages when the discipline they give to each other, if long left to themselves, works extremely ill. No doubt more aiming at independence from the first might obviate this often, but not invariably. In after years Mrs. Sewell learned the power of a wise and careful nurse through one who entered her son's household as a girl of eighteen, brought up all the family with devoted care, and still remains their loved and honoured friend. The reminiscences quoted above say—" When Mrs. Sewell began talking of J.'s goodness, she did not know how to stop." Mothers who have not the means to secure such priceless help, however, may find much encouragement both in the foregoing letter and in the following:—

"What strikes me as the defect of Taylor's 'Home Education' (it is long since I read it) is its impracticability. The child is to be constantly surrounded with perfect teachers; he is to be supplied with everything, and to battle with nothing. I cannot think such a system could form a dauntless, persevering, independent character. I remember this was my impression when I read it. I thought there were invaluable things in it, but that as a whole it was impracticable and undesirable. The book I value above all others as a help is Edgeworth's 'Practical Education.' It has nothing to do with the religious formation of character, but simply moral and intellectual training."

"In education, it is a child's *moral* nature you train. Virtue, the highest, purest, loveliest, is what you want to train them to. Now, I believe this is very much done by expecting it—in feeling sure they will be what is good and beautiful:—to raise a high ambition after beauty, truth, honesty, &c., &c., by showing them how intensely you admire and approve of it, how earnestly and hopefully you believe and expect that they will be everything you wish. Let everything be stimulating, animating, affectionate, nothing depressing. Oh! children do answer to this treatment: their simple hearts are made to glow and stretch out towards a noble, loving discipline. Expansion is the law of their nature; they delight in it."

In the same line of thought, though not applying only to children, is the letter that follows:—

" Never let any one leave you discouraged; if you do, it arises either from cowardice, selfishness, carelessness, or meanness. We should always plume each other's wings, if there are any visible; if not, find them out. Find out their inner bias, and let them know you have found it out. Never flatter or feed self-satisfaction, but as far as you honestly can, show an appreciation of the work of others. This feeds growth, hope, power, and happiness. Horses and cows bite one another for comfort and sociability.

"Let praise be distinctive, not general. If a woman has bravely passed through a great trial, call her brave. If you come in contact with a man who cultivates his garden well, give flowers and seed, and beg some of his— acknowledge a mutual taste. To a little worker toiling with unaccustomed thimble and needle, select for especial, hopeful admiration the best stitches. The same with writing. In a copy-book, be sure you find out one good letter. Don't be mean; notice it, and point out its beauty —put a mark under it; others will be made like it. Let nothing good pass unnoticed; do not fear giving a full measure of commendation. A general slur, or merely indiscriminate praise, will beat down, not up.

"The power of generous appreciation has to be developed in oneself; to be an efficient power, it must be discriminating. The words you speak must have their roots in your own heart, or they will be only barren words. Mere formal speeches may depress,—they never exhilarate, and for all good, they leave things as they find them. Do not lose the key that might be used to open prison doors, and not only open the doors, but unfasten the chains.

"We are too apt to freeze in imparting knowledge.

We are told that the sweetness of the lips increaseth learning, and that pleasant words are as an honeycomb, sweet to the soul and health to the bones, adding both joy and strength, hope and power."

No one acquainted with Mrs. Sewell will say, in reading the above, that she preached what she did not practice. How many on the brink of despair she has been the means of bringing back to trust and hope! I remember her saying, "We are too much afraid of praising people—I mean appreciative, really deserved praise. Life in this difficult world has *great* discouragements. I have met with many more people who need lifting up than taking down.'

In conversation she was careful not to smother the thoughts and observations of people with whom she was conversing ; on the contrary, they so grew in her hands that under her management they seemed to go on gathering in importance. This was the more observable when she was with children, or comparatively ignorant people. Her quick sympathies enabled her to discern when there was more on the speaker's mind than he had the power to express. A few judicious questions would bring to the surface that which had been vainly struggling for existence. Young people would leave her with bright faces, rejoicing in their new-found capacity of making themselves understood, and the ignorant would be cheered and encouraged by the thought that though they were ignorant now, they need not remain so for ever. There are few

THOUGHTS ON EDUCATION.

things for which the poor and the young will feel more grateful than for any revelation we can make to them of powers of their own, which a little more courage and industry on their parts would enable them to put out to advantage.

Over and over again, in letters to parents and teachers, come entreaties that they will qualify themselves to make children acquainted with Nature, and descriptions of the pleasure of walks with open eyes, and little basket ready to bring home treasures for examination, "so unlike the poor little things who walk hand in hand and see nothing."

"When children have once got hold of Nature, and their mother will animate and help them, they want no toys. It is such a delightful task that I really almost envy a mother who has it for her work and duty."

"Self-denial for some special object which a child can understand as worthy of it, is an excellent discipline for him."

"A handful of good life is better than a bushel of learning."

"I have no doubt myself that it would be good for boys generally if they were, up to ten years of age, under the care of good, intelligent women. They need the affections trained and developed to make good domestic men. The training in boys' schools is in most cases antagonistic to this."

I add fragmentary recollections of conversation:—
"I do not remember ever having to give my

children a more serious punishment than the withholding of a kiss at night. That was enough to send them to bed with tears and sobs. When it happened—it was very rarely—as soon as I could swallow my own grief, I think my uppermost thought was the earnest desire that they should grieve as much to break God's commandments as they did to break mine. I used to try and impress upon their minds that trouble must always come of living at variance with any of His commandments. *Because* He wants us to be always happy, He could no more allow disobedience in His family than mother could in hers."

"No true parent will ever doubt that our Heavenly Father 'delighteth in mercy,' and that judgment is 'His strange work.' When I have been reading in the prophecies of the heavy judgments on His 'rebellious house,' I have watched with Him, as it were, more than one hour, in deep sympathy with all the anguish this needed severity must have cost Him. If we had no written word for it, my mother-heart would make me quite sure that 'He will not always chide, neither keep His anger for ever.'"

"We sometimes see a pathway closed to the public, and a notice put up that whoever attempts to use it will suffer a penalty,—by order of the owner. A child might easily have it so impressed upon him not to go there, that, with the fear children have of policemen, he would scarcely dare to turn his head that way as he went by.

"How many of Satan's by-paths, which cannot be entered without disaster, are forbidden 'By order of the loving Father who is on the watch that His children shall do themselves no harm!'"

"The Book of the Law must be one of our earliest lesson-books with children. Under the Spirit's guidance, practical illustration will rivet a child's attention, and every lesson will deepen the feeling that it is an evil and a bitter thing to sin against God. Tell him, too, that the lesson he is learning to-day will never be changed, even if he should live to be as old as grandfather; he is learning something for all time. And let the example of Christ be kept before him as the model of perfect obedience to the will of the Father."

One morning, in looking over an American paper, (I think the *Sunday-School Times*), we came upon a story telling how the hymns and Scripture taught by a Christian mother who died when her little boy was ten years old, came back to his memory when he was ninety, with a force that made him a new man, without the help of another word from human lips. Mrs. Sewell remarked that this was a literal fulfilment of the promise, "*When he is old he will not depart from it,*" and went on to say that it was with her children at her side that she first woke up to see the wonderful adaptation of Scripture to meet every want and impress every duty of life. She said, "Whenever I wanted to correct anything wrong, or to help them on to some higher level, I tried to put everything I said upon some foundation truth from the Bible. Sometimes I had to wait for it. I have tarried before God day after day, asking Him where I should turn for the light and teaching I needed, and with all my heart I testify that 'they who wait on the Lord' not only 'renew their strength,' but find what they seek. Then when I spoke to my children about what God wished them to do, or not to do, they knew that the God who was telling them to 'do all things without murmurings and disputings' was the same who had taught the little bee to hum, and painted the flowers in such lovely colours; and the teaching from His Word came to them in the way of its being an honour and a privilege that the great Lord and Giver of Life should remember to tell us how to behave to one another;—and what a happy thing it was that we could really know for certain what He would like us to do."

"I always felt such confidence in teaching from the exact words of the Bible, because the Spirit that all true life comes from, can honour His own. Catechisms and Creeds always seemed to me like bones separated from the flesh; they may be well enough in their way, but I could never get on with them, nor feel the need of them."

"Then do you think we could dispense with Catechisms and Creeds?"

"I would not say that. I am not so much talking against them as saying that there is something better."

"But how many mothers do you think there are

who take up the Bible as you have done, and make a kind of lesson-book of it, without needing any other help?"

"Oh, I hope there really are a great many; but my heart is always crying to God that He would send us many, many wiser, holier mothers, who will not make over teaching their children to other people, but count it the highest of privileges to do it themselves. I am afraid the world will never be much better than it is until God sends us more Heaven-taught mothers."

And after a pause, "Yes, I suppose we must have Catechisms while there are comparatively so few mothers who think for themselves, and wait upon God for light and power. But I think, if I had to use a Catechism, I would rather have one written by a mother than by a Westminster divine."

This conversation expresses to what was perhaps the deepest longing of Mrs. Sewell's heart. More good mothers she desired above every other good. When some allusion had been made to what she considered our national crime, in allowing temptations to drink to multiply under the full protection of the law, she said, "If there were better mothers, my dear, there would be better statesmen." She used to say that if our systems of national education were as perfect as an angel from heaven could make them, the material on which they had to work was so hopelessly gnarled and twisted in its early home growth, that to persuade it to take a new direction was little short of a miracle. A manufacturer determined to send out the best goods selects his material with great care, promptly rejecting everything that comes under the stamp of "damaged." When we think of the quantity of damaged material which daily presents itself at the doors of our Board Schools, we cease to wonder that the results of our educational efforts are so often disappointing.

"We see the *success* of bad training on every side," Mrs. Sewell said. "We needn't doubt the success of good training if we could but get as much of it. The overwhelming evil all about us corresponds to the bad seed sown in children's hearts. It is just what we might expect: like produces like. We spend our philanthropy in trying to make good what need never have been so bad."

And at another time—"I have always been so thankful to God for making me a woman. It is worth while being a woman, for the sake of having the first word with the children. I have no ambition at all to get upon the world's platform and fight for its prizes. I love the quiet, spiritual work God has appointed for women. I would rather train up a little child to love and serve God and be a blessing to his country than do anything else. But women should cultivate a spirit of great sympathy with men, who have to face the world and fight its battles. We cannot help them much at their work, but their contact with the world is likely to engender a cold, hard, selfish spirit, and that is best corrected by contact with the refined and spiritual. They need to come under the influence of those who can show the crookedness of the world's policy by placing by its side the straight line of the law and commandments of God, *which never change.*"

With these convictions, it will readily be understood that she took a profound interest in Mothers' Meetings. She used to speak of them as the "foundation educational movement of the day." "The destinies of our country are mainly in the hands of the fathers and mothers, and were we as loyal and patriotic as we ought to be, we should think no effort—no painstaking—no teaching—no prayers—nothing—too much to contribute to the cause of lifting the home life of our country on to a higher level."

In the concluding chapter of "Thy Poor Brother" Mrs. Sewell writes :—

"What a halo of hope is round these Mothers' Meetings! To my mind they offer the fairest prospect we have for the elevation of the lower classes. It is acknowledged by all thoughtful people, I believe, that the education of the home is more powerful than that of the school or pulpit in forming the character of children, and the children are our hope for the future. That this hope may not be changed into despa'r is the great object of these meetings; and they appear to fit with a peculiar nicety to the present requirement, by affording to mothers instruction and comfort, and helping them to help themselves. I trust their present high aim, thus to benefit the whole nature—body, soul, and spirit—may be fully upheld, and that they may never become simply clubs, or working and reading meetings, but that, full of love and hope, they may spread over our country and fill it with healing and happiness."

As time went on, and these meetings became more general, Mrs. Sewell had to own that her hopes were too often unfulfilled. Ladies about to undertake this work often applied to her for advice, and she said, "They seem to me to have so little idea of what *may* come out of getting the ear of from fifty to a hundred poor women, perhaps for two hours every week: *women*, whom God has given the most responsible work in the world; and they want teaching in so many ways, there is not a moment to be lost. Those precious hours! how few, comparatively, make the most of them!"

I told her of a little plan which I had found useful. After the Bible lesson, I would select a verse of Scripture, and read it over carefully two or three times, giving them the chapter and verse, which some who had pencils wrote down. Then I would say, "I am going to speak of this verse as though I were talking to your children. I shall try to suppose that none of you are older than fourteen—most of you much younger." I then went on to make as simple an explanation as I could of the verse chosen, and at the end I said, "If there is anything in this lesson I have not made clear enough for your *children* to understand, ask me, and I will try to make it plainer." I advised them on a Sunday morning to get their husbands, if possible, or one of the older children learning at the school to write so nicely, to make copies of this verse in a clear text hand, and give it to each child to prick before learning it. Then perhaps just after tea might be a good time, when they were all sitting together, for the mothers to tell them as much as they could recollect of what I had said.

Whatever else that went on in the meeting failed to get all the attention it deserved, not a word of this little lesson seemed to be lost. Mothers will learn hard for their *children*—they believe in instruction being good for *them*. Not a stitch of work was ever done, or an eye diverted from the speaker, until the lesson was over. The mothers would often bring me the texts to show me "how nice the little ones have pricked 'em."

Mrs. Sewell took up this idea with all her usual ardour in making much of the suggestions of another. "Now I do call that a good stroke of business," she said. "There are the fathers and mothers, older and younger children, all set going together, and all over a little verse of Scripture. I was reading the other day of a district in London where about 700 women attended the meetings held on Monday afternoons. Now supposing the ladies who superintended these meetings were to combine and give the children lessons, each week, from the same verses—why, it might set all the women, some of the men, and most of the children thinking and talking on the same subject, and as it would be about 'the word which does not return void, but accomplishes that whereto it was sent,' what a mighty power for good it might become in a neighbourhood!"

"Our poor women here so seldom get out to a place of worship," she continued; "and when they do, so often there is nothing for them! In a mixed congregation, a great deal of the teaching *must* go above their heads. Mothers' Meetings ought to make up for this."

In 1856 her own loved mother passed away. Mr. Philip Sewell was in England for a time, and his family paid a long visit to Grayling Wells, but "grandmother" left no strong mark upon the children's memories at that time. "Grandfather" was the hero of the day to them, far more an adept in pleasing very little ones at play than the earnest grandmother. It would not have come into her mind to put little bits of cheese on their biscuits and call them "horses with riders," or do a host of other playful things by which the dear grandfather was fondly remembered. With all her wise thoughts about the care of little ones, and her delight in watching them, Mrs. Sewell did not attract very young children as many old ladies do. I think she was never enough of an old lady for them, and was more sought by their caretakers, who found her a delightful counsellor. With any child left entirely to her care, she would no doubt have quickly established relations of sympathy almost if not quite as perfect as she had with her own children: but in a slighter acquaintance, her instinct for being side by side with her companions and drawing them to her own level, did not quite meet the requirements of the baby stage.

The years spent at Hayward's Heath and Chichester seem to have left fewer traces than any other part of Mrs. Sewell's life. One or two valued friendships were made at Chichester, and she used to speak of the pleasant drives there—drives in the little pony-carriage having become part of the daily routine, for Anna's sake. These years appear to have been much occupied in a weary search after improvement in her health. Visits were paid to hydropathic establishments: Mrs. Sewell would go with her, and leave her to give the treatment a full trial. In the summer of 1856 they went to Marienberg, and there Anna was left for nearly a year. A rare cessation of outward interest and activity came to Mrs. Sewell in this time of her absence, with the result of unfolding a long-hidden power: in her sixtieth year she began to write verses, and felt the power growing as she wrote. It was the discovery of a new existence—a new era, though it came as quietly as the leaves unfold in spring.

The earliest letter of hers which has come to hand was written not long before the removal from Chichester, to a friend who had gone to stay temporarily in a place recommended by her:—

To Mrs. R.

"GRAYLING WELLS, *April* 19, 1857.

"I am so glad I mentioned that place to you, because it seems to have been quite right. I wrote to you then on the spur of a sudden impression. These sudden impressions are not to be neglected; they may be a little piece of the wonderful mechanism of Providence.

"Anna's back and chest are better, feet quite lame, and her head not much better: still, in many ways it will have been a great benefit. She has made dear and valuable friends, and gained a great deal of experience, and seen much variety, which, to such a prisoner as she is, is a great advantage. I expect she will return in May, should nothing unforeseen prevent it.

"I think how your dear children are enjoying running about in the country. Depend upon it, there is nothing better than making young children naturally happy, not overstrained in body, mind, nor in a precocious religion: let them develop naturally, and watch and train them.

"Yes, I have read Mrs. Ellis' book,[1] and advise every mother to read it, and every one interested in the present most grievous state of society in general. I have been to see her, and we had many earnest talks together. . . .

"Do not be in a hurry, dear friend. The Lord does not make haste. Upon *one* little event of our lives so many others may hang that affect other people as well, that we may safely leave Him who formed and guides the whole scheme to tell us when to go forward and when to stop. When we are in difficulty or perplexity, we are apt, I think, to feel our individuality more, and forget our membership; but it is a good and comforting thing to remember this great family circle of connected interests.

"I have had many a trouble since I wrote to you last—deep anxiety about Sarah. . . . Thank God, we have this week a better account. I have been very unwell myself, and have now a long cough and cold upon me that makes me look very shabby and feel very weak; but I am hoping to improve.

[1] Probably "Mothers of England."

"My good husband has resigned his position in the Bank. . . . We are able to live without his being in much more business than attending to his own; but I am afraid he will find leisure wearisome. We shall have to be more careful, of course, than we have been, and that is never very pleasant, is it, dear? But blessings abound, as you see."

I have thought it best to pause, on the threshold of Mrs. Sewell's literary life, and devote a chapter to it, before proceeding with the history of those other parts of her life which ran side by side with it.

CHAPTER III.

LITERARY WORK.

(*By Elisabeth Boyd Bayly.*)

"A summer bird
Which ever in the haunch of winter sings
The lifting up of day."—KING HENRY IV.

"HOMELY BALLADS"—DORKING—SPAIN—WICK—"THE CHILDREN OF SUMMERBROOK"—"STORIES IN VERSE"—"PATIENCE HART"—"THY POOR BROTHER"—"LITTLE FORESTER"—"ROSE OF CHERITON"—"DAVIE BLAKE"—"THE MARTYR'S TREE."

WHEN, in her sixtieth year, Mrs. Sewell first entertained the thought of writing for the public in verse, I think she must have felt the touch of her father's hand upon her head again, and heard his voice saying "That's right, my dear. Always hope."

The motive that inspired her is told in her own words, in the preface to the first edition of "Homely Ballads":—

"During many years of friendly intercourse with her poorer friends and neighbours, the author has frequently observed the poetry in a book to be the first part which draws their attention—that with children there is a general desire to commit verse to memory, and that the parent's ear is ever open to listen whilst they repeat the hymn, or the story which is told in rhyme.

"The author believes—and her opinion is confirmed by others intimately conversant with the minds of the working classes in different parts of the country—that there exists among them generally an instinctive love of simple, descriptive poetry, and that both morally and intellectually it is of more importance to them to have the imagination cultivated and refined by the higher sentiment of poetry than it can be to those who have the advantage of a liberal education; to the one, it is a luxury—to the other, an almost needful relaxation from the severe and irksome drudgery of their daily lot.

"With these convictions, the author has endeavoured to throw some of her thoughts into the following homely verses. But in offering them as a small contribution to the working man's library, she is conscious how slightly they express her earnest sympathy and interest—her heart-felt admiration and respect for the noble-hearted, patient, and industrious workers in our native land, by whose unceasing toil the more wealthy are exempted from similar labour, and are surrounded by the comforts and enjoyments of life."

I have heard no one ever mention Mrs. Sewell's having previously written verses as an amusement. She saw a thing that wanted to be done, and when she had time, thought she would try if she could do it herself, and found that she could. This appears to be the history of her discovering her vocation, after threescore years of training for it by using her imagination as a power of sympathy.

She described to me how the emptiness of her life in Anna's absence tempted her on to write, till several ballads were accomplished. "And then I showed them in fear and trembling to Henry King," she said, "and had to sit by while he turned over the leaves, till at last he looked up, and said, 'This will do.'" To the last she would dwell on the pleasure, the charm of being criticised and praised by him. Compliments, of course, she disliked,—"Though it's nice to have things said to you that are *all but* true," she said; but approval from Mr. King was precious indeed. "He was the most refined man. In everything—words and binding and paper—his taste was perfect. He always knew just the right thing to do with one's things, and what the title should be."

I do not know whether his verdict was given before or after Anna's return from Germany in May. This was a gala-time for mother and daughter. Anna's health had much improved: for once they were able to walk about together. They took a fortnight's holiday at Dorking, ever memorable as a little space of unclouded happiness —a "delicate plain called Ease where they went with much content," though "they were quickly over it, for it was but narrow." The weather was delicious; all day long they walked and sat among the spring flowers, revelling in the beauty of that lovely place; and when they came back to their lodging in the evenings, they were so intensely interested in Carlyle's "Past and Present" that they could hardly persuade themselves to go to bed, and drank coffee to drive off sleep and lengthen each delightful day. Twenty-five years afterwards, Mrs. Sewell would speak of that book with enthusiasm.

The "delicate plain" passed, they went home to plunge with eager interest into the revision of all that the mother had written in her solitude. "My Nannie has always been my critic and counsellor," said Mrs. Sewell long afterwards. "I have never made a plan for anything without submitting it to her judgment. Every line I have written has been at her feet before it has gone forth to the world."

Anna Sewell had the artist instinct for form strongly developed. Her pencil drawings from nature, full of truth and spirit, are remarkable for excellence of composition; if she did not edit her landscapes, she had a genius for seizing the right point of view, and figures and objects were put in exactly in the right spot; this same gift of form made her an admirable critic of manner and arrangement in word-painting. She was not a lenient judge. "Oh, if I can only pass my Nannie, I don't fear the world after that," Mrs. Sewell said, accepting her own child's criticism with eagerness;—I was going to say with entire humility, but it was more a fine ambition that made her so ready to take a hint from any one—a craving to be as near perfection as her powers could attain. If a thing was not good enough, it must be made so; and her industry was inexhaustible: one cannot conceive of her ever saying, "I can't be troubled to go over it all again."

In the autumn of 1857 the family paid a visit to Mr. Philip Sewell at Santander. This opened a new world of beauty, leaving pictures stamped upon Mrs Sewell's ardent mind; but as an instance of the superior force of early impressions, I cannot recall a single lyric, not even a simile, in all her verses, which would betray that she had been in the land of the myrtle and orange-flower. This may be partly because she wrote for English folks who had not travelled abroad, and in composition, her audience sat with her: she was as sensitive to the impression she was to make on simple readers as though they had been ranged about her in bodily presence.

Meanwhile it had been decided to leave the house at Grayling Wells. What led the family to their next home at Blue Lodge, Wick, is now forgotten. If a hope of economy was the motive, it proved fallacious, for the inconveniences of the place made it anything but cheap. The house was within a drive of either Bath or Bristol. It stood between the villages of Liston and Wick, a long way from either, and required additions and alterations; but whatever the leading that brought her there, Mrs. Sewell always looked back on it with deep thankfulness, for besides the work of blessing that she and hers were able to carry on for the poor within their reach, this lonely place proved the very spot for authorship. Here all her chief works were written—"Mother's Last Words," "Our Father's Care," "Thy Poor Brother," "Patience Hart," besides many little stories in verse; and active visitation of schools and poor, night school, and temperance work were carried on. When some one expressed astonishment that so much work and so much writing could go on together, Mrs. Sewell said, "Our time was not all cut up into bits with people, as it is here" (at Old Catton). "Every one who came to see us had to climb up a long steep hill, so that they had to be very much in earnest to do it. We could take our own times for going to them, and so we got through something."

While the alterations proceeded, Anna seems to have been away from home, and Mr. and Mrs. Sewell put up with very small quarters, with their worldly goods packed up, and a makeshift household staff, judging by the following extract from a letter evidently despatched when the writer had composition fever upon her:—

"I must write my precious one a letter to go to the post when my young woman goes to chapel at Wick. I cannot call her servant, domestic, or help yet, because I have not proved these virtues, but she may not turn out quite so bad as I fear. Having constitutionally no method, and much self-conceit, she has great obstacles in the way at present. I will tell thee a funny little instance, amongst a number of the same kind yesterday, which will make thee laugh. I told her to boil a little rice, thinking she would tie it up and have done with it. She came very catechetically to ascertain if I had a little diaper bag to boil it in, and stood informing me that she had always been used to a diaper bag, and did not think rice would look well without one; and so, while all the great outlines have to be made, she keeps worrying me about the minutiæ, always supposing I 'have not such and such a thing.' It is very laughable to hear how she goes on, but very provoking, and she will make me a saint or a sinner according to the measure of grace and patience."

Notwithstanding, the work went on. Mrs. Sewell loved to compose out of doors, but it must be on a straight walk or road. "A crinkle-crankle walk is dreadful," she said; "it cuts off all one's rhymes." There was a long straight walk in the grounds at Blue Lodge, and there she paced up and down under the leafless trees, and made her verses.

"Homely Ballads" was "printed for private circulation" by Smith, Elder, & Co., early in 1858, and met a reception that encouraged the writer to put out all her powers. When her sisters read it, they said, "We always knew that Mary had it in her, and now it has come out."

In "The Rose of Cheriton" the old man says—

"I am no poet, sir, but there are times
When these old memories almost run in rhymes.
I've often thought that poesy was given
To comfort mourners on their way to heaven,
To let them find, all plain and fairly writ,
The feeling that no common words will fit."

The writer of those words had felt them. She used to say that her versifying was not poetry. "I have a knack of a rough sort of rhyming that serves my purpose," she said, "and all the Byron at Friends' Meeting trained me well in rhythm—that's all." If one may presume to set up an opinion against hers, I should say that touches of very lovely poetry are scattered among her unpretending verses, but fewer in "Homely Ballads" than in later works; she was only beginning to try her wings when those were written. The language is strictly and intentionally "homely." It was remarked to one of Mrs. Sewell's grandchildren that "mirk" would have been a better rhyme than "dark" in one of her "Stories in Verse." "But grandmother would never have used that word," she said, "because it is not one that poor people are accustomed to."

The subjects and sentiments are homely too. Mr. John Wright's comment on the book was, "Why, Mary! what company have thee kept?" But it is homeliness idealised. In "The Young English Gentleman," the writer names a list of great folks—King, Duke, Bishop, Squire :—

> "But I have seen another man,
>   A man who pleased me more,
>   A little English Gentleman
>   Within a cottage door."

And a picture follows of a little gentleman, twelve years old, whose

> "Soul was full of honour true,
>   And ready was his arm."

But though Mrs. Sewell gave honour due to brave boys and men, it was for the poor, brave working woman that her heart spoke loudest.

"The Working Woman's Appeal.

"Amongst the hard and cutting things
   Poor women have to feel,
When poverty is serving out
   Their lean and hungry meal,
Is the unthinking ignorance
   Of some we call genteel."

The speaker goes on to describe her life in service at Squire Goldiman's, with lavish abundance of everything to use and waste, and then the contrast, when she married a man with ten shillings a week.

"I know it may, and has been said,
   I'd but myself to blame;
I might have lived a single life,
   And not have changed my name.
Well—I may have my thoughts of that,
   My betters do the same."

She has heard gentlefolks called *great* for bearing a reverse of fortune manfully, and thinks it would be only fair to give a poor woman credit too, when she makes the best of her lot:—

"I know it needs a noble heart,
   A spirit true and just,
To want a hundred little things,
   And never go on trust.

"I know it needs a strength of love,
   And naught of selfishness,
To eke the little victuals out
   That all may have a mess,
And hardly touch a bit yourself,
   Though faint with weariness.

"I know it needs the patience
   That a martyr may require,
To wash without a copper,
   With a pot upon the fire;
The chimney-smoke all driving down,
   And smuts as black as mire."

And just when her spirit was sinking under the trials of a washing-day, came Mistress Goldiman, to see "her humble servant, Anne," all in silk gown and lace bonnet.

"Oh deary me! she could not sit
   Upon my smutty chair.

"She only knew of cottages
   That poets write about,
Where work is pleasant exercise
   Both in the house and out,
And children all have curling hair
   Like cherubim, no doubt.

"Mine never could come up to that,'
   However much I tried."

And so the lady lectured her—

"On many things
   She said I should have done;
And many other things, she said
   I should have let alone."

. . . . .

"The worst revenge that I would take,
   The only one I'd seek,
Would be, that Mistress Goldiman
   Should manage here a week;
And after that experience
   I'd like to hear her speak.

"But still I often blame myself,
 When I reflect again
How wastefully we used the things
 Of Squire Goldiman;
I wish I had a quarter now
 Of what I wasted then."

Yet the spirit that aims at elevation by levelling what stands above it, was wholly repugnant to Mrs. Sewell: she thought it such a want of self-respect. In her "Two Noblemen," when the noble young cottager goes to see the young lord whose life he had saved—

"His face was so honest, his step light and free,
 No servile behaviour or speeches had he,
  Indeed he forgot he was poor.

"He had not that paltry and pitiful pride
 That looks upon toil as a thing one should hide,—
  He knew 'twas his lot upon earth.
 And when in the nobleman's presence he stood,
 He made him the very best bow that he could,
  As due to high station and birth."

And the ballad next to "The Working Woman's Appeal" is "Mrs. Godliman"—a poor woman's story of a mistress she revered.

"I've heard folks say—(I'm sure I hope
 That they may be forgiven)—
That not a feature of her face
 Was beautiful or even;
If they weren't beautiful for earth,
 I know they were for heaven."

These lines recall one peculiarity in Mrs. Sewell's

æstheticism; she had small interest in beauty apart from character. Wild plants in the hedgerows, forcing their way through difficulties, were much more interesting to her than prize specimens at a flower-show, and in human faces, she looked for histories in the old, and capabilities in the young, rather than for shape or colour.

A letter written at the close of 1858 says— "The testimonials I am constantly receiving of the Ballads are most gratifying and encouraging. The other day I had the thanks of a missionary's wife in London from herself, and, she said, in behalf of all the poor women who

> 'Wash without a copper,
> With a pot upon the fire.'

Was not that pleasant? You ask, 'What next?' I have another ballad, to be published at the right time. I have also been writing a tale in verse (very simple) for little schoolgirls."

This tale, "The Children of Summerbrook," was published in July 1859 by Messrs. Jarrold of Norwich and London. Mrs. Sewell had still many ties with the old cathedral city where the disgrace of owing a penny had burdened her mind; the Jarrolds were publishers for the people, and for the people she wrote; while ever cherishing the friendliest regard for her first publishers, she made the change, which proved to be a wise one. Mr. Thomas Jarrold, in particular, took the warmest interest in all her writings, and his death, shortly before the appearance of "Black Beauty," was a heavy loss to her: she clung to old friends, though always ready to make new ones.

"The Children of Summerbrook" shows a distinct advance in artistic power. Like Mrs. Sherwood's little twopenny stories, it is complete of its kind, with opening scenery, marshalling of characters, a critical epoch when events tremble in the balance, and a triumphant close. Dashes of poetry too, of the very simplest kind, begin to glance among the lines.

> " Now little Nelly plays alone,
> The three play there no more.
>
> " Their happy faces in this world
> Will never more be seen ;
> Their nimble feet will bound no more
> Across the village green.
>
> " For they are gone to Paradise,
> Where comes no toil or pain ;
> And oh ! they would not like to live
> In Summerbrook again."

It is said that every writer of fiction writes one story which contains his own. Mrs. Sewell's personality was too much exhaled into that of others for her to do this; but she wrote what she herself had felt most deeply and delightfully in life, in the story of a good, generous boy and girl, who worked like trumps to help their mother, and overcame evil with good among their schoolfellows.

> " George was the prince of boys ! morn, noon, or night,
> Whate'er he had to do, 'twas always right.

No murmurs, nor excuses, nor debate
That 'twas too early, or it was too late;
For when by George his mother's will was known,
In little time, his mother's will was done.
And as to Mary, that dear girl and he
Were just as happy as they well could be."

A naughty girl supplies a shadow to the lights, —points the moral, and gives goodness the chance of a battle and a victory: the crowning triumph arrives when the father comes home from sea on Christmas Eve, to find his wife looking ten years younger, and all the children's doing!

"A moment's pause of grateful joy,
Then round the board thy met;
If there be greater happiness,
I have not seen it yet."

And that was the end.

Archbishop Trench says of Landor, "Most of his poetry has no *claws*." No one could say that of Mrs. Sewell's;—unless perhaps herself, for, writing as she did between the ages of sixty and seventy-five, she had to contend with the declining verbal memory of advanced years, and unless she could write down a rhyme when it struck her, was apt to lose it.

The ballads now collected under the name of "Stories in Verse" seem to have been written next. In these again we trace a distinct advance in facility of expression and fancy. The Muse kept captive for nearly sixty years, took a little time to acquire freedom of movement; but certainly it had learned to tread lightly when "The Chaffinch's Nest" was written.

> "Adown a green lane, seldom travelled by man,
> A bright little brook in its cool current ran;
> For many long years it had trickled that way,
> And never had loitered by night or by day.
> By starlight and sunlight it glided along,
> And sang to its neighbours the very same song;
> And when the deep dark over all of them fell,
> It still had the same pleasant story to tell.
> But whence it had come, or the words that it said,
> Were thoughts that ne'er puzzled a passenger's head;
> Though still, where the little brook trickled along,
> The flowers grew bright and the rushes grew strong."

In a large elm-tree beside the brook, "two sweet little birds" decided to build their nest.

> "They neither had gimlet, nor hammer, nor saws,
> But only their beak and their dexterous claws.
> But sensible workmen, 'tis said as a rule
> Will hardly find fault with the commonest tool,
> And these little workpeople never had thought
> That new-fashioned implements need to be bought.
> So away they were flying, away and away,
> To fetch and to carry the whole of the day;
> And then in a branch of the sheltering tree
> They both were as busy as busy could be.
>
> . . . . . .
>
> And oh! what a spirit they had in their work!
> From earliest dawn to the evening dark
> It seemed only pastime and pleasure to be,
> So gaily they worked in the shade of the tree.
>
> . . . . . .
>
> The ivy-leaves hung as a green folding-door,
> And now the small architects' labour is o'er.

"Next day came a joy too delightful to tell,
One should be a chaffinch to write of it well,—
A smooth little egg was observed in the nest,
Laid soft in the warmth of the mother bird's breast."

And so on, through the cycle of the highest delights a little bird's heart can know, until a cruel moment when two thoughtless boys came by, found out the nest, and stole it away, and that little centre of perfect happiness was ruined.

Against a graver ruin and blight of the sweetest of joys, a warning voice is continually uplifted in these ballads: we hear it even in the happy story of the fisherman's foundling, and over and over again, with a remarkable union of plainness of speech and reticence, it sounds the danger-signal on what Robertson has called one of the "two rocks on which the soul must either anchor or be wrecked—its relations with the sex opposite to itself." As a woman, the writer gives her counsel chiefly to her own sex, but there are beautiful little touches on the other side of the question. She is not prudish: she can enter into the Sunday bliss of straying in the Lovers' Lane.

"Stray on, young hearts, the Sabbath-day may be
The day most fit for vows of constancy;
For marriage is a blest and holy thing,
Round which the purest joys of life may spring.

"But see 'tis holy—see 'tis good and true."

Nor is she content with a general caution: she notes the first false step.

"She'd steal away to take a walk,
And thus her work neglect,
And stand outside the door to talk,
With little self-respect."

As earnest and faithful is the warning against intemperance, and sloth, waste, shirking, and begging are treated with wholesome scorn. Perhaps some of the quarrels at Wick and Liston gave birth to "The Little Schismatics; or, Irreligion"—a smart take-off on the way in which neighbours who have been friendly, through splitting straws—

"Will then another little chapel raise,
And pass each other in the public street."

All these works have kept their favour with the public. "Homely Ballads" is now in its fortieth thousand; "Children of Summerbrook," thirty-third thousand. "Stories in Verse" was not published complete until 1869, since when 19,000 copies have been printed; but the ballads had been selling as Household Tracts long before that time. "The Lady's Dilemma," describing how a lady found all the young people in a village too learned to make a set of shirts, is very amusing.

The next flight was to be the longest. In November 1860 "Mother's Last Words" appeared, and had a sale unprecedented in the history of ballads. It has now reached one million and eighty-eight thousand, in addition (I believe) to its sale, bound up with "Our Father's Care" and "The Children of Summerbrook," in a little two shilling book called "Mrs. Sewell's Ballads for Children." "Our Father's Care," the story of a little water-cress girl, followed in 1861, and is now in its 776th thousand. It is unnecessary to describe stories which any one can get for twopence from the nearest booksellers. They have *claws*.

An old friend of Mrs. Sewell's writes :—

"We were walking together in the fields one evening when I was on a visit to Blue Lodge. It was just after 'Our Father's Care' had been published, and every post was bringing her letters referring to it—some from sympathising friends anxious to know how they could befriend little Nelly, and all of a character to gratify the vanity of the authoress, if she had any. So much was she made of just then, that I said to her quite playfully, 'I hope they won't spoil you.' 'My dear,' she replied, turning on me almost reproachfully, 'I have *nothing* to be proud of; it all came in answer to prayer.' 'Yes,' she added immediately after, 'even the rhymes.'"

It is interesting to see what a great variety of people, of all ranks and ages, found a charm in these ballads. Mrs. Sewell did not hoard reviews of her own works with the same care as she did those of Anna's, but from among those preserved, I copy the following from a very lengthened review which appeared in the columns of *The Brighton Herald*. After speaking of various kinds of poetry, the reviewer refers to that which, "abounding in the touch of sympathy, binds all hearts," and goes on to say :—

"Of this latter character are the poems of a lady, once a resident of this town, and the wife of a gentleman well known and highly esteemed by most of us in Brighton.

Yet, living as Mrs. Sewell long did in this county and town, she was not then known among us as a poetess. Now, her works are printed by hundreds of thousands, and have a world of readers. Mrs. Sewell's is essentially children's poetry—written of and for children mainly in the lower ranks of life. In the 'Children of Summerbrook' we have the incidents in children's lives as experienced in our English villages. 'Mother's Last Words' dwells on the trials children are exposed to in great towns, which Mrs. Sewell describes and illustrates, and she does it with a simple power which may be felt and understood by all ages and all ranks."

In the "Life of Dora Greenwell," the following reference is made to an essay Miss Greenwell wrote for the *North British Review* on "Popular Religious Literature":—

"She takes notice of the great hold which religious literature had gained upon the less educated portion of the community, and regards it as the revelation of deep and true devotional instinct. 'Man loves his home, and loves to hear about his way to it: the path which the vulture's eye hath not known.' She candidly acknowledges that books of the popularly religious class must not be measured by the canon of ordinary criticism. These books are written for an object, and for a certain class of people; the only question to be asked is, Do they hit or miss their mark? 'It would be easy, for instance, within the range of lyric narrative, to find a poem which, considered as a poem, surpasses Mrs. Sewell's popular ballad, 'Mother's Last Words'—hard to find one so completely answering the end for which it was written, so fraught with the secret of true pathos—that which grows out of the very nature of the thing it deals with, the pathos that is entangled and involved in life; the sadness of the streets that comes across us in the cracked notes of the ballad-singer, and in the bare feet of the forsaken child. We have seen a class of adult criminals so sunk in the strange apathy habitual to them, so stolid and indifferent, that the voice of instruction and warning seemed to pass through them to the blank wall beyond; we have seen such a class roused, interested, awakened to life, to intelligence, to affection, through the mere reading aloud of this simple story. We have known them follow its course with eager eyes, with broken exclamations, with sobs, with floods of tears."

Canon Fleming writes :—

"I read 'Mother's Last Words' in December to nearly one thousand of my poor people—it was illustrated with dissolving views; and I read the people the kind letters you wrote me when I was living at Bath in 1866, to show them something of the heart of the authoress. They were in great delight with your poem.

"On the 20th of February I am going to give a reading for the orphans, and among other things I am going to read your Ghost Story. It makes an admirable reading."

The captain of a ship writes :—

". . . I may add that your little books are great favourites among seamen. I have often been asked to obtain them for different sailors. Some very rough fellows have been greatly impressed for good by our readings."

A young man, wishing to do good, had undertaken a Sunday class of wild town lads, and could do nothing with them. When "Mother's Last Words" came out, he tried reading it aloud to them, and they were spellbound. They begged to hear it another time, and he read it over and over again, Sunday after Sunday, thankful to find anything that would keep them quiet.

Although the ballad has continued to sell, it is

now so long since it was in everybody's mouth that the present generation of Sunday-school teachers are often unacquainted with it.

Some time during these years appeared the only one of Mrs. Sewell's ballads which seems to me inadequate to the subject treated, "Poor Betsy Rayner; or, The Power of Kindness," a story of the rescue of a drunken woman. I well remember looking forward to it, and thinking, with a child's exaggerated hopefulness, that something *was* going to be done for drunken women, for Mrs. Sewell would write for them; and how sad the disappointment when it came, and even Mrs. Sewell had "healed the hurt of the daughter of my people slightly"! It is a very pretty story of a neighbour who watched, and left the door ajar for a drunken woman, cast out from her home, despised by all, until the good Samaritan took her in and fed and cheered her—led her to the Fount of Strength, and saw her started on the better way; but there is not a glimpse of the agony and bloody sweat of that poor thing's conflict, and the neighbour's for her sake. How many times had I seen the door, not left ajar, but thrown wide open,—and the poor wanderer came in and wept and was comforted; stayed a while, and went out again—to the public-house. "Oh ma'am! don't, don't — I can't help it. They won't always go home with me. I can't pass them publics by myself, and they won't always go home with me." With that cry in one's ears, what was the use of talking about kindness, when it was physically impossible to watch with the tempted creature day and night? And she was one of a hundred thousand. We are all agreed in making it a crime to supply intoxicating liquors to native races in our Australian colonies: a mass of human beings in our own land, probably more numerous, certainly with far greater capacity for good or evil, are quite as much in need of protection against their own weakness.

A quarter of a century has passed since then, and in that time I have seen many drunken women reformed; but stronger than ever is the conviction that in the struggle with confirmed intemperance, human kindness and tender mercy are as tow in flame. We need them indeed—at their highest; but only a Power transcendently beyond them can avail aught; and to bring one of these marred souls in contact with it, one must be ready to be crucified with Christ afresh.

Mrs. Sewell profoundly realised the horror of our nation's curse, but at that time she had, I think, had little to do with drunken women individually. She had very early attached herself to the Temperance movement, perhaps influenced by her early acquaintance with Sarah Stickney, who, as Mrs. Ellis, was one of its pioneers. Like so many others, this friend passed away before her, and no gleanings remain of the correspondence between these remarkable women. It must have been a treat to hear them converse—"Sarah,"

with her graphic power and unquenchable fun—
"Mary," with her racy, pithy sayings, and gift of
acute comment rather than repartee. They would
both have been very much astonished if any one
had told them in 1845, or 1850, that Mary was to
write books likely to outlive Sarah's. They had
many things in common—exuberant life, strong
public spirit, love of poetry and all beautiful
things, a very simple way of carrying their honours, and generous pleasure in the achievements
of others, especially the young. In looking back,
the great difference one sees is, that Mrs. Sewell
had had a good mother and a joyous childhood—
Mrs. Ellis was a motherless child, and the trace
of having

"Felt a mother-want about the earth"

lingered in her, even to those happy closing years
when the husband she had so nobly spared to the
public service returned in safety, and friends and
neighbours made such rejoicing over it that she
said, "It is quite an airing time for my best cap."

Mrs. Sewell next tried her hand at prose.
"Patience Hart's Experiences in Service" came
out in April 1862, and was a great success. Whoever has read it with a class of girls cries out for
another like it. Patience Hart is a girl of spirit.
Here is an instance, when the grocer's young man
begins to pay his addresses to her.

"He asked me if I were not the young lady from Mr.
Freemantle's. I said no, I was the kitchen-maid."

After a few more attempts at compliment, he found an opportunity, when no one else was in the shop, to make her an offer of his hand and heart.

"I just asked him how old he was. At this he coloured and looked sheepish, but he said he was between nineteen and twenty.

"'Well,' said I, 'I am between eighteen and nineteen. In a few years we shall be grown up, and I have made up my mind not to think of marrying till I am five-and-twenty; so if you hold in the same opinion so long, and like to ask me then, I can turn it over in my mind.'

"At this he laughed and looked very foolish, and I think that will be the end of his courtship."

She also has some observation :—

"Mary and I were just different: I used to pepper up, and she used to sulk. However, neither the one nor the other will do in service; I have found that out. Servants must not have tempers at all; that is the perquisite of the master and mistress, so far as I can see."

The book was written in the form of letters from Patience to her mother. One of the few criticisms on it came from Mrs. Ellis, when some one observed what remarkably good letters Patience wrote. "Yes; I don't know that I should have liked it, if I had been her mistress," she said, "to have a servant with such a gift for writing long letters about all that went on in the house." When the book had run through a sale of nearly 33,000, the publishers brought out a revised "Patience Hart," not in the form of letters, and slightly modified to meet the wants of the present day.

This was after Mrs. Sewell's death, and the revision was made by some of her family.

Her next book was undertaken with grave searchings of heart.

To Mrs. R——.

"Wick, *June* 1862.

"I will tell you what I am thinking of writing (quite a little book) on Visiting the Poor. Our mistakes on this matter have long burdened my mind, and if I can find time this summer, I should like to say my say. Do you not think *somebody* should write something on the subject very definite, if they could? Tell me what you think. I feel that it is a very difficult and delicate subject, only so very important, because there is such a mass of good works now, that literally many of them do no good to anybody—often the reverse—and cost so much, and yet, in one way, not enough. But it seems as if time would be wanting to me: we are so hard run in many ways."

The four previous years had seen the development of three agencies, then new—now part of the ordinary machinery of the service of the poor—Mothers' Meetings, Bible-women, and Temperance work for men, conducted by ladies. They were brought into notice by three books, written by Christian women who simply made known a mode of service which they had tried themselves, and found useful. Close on the Temperance work followed the cry for "a public-house without the drink," and the great coffee-house movement was set going. A few months before the date of the above letter, the need of this had been profoundly impressed on Mrs. Sewell's mind by the experiences of an evening spent with a city missionary in visiting public-houses in London. She alludes to this in the following letter to her son :—

"*March* 1862.

"Thy last letter asks the questions which I am continually revolving in my own mind, and have been ever since I spent my evening in the gin-palaces. I did not go into the worst, nor at the worst time: I thought I should be too much frightened to profit, and that my imagination could carry the picture to its fuller dimensions—but the question is, What are the working men to do? where to go? ... They cannot all be driven home, and prayer-meetings and reading-rooms, even if abundant, are not to their present taste. My sympathies are so drawn out to the poor fellows, under their dangerous necessities, that I feel impelled to write something, if I did but see my way to handle it well. ... Now tell me thy thoughts and cogitations upon this matter, which thou must be witnessing in all its phases all the day long. What is the way of escape? What *ought* to be done? I think we should set up our standard at *what ought*, and only come down to *what can*."

The outcome of her cogitations was that she started a vigorous Temperance work, and ultimately opened a little Workmen's Hall, among her own neighbours; and she wrote "The Rose of Cheriton," and a chapter in "Thy Poor Brother" called "The Monster Evil," in which she tells a little of the experience of that terrible night in London. "I wished to see the monster face to face, that I might know how to sling my little stone at him," she writes; and adds, "That was a night much to be remembered by me."

Once a year the Hebrews were commanded to offer a goat to Azazel—a type, we may suppose, of "Christ handed over to Satan for the bruising of His heel."[1] On that winter night, the humble follower of Christ passed under the touch of Azazel for her people's sin, and ever after bore his marks upon her tender heart, in memories of sin and horror branded there to her own unspeakable torment; but, like her Master, she rose up endued with power against all the power of the enemy. She hardly ever spoke of what she saw there. "I couldn't let it pass my lips—not some things; but *how* it comes back upon one!" she said twenty years afterwards.

"Thy Poor Brother" is written in the form of letters to a friend supposed to have a district and be rather at a loss what to do in it. A faint, discouraged worker taking it up would feel instantly that it was "not written on velvet cushions for those who are treading with bleeding feet on thorns." It is, in fact, the history of what Mrs. Sewell herself had done and suffered for the poor, —its wisdom wrung out, drop by drop, from sorrows felt as though they were the writer's own. Often she draws openly from her own experience; where any singular act of loving-kindness is recorded, she says "a lady" did so and so. She was the "lady" to whom the poor crazed woman fled, and whose first alarm (she had very little physical courage) was swallowed up in compassion and entire faith that God had heard her prayer, and would make her instrumental in the poor thing's restora-

[1] Hengstenberg.

tion—who took the dangerous lunatic into her own family, and was privileged to send her home again at last, perfectly restored, to her wondering, grateful husband and children. "Do we inquire how she could afford the time and the expense ?—rather let us ask how any of us can afford to exist upon this earth without the luxury of doing good," she writes.

To a Friend.
"*November* 30, 1863.

" . . . I wish you were fully escaped from Doubting Castle—it is a miserable place—and, moreover, you have no business there, and ought, by all that is fair and honourable, to come out. Anna will keep a little dark room in that same old castle, where she sometimes goes and bemoans herself; and I scold her, because the place is let to quite a different sort of people to you and to her, and you should not give them any countenance by keeping them company. Do come out ! . . .

"'Thy Poor Brother' is at last come into the world, or at least I suppose it will on the 1st of December. I have ordered a copy to be sent to you. Do let me know how you like it *directly* you have read it. Sometimes my heart turns quite over, in thinking about its reception, for there are so many thoughts afloat upon this subject, and so much experience has been gained, that it seems almost presumptuous to have given mine, out of my little nook —but now I must bide what comes. . . .

"You have indeed had a succession of troubles and anxieties. It is marvellous what we do pass through and overcome through its being meted out by the hour and day, and by having Hope instead of Certainty to keep us company."

The book was very warmly received, and highly valued, but considering the immense number of district visitors and the wonderfully helpful suggestions it contains, nine thousand copies seems a very small sale by this time. May it be multiplied tenfold! I believe all her most thoughtful readers consider it the best book that Mrs. Sewell ever wrote.

Her next was a contrast—"The Little Forester and his Friend," being Mrs. Sherwood's story of "The Little Woodman and his Dog Cæsar" rendered into verse. The Muse had quite a holiday in writing this sylvan story, where every one gets good at last, except the killed wolf; and the woodland pictures are full of poetical touches.

In the end of 1864 the family removed to Moorlands, near Bath,—a home nestled in the curve of the hillside, giving the impression of a place shut out from human ills, and open only to sweet flowers and sunshine. In this green Paradise, Mrs. Sewell set herself to write "The Rose of Cheriton." She had never shrunk from handling sad subjects when they were laid upon her, but this was the saddest work she ever did—a story of the ruin wrought in a single household by strong drink. It was very highly praised, but never had the same "run" as her shorter ballads—partly, no doubt, on account of its higher price (sixpence), but also, it may be, because the indictment against strong drink and the liquor laws breaks in jarringly upon the finest poetry she ever wrote. The argument is splendidly put,—terse, strong, balanced,—passionate, yet worded with the utmost regard to fairness—a quarry for Temperance speakers to dig in for quotations,—but it *could not* be poetry, and unfortunately, a long piece of it comes in to interrupt the old man's tale, and breaks the spell.

It begins with the setting sun.

" The quiet landscape caught his bright farewell
Ere the dark shadows of the evening fell ;
The gliding river and the broken sedge,
The pollard willows by the water's edge,
Smiled for a moment in the passing gleam ;
Then sighed the sedge, and darker flowed the stream."

In the calm of twilight, a sudden turn brings to view an empty, desolate farm-house. An old man standing by tells its story, the first part drawn, as we now know, from Mrs. Sewell's own earliest memories of happy farm-house life. This is in her usual style—fresh, graphic, shrewd, but touched only here and there with poetry. The music comes with the sorrow: the spell of her own tale laid hold upon the writer, and her wonted literary canons could not bind her. Space ought to forbid quoting, but one little passage must be given—the night the mistress died.

" She said,
'Open the window, I can hear his tread.'
They flung it open, just to please her, sir:
They knew her hungry hope deluded her.
She listened heedfully, and then she said,
'Shut it again, and turn me in the bed.'
And they do think she slept a little while ;
And when she woke, they say she had a smile
Upon her face, as though she might have been
Over the river, where the fields are green.

"He did not come. I waited hour by hour,
As I had done a hundred times before.
'Twas wondrous still. . . .
The yellow ash-leaves fell upon the ground
Before my face, without the slightest sound.
The oat-grass shivered like a human sigh.

. . . .

The nurse looked out and beckoned, I could see,
And called me to her, speaking mournfully.
'Your mistress wants to see you, lad,' she said,
'You follow me.'
    I did, sir, to the bed,
And there my mistress lay, as meek and low
As a white lily on the drifted snow."

One more, from the temperance argument :—

"Paul was sincere, sir, and 'tis right to think
That these good men don't see the harm of drink,
And so preserve a conscience fair and sound,
Though seeing men and women haled and bound,
Shut in the prison-house, or left to sink
In the o'erflowing sea of maddening drink.
But in my thought, the scales are on their eyes,
And if by some miraculous surprise
The naked truth should flash upon their sight,
And every drink-shop stand in sudden light,—
Astounded with the horror of the view,
Their cry would be, 'Lord, show me what to do.'"

She wrote that which she knew. Every line in that argument burns with the fire that kindled when she stood in the drink-shops herself. It is very difficult to realise that this poem was written when the author was nearly seventy years old.

Another sorrowful subject was tenderly handled

in the ballad called "The Lost Child," founded on the true story of a lost girl stealing home at night, and finding the door on the latch; it had never been locked since she went away.

Mrs. Meredith, the well-known prisoners' friend, writes of the women in Brixton prison:—

"In my interviews with them, finding it hard to bring their minds to facts, I bethought me to try your words on them, and with much prayer, sat down to read to six of them 'The Lost Child.' It affected them all as I expected it would—we all wept, but there was one who had turned almost to stone, and was a creature rather than a girl; she broke down completely, and begged me to see her alone.

"You have no idea what a true, good work your little ballads do to these poor folk."

From a Hospital visitor:—

"I am now engaged in reading to the sick and suffering in a Hospital, and I am so delighted with the effect of your poems that I shall circulate as many of your good and excellent books as possible, besides sending them to clergymen for their country parishes.

"A good chaplain informed me he sometimes reads your ballads instead of preaching a sermon to his congregation of prisoners. You do not willingly make people weep, but he says, 'Many of my audience as they listen are in tears, and all look interested, and they will ask me to read the same again.'"

"Davie Blake" was written at the urgent request of Mrs. Sewell's friend, Captain Toynbee. It lacks the peculiar charm of her English country ballads, but sailors liked it. With her usual industrious humility, she asked to submit it to a sailor's criticism before publication. "I am almost ashamed to tell you that at seventy-five I have been writing verses again," she wrote; and concluded, "Please tell Captain B—— that I have some facility in alteration."

It was certainly surprising that, at that age, having had scarcely anything to do with sailors all her life, she could so throw herself into their troubles as to wake an echo immediately in seamen's hearts. Their wrongs had long lain heavy upon her. After the ballad come fifty-three pages of prose called "The Sailor on Shore," dwelling on the fearful risks and temptations which surrounded him. The little book did its share towards bringing about the many improvements which recent years have seen effected in the lot of Poor Jack. "There's Help at Hand," a pretty story of Hop-pickers, came out in 1875. It was the last bit of entirely fresh work; but one more little book was yet to come, as related in the following letter:—

"In searching for something else, I found an old Ballad, many years old, and quite gone out of my mind; this has served as a playground for my thoughts, when they did not know where else to go for diversion.

"I think it must be nine years ago, a clergyman, quite a stranger to me, came from the neighbourhood of London to persuade me to put the history of William Hunter, the young martyr of Brentwood, into Ballad measure. I did not take to the idea, but he was importunate, so I promised to try. I was going to Lowestoft, hoping to lose a bad cough. I went in company with Fox's 'Book of Martyrs,' and while walking about there alone, I manufactured a great many verses (I was not inspired). When

I returned, I read them to my darling, who, with her usual frank criticism, pronounced them 'not up to the mark;' so I put them away and forgot all about them, till they accidentally turned up a few months since, with other things. In reading them over, I felt some motherly yearnings towards my weakly offspring, and set some of the bones, strengthened some of the weak members, and stuck in a few feathers; and now my grandchildren pronounce it fit to be dedicated to them! It seems too ridiculous for an old woman of eighty-three to be publishing Ballads—don't you think so?"

This little poem, "The Martyr's Tree," came out in 1880. Readers will probably agree with the daughter, exacting in her love, that it is not quite "up to the mark" of Mrs. Sewell's best work, though it has many very graceful and tender passages. The hand and brain she had so long spurred to do their utmost, began to shrink from heavy tasks: this was her last new publication in verse. In the last winter of her life she wrote a tiny book called "Sixpenny Charity"—a plea for regularity in giving help to cases of chronic poverty, were it only to the amount of sixpence a week, that the receivers might count upon it, and have a little sense of thrift in managing accordingly. Then the pen was laid down, and she who had always had so much more of music in her soul than her highest efforts could express in words, was

"Taught in Paradise
To ease her breast of melodies."

CHAPTER IV.

BLUE LODGE—LIFE AT WICK.

"In any circle, the gentle influence of one loving soul is sufficient to breathe around it an unspeakable calm ; it has a soothing power, like the shining of the sunlight, or the voice of doves heard at evening :

'It droppeth like the gentle dew from heaven
Upon the place beneath.'" —FARRAR.

THE first letter that has come to hand written from Blue Lodge has a particular interest when it is remembered that, in after years, Mrs. Sewell always gave her residence in that solitary place the credit of having allowed her literary faculty to develop.

To Mrs. R——.

"*December* 5, 1858.

"How many hundred times have I said to Anna, 'Oh, that dear Mrs. R——, when shall I write to her?' but I do not remember ever in my life being so occupied. . . .

"It grieves me to find that you have got into a damp situation. I cannot bear to think of that willing body of yours being unfairly treated ; it is direct injustice, to which a severe penalty is attached, and the judgment is pretty sure to come.

"We are situated just the reverse of you, on a high hill which is frequented more by the wind than fogs—though a number of fine trees round us offer a pretty good screen : it is remarkably healthy, and almost as inconvenient as it can be. It is a long way from *everything*, with neither postman, carrier, omnibus, nor rail, neither shop, needle-woman, nor charwoman to be had, so that everything has to be done and obtained with the greatest difficulty. For instance, our letters every day take two good hours to get and post. We are two miles and a half from the school, &c., and the roads almost impassable in some parts for our chaise, and entirely for foot-passengers in winter wet. And adhesive clay and ruts to break the springs, which was the case last week! You will naturally say, Why did we come here, almost 'out of humanity's reach?' Well, dear, humanly speaking, it was a great mistake, a mistake through and through; but as we allow not of the word 'chance' in our dictionary of Providence, so we do not believe we are out of the way of usefulness and blessing; and though we may be put out of the way of *temporal* prosperity, there is no reason why we should be out of the way of *spiritual*, but rather why we should be *in* it; and I still hope and trust that the bounds of our habitation have been fixed for us in love and wisdom, and that we shall by-and-by see that it has been good for us to be here.

"We have settled in a thoroughly neglected parish, where there have been many changes and quarrels, and now for some time everybody has given it up, not being able to pull together. There is *one* sermon from the curate on Sunday, and that is all he does for the souls of seven hundred parishioners. There is a Sunday and day-school, but which no one but the poor discouraged master ever entered. This broke our hearts, and we determined to put forth our strength, with the Lord's help, to do something for them. There was not a tract or book for any one to read, nor any Bible to be purchased. This we felt must be mended also, and therefore, dear friend, as we have taken all this upon us, you will not be surprised, with writing, needlework, and all the *et-cateras* of housekeeping, that we should have little leisure time. We are rather afraid that we have engaged with too much for our strength, but the cry seemed so loud, 'Come and help us,' that we were anxious to try. To-morrow our Lending Library will open, with a good number of subscribers, and beautiful books. It has been a difficult business to set it off. We were strangers, and the clergy were very suspicious of us, fearing we were Dissenters, and as we have taken in three parishes, we have three clergymen to deal with. We determined to hold to broad catholic foundations—they were no broader than the Church of England. We are surprised at what we have gained, though James's *Anxious Inquirer* was cast out, from the name of the writer. We feel that we have had more help and wisdom than our own, so we thank God and take courage. Dearest Nanny is quite lame, and her head very weak, but according to her measure she is very active; and her back being strong now, she can ride alone on the pony to the school often in the week. My good husband is pretty well, but I often grieve over him in this very secluded place: there is no one to speak to but the ploughmen. Do bring your boy up to some handicraft, whatever else he may be. The wasted hours of most men would do almost half the work of women."

Then follows the passage already quoted about a "tale in verse for little schoolgirls."

From this letter, and others which follow, it will be seen that Mrs. Sewell's work as an author did not make her neglectful of either the poetry or the prose of actual life. There are many poets who never in their lives write a line of poetry; the music that dwells within them manifests itself in the sweet and graceful actions of their lives, in the tones of the voice, in the readiness to discern and adopt the good and beautiful, from whatever source they may flow. These are the *élite* of the world, in whatever station they may be found.

The following recollections bear testimony that,

even apart from their work as authors, both Mrs. Sewell and her daughter belonged to this high class. Though the visit mentioned was paid in 1863, I insert them here, as they describe the house and surroundings at Wick. They are contributed by the friend most intimately acquainted with Mrs. Sewell's literary life, herself known as a poet, and with a critical faculty which made her sympathy a practical and highly valued help to her fellow-worker. "F. always saw exactly what was wrong," Mrs. Sewell said; "and she could say it, not in my blunt way, but so nicely!"

"It was just thirty years ago, in the winter of 1858, that we first made the acquaintance of the Sewell family. They were then living at the Blue Lodge, near Wick, between Bath and Bristol. Even now, whenever my mind turns without effort of will to revive their images, they present themselves framed in those old surroundings rather than in any more recent scenes. No one who knew the mother and daughter will wonder at this. There was about them both such a rare distinction that the first impression they made was not only lasting, but lastingly localised, clearly seen through all the accumulated treasures of a long after-friendship. This distinction is hard to describe. It was not mere intellect, or mere goodness, or even mere nobility, though it had much of all these in its composition. Perhaps some impression of it may be conveyed by saying that it was the general effect produced by uncommon intellectual powers, combined with still more uncommon integrity and simplicity, and directed by a 'charity' that can only be fittingly described in the words of St. Paul's inspired lyric. In speaking thus I include the daughter with the mother, but must now confine myself to the dear memory of the latter.

"To begin, then, with the intellectual powers. When my husband first saw Mrs. Sewell, he was struck with her likeness to the late Lord Lyndhurst; and as we look at his bust now, and compare her photograph with it, we see the same massive mouldings of brow and temple—unmistakable signs of great capacity—and the same firm outlines of cheek and chin—equally unmistakable signs of tenacity of purpose. But the mouth, so sweet and sensitive, for all its strength, is of a different cast to that of the great Chancellor. 'Clever' is about the last word expressing ability that one would dream of applying to Mrs. Sewell. Nothing so showy in its suggestions would fit the case; yet *clever* she was, in a very emphatic and varied sense, with a cleverness that worked not only through reason and imagination, but through eye and ear and delicately constructive fingers. When long past eighty she embroidered flowers exquisitely in coloured silks, from nature. Indeed, no one who knew her could conceive of her taking any inferior pattern. Like all effectual people, she was accurate and thorough. Life being too short for this exhaustive knowledge of many regions of thought, she was content to leave some subjects untouched altogether, of which people much inferior to her acquire a smattering that passes in society. Her intense truthfulness and the concentration of her energies on practical aims, alike led to this result. Her judgment was admirably sound, when not interfered with by her sometimes too enthusiastic confidence in her fellows. If now and then this involved her in bitter disappointment, it much oftener increased her usefulness and happiness.

"But even more conspicuous than ability were the integrity and simplicity which characterised Mrs. Sewell. She had as great a gift for being *herself* and for saying 'the thing that is' as the mass of mankind have for attempting to be some one else, and for saying 'the thing that is not.' The word 'unconventional' springs to my lips when I think of that lovely mother-daughter pair of twin souls. Yet it will not do—for it has gathered a taint of the uncouth, the rough, the careless in household ways, the brusque and eccentric in social life, and from such blemishes they were wholly free. They could not be anything but dignified and courteous, for their inner being inevitably revealed itself thus, without effort and under the most simple and natural forms. The 'plain living' which they loved to associate with 'high-thinking' was marked by exquisite order and nicety, such as one rarely sees. Yet all seemed to spring up naturally around them, with no petty anxieties or fatigues to themselves, and no worrying of dependents. All was lovely calm, yet full of cheerful activities that never jostled each other. Our first visit to the Blue Lodge was early in winter, in the flowerless season, and there was no greenhouse from which to supply the vases in the drawing-room; but I well remember the tasteful arrangements of ivy-sprays that filled these, and adorned odd nooks and bare corners. The room was a large and lofty addition to an otherwise very modest house. It swallowed the Chichester furniture at a mouthful, and gaped for more. But a skilful use of Indian matting, a judicious placing and draping of spare chairs and tables from other rooms, and above all the introduction of Anna's spinning-wheel, had banished all bareness, and given the same air of distinction and simplicity to the room which was so striking in its inhabitants.

"It was, however, by the last and noblest of the characteristics I have ventured to enumerate as combining to produce this note of 'distinction' that Mrs. Sewell was most widely known, and it was this which formed the keynote of her whole character and course. The 'charity' which 'seeketh not her own,' which 'suffereth long and is kind,' which 'beareth all things, believeth all things, hopeth all things,' was the inspiring motive of her life, and the atmosphere in which her whole being moved. She had a profound appreciation—an appreciation which cost her unspeakable suffering—of the miseries of others. The miseries of biting poverty, still more those of vice and ungodliness, were terrible to her heart and imagination, and she found no rest save in using her powers to the utmost in remedying them when they came within reach of her living presence or her pen. She recognised that the mission of the Church of Christ, in the individual as well as in the body, is to supply channels through which Divine Love may reach the need of man. She was no socialist, no democrat;—but she courageously recognised the grains of truth hidden in socialism and democracy at a time when such recognition was rare in religious circles, and involved loss of caste, and loss of confidence among many whose good opinion she highly valued. Nor did her benevolence rest only on man as the head of creation—it flowed down to the skirts of his garments in the animal world. In this sphere, as in the higher one, her strong imagination wrought as the handmaid of charity, and gave her a quick discernment of the capacities and claims of the lower creation. It was indeed a fitting thing when the daughter of such a mother roused herself from the languor of sickness to compose 'Black Beauty, his Grooms and Companions,' that most charming and graphic bit of animal autobiography. Almost at once it rushed into a popularity undreamed of by its author, as she jotted down her thoughts in pencil on chance scraps of paper, lying on the couch soon exchanged for the little white bed from which she never rose again. Standing beside that bed in the empty, silent room, in 1882, Mrs. Sewell told me that the joy of the success of her book had been almost too much for Anna's delicate frame. But the devoted mother could rejoice, even in the midst of the anguish of parting, over the welcome given by thousands of readers to her darling's dying work. Truly in their lives there abode, and were fully manifested, 'faith, hope, and charity,' but the greatest of these was 'charity.'

"To return once more to the Blue Lodge, where I spent three delightful days in the summer of 1863. There was a long, straight walk down one side of the grounds, overarched with trees, associated in my mind with eager discussions of literary work and larger matters. 'Thy Poor Brother' was in the press, and we were busy with the proofs, now in the drawing-room, now in the summer-house, and now breaking away from pen and ink for more discursive talk as we paced up and down in the shade of the Long Walk. Towards the end of my short visit, Mrs. Sewell claimed my promise to read to her portions of a manuscript of my own, and I enjoyed the great advantage of her criticism. On leaving, Mr. Sewell drove me to the station. He was a most kind and courteous host, ever ready to welcome the friends of his wife and daughter. Both then and afterwards, I was struck with the patience and cheerfulness with which he bore the reverses of life.

"Of how few of us can it be said that our judgment of the character and work of others is, if anything, too favourable. But I think no one admitted to dear Mrs. Sewell's intimacy would hesitate to say that this was the case with her, where her heart was once thoroughly interested. Her vivid imagination detected the 'divine idea' of the individual and of the work through a thousand faults, and she esteemed her friends and their achievements accordingly. As a critic of details, however, she was keen and outspoken. Suddenly, in the midst of impassioned recitation or reading, she would grasp her grateful victim's arm, and bring all ruthlessly to a stop. Then, looking round half impatiently, one would see a grave, questioning look, and after a few seconds' pause would come the query, 'Is that quite —— ?' or, 'Isn't that rather —— ?' so and so, as the case might be. Her straightforward, unflinching attack on literary self-love was a compliment to sense and temper, and her judgment rarely failed to commend itself more or less to even the most sensitive and irritable artist in words. Meanwhile Anna would appear from time to time at the garden door of the house, shading her eyes with her hand, and trying to discover our whereabouts, anxious to meet any possible want or wish of her mother's. At that time a weakness of the limbs confined her much indoors, except for the almost daily drives with her mother to the village, to visit their cottage friends and superintend the workingmen's club they had established. These drives often fell on cold and wet winter nights, and I remember Anna's gentle triumph in having falsified her friends' predictions of physical harm to herself from the exposure, her mother gaily adding, 'In fact, we've come to regard night drives in an open carriage in bad weather as a positive cure for delicacy.' At the time I speak of Anna, was, unable to stand for more than a few seconds at a time, though she moved freely about the house. Wherever Mrs. Sewell and I might be working at our proofs, or discussing questions they suggested, if household affairs brought the daughter to her mother's side, she was obliged to kneel on the nearest support for the minute she remained. But her general appearance had little or nothing of the invalid, and the calm radiance of her expressive face was remarkable. My husband chancing once to meet her in a shop in Bath, came home, saying, 'I've just seen Anna Sewell's beautiful face.' And beautiful indeed it was, with the beauty of nobility and purity.

"From the time of our first acquaintance Mrs. Sewell and I kept up a constant and sometimes frequent correspondence, Anna often writing for her mother, and often, too, on her own account. Although my dear friend was thirty years my senior, there was never a hint of *de haut en bas* in her communications by lip or pen, or any disposition to dictate, even in reference to those labours for others in which she was so incomparably better versed than I. No doubt the fact that the reigning friendship of her life had been with her own daughter, made it natural to her to put herself on a level with the comparatively young and inexperienced. But her native grandeur of generous sympathy was the radical cause, as it was the cause of her having been able to form and maintain that friendship itself. Her letters abound with proofs of these things. I send a few of them, though not without reluctance. They are very sacred to me. But it is high time that she should be better understood by the large public who delighted in her ballads, and by those unknown fellow-workers who have again and again found that her 'homely' verses could move hard hearts and soften seared consciences that scoffed at anything more didactic.

"At Moorlands we met more than once. My last visit was at Old Catton, near Norwich, in 1882. Husband and child were both gone, and this first actual vision of my now aged friend, in her desolated home, was inexpressibly touching. I cannot trust myself to attempt details. Yet the natural force of the brave spirit was unabated, her mental powers were as fresh and vigorous as ever, and her faith and hope were strong and bright.

As to earthly ties, she had the happiness of being near her son and his family, and not far from her three surviving sisters. The main business of her life still lay among the poor, the down-trodden, the neglected, and she discussed plans of amelioration with all her old ardour, though with less of sanguine expectation. Her garden was still an object of interest. A fern-wall had been already completed, and formed an exquisite piece of embroidery in living foliage, and she was planning other improvements to be carried out in the autumn. The ground lay chiefly at the back, but there was a strip in front, between the house and the road, laid out in beds filled with the gayest flowers. This was 'Anna's garden,' dear Mrs. Sewell told me, expressly designed and kept up for the pleasure of the toiling artisans of Norwich, whose Sunday afternoon walks led them in large numbers to Old Catton.

"Two years later, in 1884, my beloved and honoured friend passed out of sight into the blessed place prepared for her. The hope of a dim and vague immortality in the race would never have satisfied her unquenchable spirit. Nothing short of admittance to the nearer presence of her God and Saviour, nothing less than a thorough and personally conscious awakening in His likeness, could meet her need and longing. There, and in that perfected state, we believe she is serving still, free from the embarrassments and limitations which exercised her patience here. But the lesser immortality is also hers. Not only does she survive in the hearts of friends for whom her vacant place among the things that are seen can never be filled, but she lives also in the 'choir invisible' of those who have served all future time in serving their day and generation, and whose works of love and mercy do most emphatically follow them."

The "air of distinction," so well described here, was noted by every one. My children used to call it "Mrs. Sewell's duchess look."

The Working Men's Club alluded to seems to

have grown out of evening classes three times a week for men and lads, begun by Anna, though as the work advanced, Mrs. Sewell herself took an active part in them. The lessons were by no means confined to reading and writing. On their way to the night-school, the ladies would occasionally stop at the butcher's for a bullock's or sheep's eye, and taking it with them to the class, dissect it before their scholars' astonished gaze, showing them what a wonderful and delicate organism must be at work to make it possible for us to see. Again, they would explain why the wheat-plant, on which our daily food mainly depends, can grow and thrive in seasons when many other things perish from drought; its little fibrous roots are able to push themselves down so far underneath the soil that the plant is nourished from beneath, regardless of what is happening on the surface. These lessons would draw out such observations as, "Well, it do look as if somebody were a-looking after us, and a-minding on us." The impression left was, "For that Thy name is near, Thy wondrous works declare."

One of the happiest results of these lessons was that they introduced topics for interesting conversation into village life. The men were proud to pass on their newly acquired knowledge—it was something to talk about to wife and children at home, and many coal-miners (Wick is a mining district) and agricultural labourers woke up to see that their lives need not necessarily be monotonous, whilst they could "regard the works of the Lord, and consider the operation of His hands."

Another effect of this frequent intercourse with these "Poor Brothers" was, that the men became more considerate and helpful to each other. Those who are not well acquainted with village life can scarcely realise how often suspicion and petty jealousies will shut out friendly intercourse. The power of mutual help was throughout life a very uppermost thought in Mrs. Sewell's mind. In "Thy Poor Brother" she speaks of a dear old widow who said to a young lady friend, " Oh, Miss, what a *back* you are to me!" "Not a *bank*," the writer comments, and continues:—

"I believe the unpauperised poor would generally feel more security supported by a back than a bank—by warm heart sympathy than by money aid. I often think of that old widow's expression, and feel that we all need the *back* of mutual friendly support. I have sometimes looked upon a cornfield, waving and rustling in its summer beauty, and fancied it the type of what we need from each other in this world. Those slender individual stems, alone, so feeble that the slightest blast will bring them to the ground—backed by each other, so buoyant, active, and mutually helpful that the sweeping blast only moves them to sing together a louder chorus of universal confidence. Oh, I have thought, there is nothing in common troubles that would hurt us much, if we stood together in the sight of God, with our friendly arms supported and supporting each other. . . . But oh! how many feeble stems are broken and piteously trodden down by the roadside because there is no back—no friendly human arm to stay upon!"

From several allusions in letters, it seems probable that Mrs. Wightman's book, "Haste to the Rescue," had something to do with stirring up Mrs. Sewell and Anna to begin aggressive Temperance work at Wick; and with a view to developing this precious spirit of mutual help, they formed a little Brotherhood of working men in connection with it. These men immediately asked Mrs. Sewell to become their president. Her friend Mrs. R——, who has preserved several interesting letters on the subject, well remembers the deep feeling of responsibility with which she consented. She had not sought any "rule or authority among them;" but she felt that it would discourage them if she refused the post. The following letters refer to this :—

To Mrs. R——.

"WICK, *April* 1, 1862.

"We are very busy indeed, but we are very much blessed, so that we are neither harrassed nor worried. Our Temperance Cause, we think, is going on with manifest blessing. . . . Our little band of Brothers work beautifully with us. I have had a bad influenza cold that has kept me in the house more than a week, so they all came here for our meeting—Brother George, Timothy, and all the others—ten of us. We had such a nice meeting in talking over the subject and making arrangements. I began with reading a small portion of the Scriptures and prayer; and George B—— ended with prayer, and they all sang a hymn—and then they had coffee, cocoa, and currant cake, and we were very happy together. The worst of it is, they have determined that I shall be the President and address them, and take the particular management of the business. I don't know what to do. I feel so utterly unqualified. I have put off my *headship* for the present, and told them that we must meet to edify and strengthen one another, and to keep together those who may sign the pledge and join the Society. A tradesman here has quite given up drinking, and is using all his influence on our side. Mr. C——[1] is most kind. He is, I understand, trying whether he can do without stimulants. I think we shall have a pretty many to sign amongst the working men—and if all the clergymen come who wish to do it, we shall have on our platform four of these dignitaries, besides the speaker! Is it not wonderful? We are not *anxious*, because we keep putting every step entirely into the Lord's hands, to manage it for His own name's sake.

"Now I must tell you a wonderful thing. The week before last we were astonished by a visit from *Mrs. Wightman*. She was staying with a relative at B. who is very ill, and hearing that the author of 'Mother's Last Words' lived in the neighbourhood, she drove over. She was so pleasant, and gave us valuable advice and information about our 'little cause.'"

To the Same.

"*June* 1862.

(After a passage previously quoted, about writing a book on "Visiting the Poor.") "Last week, on Whit-Tuesday, we gave a Tea-meeting to our pledged abstainers—I suppose about a hundred and twenty. We had tables on the lawn, and a capital cake and bread and butter. After tea we adjourned to the little spacious barn which had been prepared for the occasion, and had an excellent meeting—Mr. C—— in the chair. Mr. Charleton, an excellent Quaker, and two Methodists, working men, addressed us in very telling speeches—an Independent minister and a clergyman of the Church of England were in readiness to speak, had there been time. So you see we are not sectarian, and I hope and trust we may not be

---

[1] Probably the clergyman whose church Mrs. Sewell and Anna attended while at Wick.

so, or else I feel that the large measure of blessing that we have received in working together as brethren will be likely to leave us. Love and union is all my aim. We have formed a Band of Hope, and I am thinking of a Mothers' Meeting in connection with it, which you see will pretty fully occupy our heads, hearts, and hands."

And purses too, she might have added; but Mrs. Sewell's benevolent work was never undertaken in an expensive way: she would search about for every means of "making do" with what she had at her command before spending money on appliances. She was a true daughter of the mother in whose household, she said, "there was never any waste, nor any pinch. The first thing she would do when she went out in the morning was to look out such a nice breakfast for the dogs and cats! They never had a scant meal, and yet there was never any waste."

But it was very difficult, both to her and her husband, to hold their hands from giving to any needy case. In old age, speaking of the great wisdom needed in giving away money, and the pain of refusing, she said, "I always feel *He* knows the depth of my pocket, and I have prayed that He would not send me those I ought not to help."

Money-giving, however, she reckoned a minor, though very important, department of charity: the power of a heart and a home she ranked much higher. She often spoke of the responsibilities and means of blessing that arise out of the simple fact of possessing a home of one's own,—the *back* it gives, and the duty and privilege of sharing it. A friend remembers the pathetic emphasis of her tone in describing a homeless lady, not poor, who was engaged in evangelistic work. "Her parents were gone, and her brothers and sisters were married, one after the other, till L. was left a lone woman :—and she spoke in public; and a lone woman who speaks in public is a *very lone creature* indeed."

She had the deepest feeling for the numbers of young people who flock to great cities, London especially, in search of occupation, and without the shelter of home, without friendly or motherly counsel, are exposed to terrible temptations. The following little narrative describes a kindness exactly in harmony with her spirit. The narrator was a lady living with her two servants in one of the prettiest suburbs of London :—

"'Every Saturday afternoon, about four o'clock, an omnibus stops at my gate, and I go out to welcome two young women who have come from one of the large houses of business in the City, where they have been through the week. They do not need to bring a bag, as they always find their night-dresses and other little things they may want in a drawer in the room where they sleep. Their first visit is to this little room. Then we have tea, and if the weather is fine we walk or drive, or go into the garden. Occasionally we treat ourselves to a short railway journey into the country, and come back laden with flowers, with which we brighten up our rooms for Sunday, the girls generally taking a few to some flower-loving neighbours. They always have some needlework of their own in hand, and in the winter they do a great deal while I read to them. On Sunday they attend church with me in the morning and evening. In the afternoon they often find their interest in reading to a sick neighbour, and when teachers are scarce, have occasionally taken a class in the Sunday-school. On Monday morning, breakfast has to be ready at seven o'clock, that our visitors may be in time for the omnibus that passes at 7.45. I always part with them with regret; they are so pleasant to me. I have had them in this way for two years, and I love them as if they were my daughters.'

"'What led you to take them in the first place?' Mrs. Sewell asked.

"'I was one day at their shop in the City, and had occasion to go into the show-room. So much was going on there, I had to wait. In looking about me, I was struck with the appearance of these two young women; they were both remarkably nice figures. Their "presence," as the trade terms it, must have been worth a good deal in a show-room; every cloak, mantle, or shawl looked perfection upon them. When they were at leisure to attend to me, I asked them some trifling questions about themselves, and it ended in my inviting them to come out to me on the following Saturday. That was the beginning of our friendship. The eldest is about twenty-four years of age; she is the daughter of a clergyman—her parents long dead, and she has to support herself in the best way she can. She has a sweet face, and is one of the most graceful women I have ever seen. You can easily imagine what her temptations must be. She has told me all about it. The Sunday used to be dreadful. Oh, how I wish I could shelter thousands of these girls instead of only two!'

"'Don't think of that, dear friend,' Mrs. Sewell replied. 'Keep to your two, like a true mother, as long as they need your home and your love; when *they* no longer need it, take two more. It is your personal influence over each of them individually that gives it its great value. What is wanted is, that a thousand ladies, situated as you are, should each take two; and how much the better they might be for doing it!'"

There is another class of sufferers, sometimes well provided with "houses to eat and to drink in," who are quite as deeply in need of a place of shelter, opened in some friendly heart.

In this sin-stricken world, there are to be found in every position of society, from the highest to the lowest, numbers who go mournfully down the stream of life, dragging with them the intolerable burden of a sin for which they find no place for repentance, although, it may be, they seek it carefully with tears: the memory of yielding, perhaps, to some fatal temptation—or, what is worse, having to carry about with them the conviction that they have themselves been the cause of lifelong injury and sorrow to others.

For the outward wounds and bruises, the fractures and the fevers which befall our fellow-creatures, we give large subscriptions to build Hospitals and Infirmaries; but those I speak of are "whelmed in deeper gulfs than these." Can we think of no Hospital Sunday for them?

No outward buildings, no subscriptions, will meet these sad cases. What we need is *many more* Christian men and women, so filled with the spirit of compassion which dwelt in Christ that the sinful, the mistaken, the erring, will know that they may safely stand at their feet behind them and weep. It often happens that the real dimensions of these troubles are greatly magnified by morbid introspection: the anguish that is felt is not always simply contrition—some of it has its roots deep down in a strong feeling of personal mortification. If these burdened ones could sufficiently trust any one to unburden their heavy hearts, it might result, with the blessing of God, in changing the whole aspect of their lives. Saphir, speaking of the woman who was a sinner, says—" She had entered on a new existence, distinct from that dark and starless night of loneliness and self-condemnation in which she found herself when first convinced of her sin."

It is true that the troubled conscience can find no rest until it gets to Christ; but human sympathy is permitted to do a great deal to help these burdened ones to reach Him. Christ intends His people on earth to be His representatives, and for the "little while" He is hidden from our sight, He is asking His children on earth to act for Him, and with His tears in their eyes, His love on their faces, and with voices which have caught from Him the true ring of Divine compassion, to offer to all His message of reconciliation.

I am speaking of something which can by no possibility be reduced to a plan or system. Call it Confessional (or System) and the gold becomes dross—dross of the worst kind, because it counterfeits the finest gold. Hearts which by God's grace have been filled with His own deep, compassionate love must overflow upon the dry ground, long parched with anguish and remorse, and under such blessed influences the desert may again become a fruitful field. "Confess your faults one to another, —pray one for another"—with what end? "That ye may be healed?"

In anticipation of His work on earth, Christ says, "The Lord God hath given Me the tongue of them that are taught, that I should know how to speak a word in season to him that is weary." If Christ, in His perfected humanity, could only under Divine guidance take up the difficult task of "speaking a word in season to him that is weary," what must our need be? Surely the common platitudes of being glad or sorry to hear so-and-so will not suffice, when to be qualified for His task *He* had to "wake morning by morning to hear as they that are taught." I have heard my dear friend say that her first thought and prayer in the morning usually was that she might know how to speak a word in season to the weary; and God gave her her request. How many she helped to "take heart again" will be known only in that day when the secrets of all hearts are revealed.

The following letter is addressed to a friend suffering under spiritual darkness. After reference to Madame Guyon's experience of having to be weaned even from *feeling*, it continues:—

"I have been thinking that it may be God is purifying my beloved friend so. You have been praying and longing and seeking for holiness, as Madame Guyon did. Perhaps God is teaching you in the same way, that you must be willing to *be* nothing, *enjoy* nothing, *seem* nothing, *do* nothing, but submit with a full, blind submission to suffer His will, asking no more, Why is it so with me? There seems to me a likelihood that God, who always purifies us *across the natural grain*, may have adopted this polishing process for you, working in the dark upon His precious jewel to bring it out, in His good time, radiantly reflecting His beauty. Your own nature is so lovely, so lovable, so generous, helpful, and clever, that you have, according to the common recompense of things, been the gratified, happy recipient of much love, admiration, and praise. It could not and should not be otherwise; and it may be that God is weaning you from all this—from all expectation from the creature, all expectation even from yourself, that you may be cast helpless, dry, empty, upon Him, to be filled in due time with His adorable fulness—out of your weakness to be made strong, only in His strength. These are the thoughts, dear one, that I have had. You will judge if they are apposite."

But notwithstanding all her tenderness for the sorrowing, it was to the young and hopeful that Mrs. Sewell's sympathy flowed out most naturally. "I cannot say that I *prefer* the company of old people, though I am so old myself," she writes at a later date; "I like the young spirits full of hope and animation, rejoicing in their strength, believing all things possible, and enjoying to the tip-top of their nature."

And again, writing from Wick, and alluding to a young friend:—

"This stirring world is full of interest to her. With what undaunted courage, resolution, and glad anticipation the young meet the world, and how good it is that it should be so: each one has the prize to win, of some kind. You and I know that there are blanks as well as prizes; yet we fervently thank God for our creation, and for all the blessings and all the crosses of this life, and look for the golden city which lies beyond."

"WICK, 1861.

"For the last six weeks we have had four of my little grandchildren staying with us. It is something quite new to us to have so much young life about us, but it is very charming to see the ever-hopeful elasticity, and boundless expectation, and simple faith of children. I often think of our Saviour's admiration of them, and His charge to us to be like them, and I think it must have been in some such particulars as I have named, and not so much in their innocence, which is, I think, the prevailing idea."

By that time the grandchildren were old enough to find out the charm of Grandmother's imagination. "She could not only tell stories, but *play* stories," says one of them. "There was a rocking-boat in the hall, which was a great feature. We remember the delights of the afternoon play-hour; she would play at going on journeys, when an enemy would come after us, and we all had to jump into the boat and row for our lives—just what children delight in."

To her last years she loved even to hear about the plays of imaginative children. The age which is often called "uninteresting" was the beginning of warmest interest to her.

The following extracts from Mrs. F.'s journal while visiting Blue Lodge may be interesting for the graphic picture they give of the surroundings in which Mrs. Sewell's chief works were written:—

"*Monday, July* 27, 1863.—Pony-chaise met me at Keynsham station. Lovely drive through quiet and sunny country. After dinner commenced reading 'Thy Poor Brother,' and went on for an hour, Mrs. Sewell reading, and I offering criticism. Her genuine modesty struck me greatly. The difference in age, and her wide reputation compared with my obscurity, made it the more striking. . . . To the MS. again before tea. Tea on the lawn, under wide tree-shadows, with beds of brilliant flowers spread all about. After tea, more MS., till moonlight drew us again to the garden. A long talk there on things in heaven and earth and ranging between the two. . . . . Delightful company!

"*Tuesday, July* 28.—The window of my room gave me the view of a sunny, park-like, upland field, sprinkled with calm tree-shadows, under which newly-shorn sheep rested here and there. Birds singing softly all about. Breakfast in a sunny parlour, which gave us through the open door the same view as from my window, and through the open windows opposite the brilliance and greenness of the flower-garden. Walked in the garden for a quarter of an hour after breakfast with Mrs. Sewell. Then she established me in her private sitting-room, with letters to write, and Bushnell's 'Inner Life.' At twelve we met in the drawing-room, Mrs. S., Anna, and I, and went on with 'Thy Poor Brother.' . . . Tea again on the lawn. . . . After supper, recited Wordsworth's 'Ode on Intimations of Immortality.' Talked of his poems generally.

"*July* 29.—Mrs. Sewell claimed my promise to read her parts of *my* MS. . . . Drove in the evening with Anna to Wick. Saw their cottage, taken for Mothers' Meetings, &c. Afterwards another spell at the MS. Set to work at criticism. Her suggestions are invaluable.

"*Thursday, July* 30.—The last day of this most delightful visit. . . . Four whiter days have seldom illuminated my life-calendar."

In December 1863 "Thy Poor Brother" came out.

To Mrs. R——.

"WICK, *Nov.* 30, 1863.

(After speaking of the expected book.) "The last week we have opened a miniature Working Men's Hall in our village, fourteen feet square. I am high busy, preparing lectures, addresses, &c. Nanny and I drive to Wick three evenings in the week at eight o'clock. Don't you think we shall get very brave and hardy before the winter is over? We have had such a very encouraging beginning."

Those who remember the mother and daughter will have no difficulty in guessing who supplied the courage for these dark winter drives. Mrs. Sewell was naturally timid, and one can quite believe in her retaining to old age "an indefinite remembrance of old John Spraggs" (a beggar-man who had been made a terror to her in childhood). Anna, on the contrary, had no acquaintance with fear—not even enough for mercy; it was impossible for her to understand the terror that would make others, children especially, tell lame falsehoods simply from want of presence of mind. She had a fine vein of Grandfather Holmes in her composition, naturally stern in her judgments of others as well as of herself, which made it the more remarkable that in her last chastened years all took notice of a more entire gentleness of spirit in her than even in her tender-hearted, impetuous mother.

But Mrs. Sewell was fearless too, when Anna held the reins. She had the greatest admiration for the quality of physical courage, which she did not possess. "But I have a great deal of moral courage," she said, after owning this; and it was true.

This was the last winter at Blue Lodge. The life there, so full of interest to the ladies of the house, was dull for the master. In 1864 some occupation adapted to his declining strength (he was then seventy-one years old) appears to have offered itself in Bath, and it was decided to remove there, and take lodgings at Combe Down until a suitable house could be found, Mrs. Sewell and Anna hoping still to drive over to Wick very frequently to carry on a part of their work there.

It was a sorrowful day at Wick when the news passed through the village that the good friends at Blue Lodge were about to leave. I have a little packet of letters in my hand written by members of the Temperance Society, night-school scholars, and others, showing with what gratitude, love, and entire appreciation they had received the kindness so freely bestowed upon them. One letter will serve as a specimen of the spirit which pervades them all :—

"MY VERRY DEAR AND HONORED LADY,—I hope you will take these few lines without offence, from the hand of one, that feels it his Bounden Duty to render to you my many thanks for all your kindness to me, and to my family, and to all of us.

"I understand to well that you are about to leave us, and I feel deep regret on account of it : tis always Good to have a friend and Bad to be without one; yet still my Jesus is precious to my soul, and I know he will never go away.

"I hope you are better. I have heard you have been Ill, and I hope dear Miss Sewell and Mr. Sewell is Well.

"Since I left wick parish, I have not had the opportunity of seeing you very often, still I have never forgott, nor never shall, your great kindness. Both you and Mr. and Miss Sewell has always a verry High Place in my affections. If I never see you again in this world, I pray that God will Bless you and prosper both you and Mr. Sewell and dear Miss Sewell. May he Crown you with Every Needful Blessing here and Crown you with Glory in the world to come. I am quite Sure he will.

"Dear Lady, I felt I could not let you go off, without

sending you these few lines. But I feel much Contrition while writing to you—my heart is full while I write. I feel like the Disciples did when Jesus was going to leave them, but I hope the Lord will still Bless us all and Bless you most wherever you go. When I think how Benificial you have been to the inhabitants of wick how they will all miss you and Miss Sewell when you are gone away.

"I hope dear Miss Sewell got home safe—when I met her in the rood to wick, I was so overjoyed I felt like one lifted out of the Body. I couldn't help my tears after we parted.

"Dear Lady, I should like to tell you a good deal but I cannot in the Space of a Letter. I am not well the cold winds upset me, and my wife has the Rhumatics. I get about as usual but my little trade is verry Bad, tis such short work Round here for men—we have been verry hard Pressed Lately with the times but still rest in the promise of our Heavenly Father. I Pray on and Fight on Determined by the help of God to get safely landed in the Better world. May he help us all to do the right thing for Jesus sake. Please to pardon my faults. We send our united love to you, dear Lady, and Mr. Sewell, and dear Miss Sewell."

CHAPTER V.

MRS. WILLIAMSON AND OTHER FRIENDS.

"Feed my lambs."

THE "next step" after leaving Wick is described in the course of the following letter:—

To Mrs. R——.

"COMBE DOWN, BATH,
July 4, 1864.

" . . . I can well believe from my own experience that you are *getting good* by being emptied of all good. When cut off from the occupations and circumstances that to a great degree build up our personality, we almost lose ourselves, and hardly know where to find up the *I* and *me;* or we get introduced to them in a very mortifying and disagreeable way sometimes, so poor and pitiful that we are astonished at ourselves. I do not know whether you feel so, but I do—I am feeling so now—a poor, empty, barren, hard-hearted, pitiful wretch; but I think I do thank God for the ugly sight: my dear Master looks so lovely, so desirable, so *needful* under such circumstances. If you and I are to be His servants indeed, we must be unclothed from ourselves again and again that He may have His own will and way *with* us, and do that *in* us which our faith asks, and our nature dislikes, to have done.

"I have no doubt, my dearly beloved friend, that you are in your right place in the Refiner's fire. . . . Precious friend! it is such a hot place—but you will come out of it unhurt, a vessel more fitted for the Master's use, as you do so earnestly desire to be.

"We are getting pretty well reconciled to our lodging life. It seemed very hard at first to be cramped up in little rooms with no garden of our own, and all strangers about us, and no welcome from the faces we met; but I believe it is a right step we have taken for the present, and that is a great help to settlement. Dear Nanny is pretty well—the fatigue of leaving all right at Blue Lodge knocked her down, and she has again lost a good deal of her walking power; but she has many advantages, with close proximity of church, chapel, schools, shops, &c., which she had not before. My goodman is pretty well, and likes his work. Combe Down is a very high, healthy situation, and the surrounding scenery is most beautiful. There are large quarries here for the celebrated Bath Stone, and many quarrymen, who need to have something more done for them than is at present the case.

". . . I am not able to write for any magazines. . . . I am sure you do not know how difficult it is to write *telling poetry*. I have such constant applications, that I believe those who do not write poetry at all think it just as easy as mending a glove—but they make a great mistake."

The quarrymen, however, were not to become the next objects of Mrs. Sewell and Anna's care, for before the close of the year we find congratulations received on having met with a suitable house, and entered on possession. For a time—how long is not clear—the mother and daughter still drove over to Wick for winter evening work, but during this winter of '64-65 Mrs. Sewell was much out of health, obliged to seek perfect quiet and rest, and this may have led to severing her ties to work which no longer "lay at her door."

Moorlands, the new home, was within a walk of Bath, a little way off the Wells road. The meadow-land attached to it sloped down to a lawn where fruit-trees grew, lying on a gentler slope in front of the house. One tall apple-tree I remember gracefully bending under its load of little red-cheeked apples. A terrace-walk beside the house was made for Anna's benefit, with a border full of brightest flowers. When this green nest was lit up with the touches of brilliant colour which its owners knew so well where to place, it became a spot to dream of for its loveliness; and the drives about the lovely neighbourhood were a never-ceasing delight to Mrs. Sewell and Anna. The banks and hedgerows around Bath are rich in varied colouring at every season of the year—never more so than in the first half of winter. Mrs. Sewell had an eye to feast on colour, and pine for it when all around was grey. The new home became very dear, although it was discovered that the previous tenant had "let things go" to an extent which made it a troublesome task to get them into sufficient order.

To Mrs. R——.

"Anna is much better; we are getting on well, working like—Trojans, shall I say? or English women? I think the last, because the cause is better, and *bloodless*. I wish you were here in our sunshine to-day. Oh, it is charming, and looks so lovely! The grass as green as an emerald, and Daisy and Fanny (the cows) chewing the cud and not seeing a hair's-breadth into the future; just switching their tails to keep off the present flies. How difficult it is to switch off our little present torments!"

At the close of 1864 "The Little Forester and his Friend" stepped into the world, appropriately dressed in green, and met a hearty welcome.

Return to "humanity's reach" brought its usual penalties and pleasures. One of the morning visits paid to the new-comers was in reality the chief event of this period, as it proved to be the beginning of a friendship which Mrs. Sewell always reckoned one of the greatest blessings of her life, with Mrs. Williamson, of Fairstowe, Combe Down. This remarkable woman had come to Bath in 1863, her husband, a clergyman, having been obliged to resign his charge at Headingley, Leeds, on account of ill-health. In a letter written years afterwards, Mrs. Sewell alludes to their first meeting.

To Mrs. Williamson.

"I remember your first visit to us at the Moorlands exactly how you looked and talked, and the exact impression left on my mind—a rest and inward satisfaction in you, and a great desire to know more, because you did not look at all like the general run of our callers. Then I had rather a fear as to whether you would take to me; but thanks be to Him who gives us our dear friends to make our lives pleasant, He drew us together, and made us to love one another heartily and confidingly, fostering it all with the golden seal of His own love, so that nothing can disturb it on earth, and nothing will be able to disturb it through the everlasting ages. I shall not be put into such a high class as you, but oh! I shall delight to see you above me, because we shall be near enough for communion, and I should never think of envying you."

Such words, and many others like them, were no polite form from Mrs. Sewell. She was most genuinely disposed to "esteem others better than herself," and this beloved friend perhaps above all others. She had a profound admiration for large executiveness and organising power in a woman. Mrs. Williamson possessed these in a high degree. A little sketch of her work, which appeared in a Bath newspaper after her death, says:—"It might literally be said that not a moment was lost before that benevolence which had characterised her residence in her husband's parish began to be exercised here. In a short space of time she had started the Home for Orphan Girls at Macaulay Buildings, and the Home for Orphan Boys at Claverton Down, each of which was conducted on the family system."

The "family system" was then comparatively untried; it had been the custom to bring up orphan children in barracks—with disastrous results, especially for girls. Mrs. Williamson aimed at making the lives of her orphans as natural, as much in the stream of ordinary life as was possible. They went out to the district school as other children did, and always had credit for good behaviour there. Her own house being very near to the Girls' Home, she was able to take an especially motherly oversight of them. Her beloved helpers

—one of whom, Miss Judell, still has charge of the Orphanage—were to her as daughters, and as lesser mothers to the children; and the little ones grew up with all the frank, trusting, spontaneous ways natural to children reared in a happy, loving home.

It was at Moorlands that I first had the pleasure of making my own elder girls acquainted with Mrs. Sewell. We found her learning to play at croquet in her seventieth year, because a friend staying with her represented that she ought to have some knowledge of a game which then occupied so large a share of her fellow-creatures' attention. With girlish briskness of movement, she threw down her mallet and came to meet us. I rather think that the study we interrupted was not much further pursued. Mrs. Williamson was to bring her orphan girls (I think the Boys' Home was not then opened) to tea at Moorlands in a few days, and Mrs. Sewell kindly asked my daughters to meet her. One of them has preserved the following recollections of the visit:—

"Jessie and I arrived to find Mr. Sewell very busy and concerned about the provender, and while Miss Sewell went to attend to his wishes, the other visitors appeared—Mrs. Williamson on her little pony, the children skipping about her, and a carriage for Mr. Williamson and two orphans—one who was not strong, and a very little one who was to have been left behind as too young to go visiting, but the other girls had entreated for her to come, and the elder ones said they would all carry little Emily in turns, and when the carriage was ordered they all wanted to dress her. I noticed how pretty they were, and Miss Judell laughed and said people often asked if Mrs. Williamson chose her orphans on account of their looks—which was the last thing she was likely to do. I suppose they are loved into good looks. It *was* a pretty sight when Mrs. Sewell stood before the house to receive them, in her black silk dress without a furbelow, and quilled net cap, and with her duchess look—Mr. Sewell bending down his tall white head to the little ones and making them so heartily welcome. In a few minutes they were scattered about the grounds to do just what they liked.

"One little child mounted the wall beside the pig-sty and sat absorbed in gazing at the pigs, to the great amusement of Mr. Sewell and his gardener. 'She'll be the farmer,' the gardener said. They were to have seen the cows milked, and had tea on the lawn, but it came on to rain, and all the out-door diversions had to be given up. It did not signify, with such a tide of good spirits flowing: there was all the fun of running to and fro from kitchen to barn with the tea-things, we helping of course, and they would stop in the rain to hold the yard doors open for us—such pretty manners in everything. At tea the great excitement was to coax Lion, the brown dog, to eat from their hands. Proud was the little girl whose cake he gobbled up—so unlike our poor children in London, whose one idea is 'I'll eat, and I'll stuff, and I'll cram.' The rain cleared off before they went home. Mrs. Sewell showed us her long flower-bed beside the level walk, full of salvias and old-fashioned flowers. She has made quite a study of placing them, but they look as if they grew just as it happened. We had a little talk in-doors in the twilight and firelight, partly about *Ecce Homo*. After Mrs. ——'s horrors at that book (she had not read it), it was very interesting to hear it discussed *pro* and *con*. Of course we could only listen, not having read it, but somehow we did not feel at all stupid for that. Miss Sewell is not as *unstiff* as Mrs. Sewell, but very kind. Mrs. Sewell walked down the fields behind the house with us to show us the short way home, under splendid trees. It was such a happy evening, Aunt E. said we ought to make it balance a great many times when we go out and don't enjoy ourselves. It seemed like Eden, everybody so good and so happy."

It was a very congenial task to Mrs. Sewell to have anything to do with or for Mrs. Williamson and her orphans. The work grew and spread, including a Free Registry for servants, shelter for them when out of place, and other things. In 1872 it seemed, for a time, as though the guiding hand would shortly be withdrawn. In writing to ask Mrs. Sewell to undertake the task of compiling the Annual Report, Mrs. Williamson says :—

"It is now more than six months that I have been laid aside from all work, solemnly warned by my friendly doctor that entire rest is absolutely needful for life; and have been waiting with folded hands, and I hope a folded will, the Master's mind concerning me. . . . As year has followed year, all our experience has testified that our God is a faithful God, and that He has more than realised all our hopes and expectations; and for myself,—whether now, or at the end of a few more days of blessed and privileged toil, I am withdrawn from it, I can leave it in the full assurance that the same Fatherly hand will hold it up, and support the true fellow-labourers who have stood at my side from the beginning, devoting themselves to the Orphan Homes as a noble life-work, and loving the children as their own.

" . . . Our little work has at least proved that small power of any kind, and weak health, if devoted with a single eye and honest heart to Him who has measured out to us both our power and health, will not prevent our obtaining great and rich blessings, not only for our work, but for our souls also."

A full tale of work is recorded in this report, but the silent service that could not show in print was perhaps even more fruitful. "Many people used to ask whether Mr. and Mrs. Williamson were not very rich, reckoning their means in proportion to what they did for others," writes one of their fellow-labourers. "Their own house was ever a refuge for the homeless and destitute of all classes, and these tried and tempted ones, under the blessed influences of this home of hope and love, often gathered up strength which served them for future conflicts. Mrs. Williamson often spoke of the benefit she herself derived from associating with people in all positions of life, differing from each other in political, social, and religious views. 'I love my children so much,' she would say, 'I might be in danger of becoming too much absorbed in them, if it were not for counteracting influences. I delight in the thought of the *many kinds* of workmen God employs in the preparation of His Kingdom.'"

Mrs. Williamson found time to read largely, and extract choice passages from what she read. She has published two little selections, "Wayside Wisdom," and "Pilgrim Lays for the Homeward Bound," which have been much valued by the large circle who knew and loved her.

I had hoped that this valued friend would herself have told the story of her friendship with Mrs. Sewell, but at the time my request that she would do so reached her, she was herself on the brink of the river, waiting to rejoin her friend on the other side. She left me kind messages, which have been conveyed to me in the following letter from her friend Mrs. Walker:—

"BATH, *September* 6, 1884.

"DEAR MRS. BAYLY,—I saw our beloved Mrs. Williamson last on Monday, July 14, four days before she entered into rest. She seemed rather stronger than when I had seen her on the previous Saturday, and immediately began to speak to me with all her usual eagerness. 'I want particularly,' she said, 'to ask you to write to Mrs. Bayly for me—she has been requested to write some account of dear Mrs. Sewell's life, and knowing how intimate we were, and how we loved each other, she has asked if I would like to supply any particulars connected with our friendship. Write to her and tell her what you know of our friendship. Tell her how it was a remarkable one, springing up in old age, blossoming late, like a tree in autumn. Tell her how much I valued her; it was not for one quality alone, it was for her rare combination of qualities; for the strength combined with sweetness; the qualities of mind and of heart. I could speak and write to her of every subject freely, without fear of ever being misunderstood. We instinctively understood each other. What I valued so much was her largeness of heart and mind; there was nothing narrow about her.

'A perfect woman, nobly plann'd,
To warn, to comfort, and command.'

Looking up at the text hanging above her bed which had been in Mrs. Sewell's dying room, she said, 'How little she thought how soon it would hang over my dying bed! Then when I rose to go (for I dared not let her talk any more) she said, 'You used to say we were like David and Jonathan, and you see we shall not "be long divided."'

"I can only add, as she wished me to do, my own

impression of the peculiarly strong link between the two. It seemed to me as if their whole natures fitted and corresponded together. When Mrs. Sewell died, Mrs. Williamson, though very calm and quiet, appeared to me to feel the loss right through her being. At the same time, she bore it with her usual courage, and would say how wrong it was to sorrow over much for friends when we might so fully enter into their joy, and into following them into the presence of the Lord.

"In reading through Mrs. Sewell's letters, I am struck with the many points of contact in the nature of the two friends, both in larger and smaller matters. There was of course, in the first place, the union of fellowship in the Lord. Beyond this, both had large, philanthropic dispositions. Both were continually planning and working for the good of the poor. Both not only pitied but loved their 'poor brethren.' Then again, both delighted in literature; poetry was Mrs. Williamson's favourite recreation. Both delighted in Nature. Dear Mrs. Williamson was never weary of gazing at the lovely views from her sweet abode. I shall never forget how she would pause again and again to seek one's sympathy in admiration of each particular point of view. The birds were her life friends. Her own nature was full of life and joy, and in sympathy with all that was pure and good and beautiful. Ever shall I esteem it one of my greatest privileges to have been much with her during the last two years of her life. In the last few months our intercourse was specially sweet, and at times quite sacred. She seemed latterly so passionately to long for perfection, she complained of herself as so deficient in love; and when I observed that her love showed itself in deeds more than in words, she answered, 'One may give all one's goods to the poor, and yet not have love.' Her almost perfected soul seemed to crave the finishing touches of holiness.

"In one of her last letters to me she wrote:—

"'I enclose the two last cards from Norwich. They tell of gradual decay, but this we must prepare for; and all we can desire for this venerable mother in Israel is that He for whom her life was spent may bid her sun go calmly down, and this I *believe He will do*, and give her an abundant entrance into the unimagined blessedness of His presence, of which we know so little, except that it is *fulness of joy*, and that when we wake up after His likeness we shall be satisfied; which we certainly never are when we behold *our own*. Mine appears every day to satisfy me less and less, but this only makes me long more and more to "be clothed in beauty not my own." Meanwhile, let us love one another while waiting for His appearing.'

"She often said she felt her powers failing, and that no one knew how weak and how tired she was. It was difficult to realise it, so indomitable was her energy, so eager and vigorous her mind, and so tenacious her memory. There seemed nothing of age about her, save its calm and mellow ripeness. There was so much romance blended with her intensely practical judgment and rich common-sense. There was such a kind, youthful enthusiasm in the warmth with which she would take up a new object of sympathy or subject of thought. How she would follow a friend to the door, and on to the gate, and even to the road, with an abounding warmth of affection that seemed as if it would not let you go."

The following lines were the last that Mrs. Williamson asked to have read to her :—

"Rest.

"I lay me down to rest,
  With little thought or care
Whether my waking find
  Me here or there.

"A bowing, burdened heart,
  That only asks to rest
Unquestioning, upon
  A loving breast.

"My good right hand forgets
    Its cunning now;
To march the weary march
    I know not how.

"I am not eager, bold, nor
    Strong—all that is past;
I am ready not to do
    At last—at last.

"My full day's work is done,
    And this is all my part;
I give a patient God
    My patient heart.

"And grasp His banner still,
    Though all its blue be dim;
These stripes no less than stars
    Lead after Him."

Among the many visitors to Fairstowe whom to meet was a delight, was Mrs. Charles, so well known to the literary world as the author of "Chronicles of the Schonberg-Cotta Family," and many other valued books. Mrs. Williamson pointed out to me a seat in the garden, under a large tree, where Mrs. Sewell had sat and talked with her. She said, "I used to leave them talking when I went out, and find them still talking there when I returned." When we think of these three women, differently gifted, but with so much in common, it is no wonder that the hours they spent together passed only too quickly, and left behind them "Sunny Memories."

In answer to my inquiry whether she could transcribe some of these "memories" for this little history of our dear friend, Mrs. Charles, though very much occupied, kindly found time to write the following letter :—

"DEAR MRS. BAYLY,—I could not indeed fail to say such words as I can in honour of one whom I love and reverence as I do Mrs. Sewell, though just now I have scarcely a free minute to write.

"We certainly need not think of her, or any of the beloved ones 'at home,' as creatures belonging only to the past. Her 'new name' we may not know, but we are quite sure she is *herself* still.

"What I remember of my brief intercourse with her is not any special incident or saying, but *herself*, the bright, calm presence embracing in it the riches of a varied past.

"It was the variety and range of her spiritual experience which were so interesting: the combination in her of the flowers and fruits of many religious zones and climates.

"There seemed to me the quiet beauty of the deeper experience of the Friends, among whom, I believe, her early training had been: the upward look, as of one listening for a voice still to be heard among us, instead of the downward, anxious groping, as of one only poring over the letters of a book. That the Voice and the Book were for her combined, no one, of course, could doubt; but this listening for the eternal teaching of the ever-present Comforter, the Holy Ghost, through which the early Friends were first awakened to so many of the wrongs and sins of our times, struck me as one of her characteristics. 'Thy poor brother' and 'Unto Me' were ever sounding through her heart.

"And then there was the fervent sympathy with another of the many companies of Christendom, the Moravians, first missionaries of the Reformed Churches, whose hearts have so especially gone forth to the outcast and the forgotten of the nations and of mankind. When I knew her, she was much in association with the Moravian Brethren, whose ideal of the Church is of a great evangelising brotherhood, whose hearts, like hers, have always gone forth to the deepest need—taking the glad tidings among the ice and snows of the Esquimaux, among the low races of Australia, to the slave and to the leper. 'Thy poor brother' was their motto, as it was hers. Wherever the need was deepest and the compassionate service truest, there she seemed to feel nearest to Him who 'had compassion on the multitudes' in their commonest wants of hunger and thirst, as well as in their highest cravings.

"For, besides all her other gifts and graces, she had most truly the gift of the poet, and therefore her benevolence could never be lost or swallowed up in a mere generality of well-wishing, and her speech could never be stiffened into rhetoric. Not 'humanity,' but each man or woman or little child, all different:—not 'masses,' but 'multitudes;'—not generalised 'brethren,' but 'thy poor brother.' The fountain of poetry sprang to light late with her; and this also had a beautiful special meaning through her for us all. The spring-time is sure to have its songs; but it is inspiring to us to know that the music never dies.

'The poet has the child's heart in his breast.'

"The sources of her inspiration were ever fresh, just because they were so deep. And real poetic inspiration was hers, stamped with the recognition of the common heart of all. Our most subtle and sifting critic * acknowledged it; and my mother has just told me how a poor dying boy in a country village was so touched by her reading to him 'Mother's Last Words,' that he sent to beg to hear them again. They were read to him once more, and with their music in his heart that night he died.

"Those few glimpses of her when we were staying near dear Mrs. Williamson were the last I had.

"But the last picture I have of her in my heart is as

---

* Matthew Arnold.

beautiful as anything can be. I think of the aged, white-haired mother sitting by her dying daughter's couch and writing at her child's dictation 'Black Beauty'—that tender, pathetic, humorous plea for the dear dumb creatures to whom St. Francis did not hesitate to extend the name of 'thy poor brother.' The daughter's last longing before she left was to leave this last plea for the creatures so helpful to us, 'groaning and travailing in pain together until now.' And the words came through the mother's lips, as it were, 'Mother's last words' to us all.

"And now they are 'awake together' in His likeness, of which we saw so much in them whilst here—the likeness of the infinite compassion which is always going after the lost, always remembering the one missing, and never content until it is found; never content with any of us until we translate, as she did, 'the least of these My brothers' into '*thy poor brother*.'"

The connection with the Moravian Church was short-lived, ending with the short sojourn in the neighbourhood of Bath, but it happened to occupy the time during which Mrs. Charles occasionally met Mrs. Sewell and her daughter. It appears to have left no deep mark—I cannot find that any form of church-life ever did, on Mrs. Sewell, after her separation from Friends. She would refer frequently to the impression made on her by individual teachers—occasionally to a very strong sense of repulsion from certain forms of worship or church government, but never, so far as I recollect, to any sense of attraction that was not personal; her heart remained with her own people.

The shadow of a coming sorrow lay over these years at Bath. Among the few letters of this period which have come to hand, there is hardly one which does not contain some anxious reference to the health of the beloved daughter-in-law. In 1866, not long after Mr. Philip Sewell's coming to reside at Clare House, Norwich, she passed away, leaving seven children.

The occupation which had led Mr. Sewell to Bath seems to have come to an end before this time. As soon as could be arranged, the family removed to their native county, and settled in a house at Old Catton, about a mile beyond Clare House, on the road from Norwich to Buxton, where Mr. John Wright and his sisters resided. This was in 1867. It was the last move; the little white house became the home of seventeen years, and round it cluster all the freshest memories that remain of a spring-like old age.

This removal gave rise to a correspondence with Mrs. Williamson, the greater part of which, on Mrs. Sewell's side, has been preserved. After reading through these numerous letters, however, I can better understand the reply given me over and over again by friends and relatives to whom I have applied for letters—"All those we have kept are so filled with comments on our own affairs, that they could have no interest for the general public." The two great-hearted mothers were never tired of talking and writing about the orphan children, but it is comparatively rare to meet with a passage that will bear extraction. Many of the subjects named, too, belong to those with which "a stranger intermeddleth not."

The letters being—like all Mrs. Sewell's, unless the receivers dated them—without date, I have thought it best to insert here all extracts containing no allusion to events which would give them any definite place in order of time.

"Orphan children are not, in a sense, like common children, being especially adopted of the Lord, and have to be cared for under all extremities. How beautifully Mr. Van Meter realises them as belonging to his Saviour! and so do you; therefore rest and get strong for their sakes, and for us all. The letter you sent me of Miss Rye's is very interesting and business-like. I am so pleased we had the pleasure of seeing her at your house, and wishing her good speed. If we can do little ourselves, it is pleasant to be in sympathy with those who are working hard. It is difficult to define what work is; I mean, what has the essential element of work in it. This will be seen when the chaff is blown away. Well the Lord knows, for His work *in* our work is the only thing that will abide when He cometh."

Writing to Mrs. Williamson of her daughter's sudden attack of illness, she says:—

"This has hindered us in our own work, but we do not now know what kind of work carries us the most surely forward. He who takes the charge of us can only tell this—He will do the best for us. I wish to leave all with Him, and neither fail nor be discouraged.

"I have tied myself up to the whipping-post every night when I went to bed, and well flagellated myself for not having answered your letter, which I meant to have done immediately on receiving it; it filled my heart with sympathy and concern for you. . . . You will not rest till all your chain is run out. It is not for me to say *stop*. This is our working day, and we know not how long it may last. You and I do not naturally take to the 'easy-chair' life; it is to me another name for the stocks. I am often reproved for not playing the part of a 'nice old lady,' but I say I have not the gift, and whilst such blessed health and spirits remain, I should not succeed if I tried."

"These bodies of ours require a deal of looking after, and are held on a repairing lease till the tenancy has run out; and then, beautiful and glorious. We may well be content in our moth-house, seeing where the door out of it opens."

"I set you, dear friend, before me, to follow, not to copy, because our work and our gifts are different—the same work and one Master, but on different parts of it. And what a fine thing work is! As I look at the few remaining years which may possibly be mine, I feel quite greedy for work, and long to fill all that is left in some way of following the Master. I long to do more of the healing, helping work, to make something better—something that is different to sin and misery; something that carries the aspect of hope in it; something that must bring me continually to Him for all the grace, and all the needed ability. Your hearty, sound, ever-increasing work is a constant stimulant and encouragement to me, and a constant subject of rejoicing. It is the good leaven which silently spreads wider and wider, embracing larger and larger circles—no flourish of drums and trumpets, but a constant chime of sweet music leading one on. I hope I shall stand near you in the Great Day, and see you with all your orphans and emigrants about you, whom the dear Master has given you the privilege of bringing to Him.

"I am glad you like Robertson's sermons, because I do, and as you say, if you are not reading with a narrow, suspicious mind, you find but little you can think wrong. What I feel is he does not give you *all*—you are ever expecting to find what is wanting, and are continually led on expecting, but not finding.

"Write to me again; my heart yearns after you. I think of your loving-kindness in sparing us your good Jenny and taking savage Nanny to train for yourselves. Say an affectionate word for me to the children of your homes, and take the love to yourself which neither best, nor dearest, nor any other word expresses."

"I forget whether you admire Bushnell's writings as much as I do. I have just been reading a sermon preached after his death, describing his character; such a great soul: such a powerful mind—so simple, affectionate, genial, and childlike. How often we find great men like little children! In Christ was his happy abiding-place.

"The sweet Lady Augusta Stanley also is gone from us. Oh I do hope God is polishing some rare jewels to shine before the next generation, to reflect His beauty and bring Him praise."

"Let all who are watching for the 'promise of the Spirit,' watching for His coming more than they that watch for the morning, bear this thought with them continually, that Christ is *now* present to their faith, to do for them all that their present state requires, and that the Spirit is also in them to perfect the love and obedience requisite to the reception of the promise of the Father: thus all that is needed is being done in the best possible manner, and as soon as the way is prepared, they will be filled with the Holy Ghost. If the vision tarry, wait for it, and wait for it with the assurance that you shall be baptized with the Holy Ghost not many days hence.

"When we are sitting together in our blessed resting-place, and have leisure, we shall be able to trace the fulfilled prophecies, and see how mercifully the hope of Christ's appearing was left for the quickening heart-cheer of *all the ages*. I wish I could feel the nearness of His coming as vividly as some do, for my heart fails me over the present state of things.

'The darkness deepens, Lord with me abide.'"

"I am thinking of thee, beloved, as I sit alone on this quiet sunshiny Sabbath, when everything around me speaks of love and beauty, the winds whispering of joy and peace; and the mystery of life seems to be fresh upon my heart. The mystery is over with those who are gone from us; their eyes are opened and their hearts are filled to overflowing, and they know what it is *to live*. Whilst the veil remains drawn to us, and the full revelation tarries, we may console ourselves with paying visits to the Holy Land, anticipating the delight with which we shall once more dwell with our partners in the battle of life. I never think of the grave; not even of my own; it only seems as the hiding-place for my old clothes."

"I have just begun to read Kingsley's Life; if you have not read it, do; it is worth anything; such thought, freshness, earnestness; such love and trust in God—such an affectionate admiration of nature and the beautiful earth and heavens. I feel my very soul fed and expanded and encouraged by it."

"What two great lazy giants Indolence and Doubt are! What miracles of liberty and joy might be wrought if they could be persuaded to emigrate and leave the land free, taking with them the large family of Hurry Scurry which are making so much fuss!"

"I often think of Bezaleel and Aholiab, and their endowment from God of the special spirit of wisdom for the work they had to do—'In all who are wise-hearted I have put wisdom.' The gift still continues to descend upon the wise-hearted. How many promises are not fulfilled because not expected—they are treated like old fashions which have passed away with the dispensation."

"... How high those ascend who rise through great sorrow, and how little the generality of people know anything of the steps up which such people climb! How few people there are who really are known, or who know any one, or who know themselves! You and I shall find a good deal new in each other. ... Oh for the new heaven and the new earth, and old friends upon it! It is a comfort to have come upon the *last times*, and not to be so long without a body as Abraham. Don't you think so?"

"I have at last roused my energies to ask how my dear precious friend is bearing on, through this most perilous and painful weather. ... It has been quite humiliating to me to find how one misery in the flesh can absorb the whole nature, and let the zeal and power of life pass into warm clothes and a glowing fire."

"Will work be ever more fairly shared?—more workers and fewer martyrs—for it is coming to this in the great strain of life and action. We could not well do without our heroes and martyrs even for good middle men and women. An impetus, an enthusiasm, an example is needed to create even these."

"A nation's sorrow and sympathy is a refining, exalting, and affecting thing. We could hardly do without sympathetic sorrow—all fine weather would make us hard and selfish."

Referring to national calamities :—

"... It is a mercy indeed that we are held in that strong Hand, and are not floating as a loose end. That which is purposed will be accomplished, and the righteous kingdom will be set up upon the earth, and the elect people will bear rule. It *will be* all right at last, and no one will have to complain, and you and I will rejoice together and praise the Lord.

"The *bitterness* is *now*, that with all our great advantages, all the honours that have been heaped upon us as a nation, and with all our opportunities to be good and to do good, that we are what we are. I think the Lord must be so disappointed in us. He may say to us as He said to the Jews, 'What more could I have done for you than I have done?' As a country we cannot *fast* for our sins; we have no heart for that, no belief in the good of it; but we might fast apart, as Daniel did, and confess the sins of our nation as well as our own."

> " When I gave thanks to God for all
> His priceless gifts to me,
> Believe me then, among the chief
> I give Him thanks for Thee.'

"Thy dear little note on my birthday fed that always hungry place, my heart! I do not know what I should do without love, it suits my constitution entirely; I think as we grow old, we do not value it less, but we expect it less, and it always comes with a glad surprise. . . . Through the exceeding kindness of my God, much love still comes to me, in each case, as in yours, giving to my old heart a fresh glow of happiness.

"Oh! what a home that will be, where all the brothers and sisters meet together, knowing, loving, and appreciating each other; each in its separate, sanctified individuality, each filling its prepared place—all *satisfied!* I shall live to see thee shine, blessed friend, and to see the troops that will come to greet thee as benefactor."

"How strange it is that so few know how to be merry and wise. *That* is to come in its full extent, and oh how much more! I think unspeakable adoration is the feeling I care to have most largely increased—the capacity for it here is so limited, and the desire for it so great. We shall be satisfied *there*—no more hunger and thirst, and that for ever and ever. It seems to me easier to think of eternity, than to think of an end—both are beyond my present powers.

"I have been thinking a good deal lately about Christian discipline, and how wonderfully the Blessed Lord can *alter* afflictions without removing them. To outsiders they will look just the same—very bad; but if His dear Hand has touched them, all the sting and heavy ache has gone out of them, and He gives perhaps the 'manifold more in this present life' to more than compensate for all He must take away. What a pity it is we do not believe more fully in the 'hundredfold more' which in His generous tenderness He is willing to give! What a pity that all the gloomy talk is about taking up the cross!"

CHAPTER VI.

LIFE AT OLD CATTON.

"What little help I have been able to give to others, my fellow-pilgrims, has, I am sure, been given largely, under God, by means of an old inveterate habit I have of looking on the sunny side of things. I am to-day more convinced than ever that it is the true side, although for a season, if need be, we are in heaviness."—DR. RALEIGH.

THE new home at Old Catton gave abundant scope for the new inmates' love of improving. The place they made so pleasant looked dreary and commonplace enough when they first arrived, in September 1867; and the change from the lovely surroundings of Bath to Norfolk lanes shut in between high banks and stiff hedges, made a sad difference in the pleasure of afternoon drives. Many of the streets in Norwich are paved with little round pebbles set on end; this gave great offence to the pony who came with the family from Bath. When he found out that there were two ways to a place, by one of which the pebbles could be avoided, he flatly refused to cross them; neither coaxing nor scolding would move him; his mistress must go round the other way. But the objects of interest around were many. Besides Clare House and its inmates, there were at first two homes at Buxton, about seven miles off, that of Mr. John Wright and the sister who had lived with him since the death of his beloved wife in 1861, and close beside it, the home of Mrs. Sewell's two other unmarried sisters—a place where she loved to go for perfect rest.

Some preparation had already been made for beautifying her own home. A rather low wall had divided its garden from the next-door neighbour's. On this a high lattice-work was put up, and creepers planted to train over it, which formed by degrees a beautiful leafy screen. A broad, sloping bed under the wall was given up to wild things transplanted from the lanes and hedgerows, making the "exquisite embroidery" of which Mrs. F.—— speaks. There, in time, grew flowers of all seasons —primroses, wood-sorrel, speedwell, wild geranium, lilies of the valley, and climbing things full of blossom in spring and berries in autumn. A little lawn rose steeply in front of the paved verandah outside the French window of the dining-room; on its brow, a straight, level walk, running the length of the garden, supplied the requirements of composition. Two large beech-trees flung their shadows down the slope, and beside every root and stump, little wild-flowers—speedwell and wild geranium— came to bloom. A thick hedge cut off the farther part of the garden, previously given over to vegetables. Mrs. Sewell had these exchanged for a second little lawn and flower-beds, and against the wall, her summer-parlour—a large greenhouse, without artificial heat, but making a shelter open to light and sunshine where she hoped that Anna would spend many an hour.

The drawing-room was over the dining-room, each taking the whole width of that part of the house, with an outlook behind over the garden and the fields beyond it to the village church and trees— in front, across the highroad to a grove of beech-trees in Mr. Buxton's park, where deer would come to lie in the cool shade. The roof of the verandah made a balcony outside the large back window of the drawing-room; there Mrs. Sewell trained flowers and creepers in boxes to make an upstairs garden for Anna when she was unable to leave that floor. A tempting lump of mutton-suet hung, enclosed in a piece of net, for the special benefit of the tom-tits who were constantly to be seen hovering about, and pecking at the dainty morsel, in no danger of being trapped, or frightened from their meal. The room itself had an old-world look, a low, subdued harmony of colour, and a scent of pot-pourri, in keeping with the quaint speech, the silver hair, and antique, old-world courtliness of the lord and lady of the home. An exquisite perception of the effect of colour was seen in every part of the house—or rather, felt: all was too simple and harmonious to have any striking effect. The paper on the walls was of the quietest tone—no showy patterns, no one piece of grand furniture to spoil the look of the rest, but plants at the windows, and flowers in vases arranged lightly, never in solid clumps; at meals, no profusion of dishes, but simple delicacies daintily served.

It has always seemed to me that there is a peculiar charm in visiting at the houses of Friends, arising partly, perhaps, from the delightful absence of all pretension and fuss-making. If ropes and pulleys have been necessarily set to work in preparation for a visitor, refined feeling keeps them out of sight. For the time being, you are permitted in the most natural way to blend your life with theirs. Friends who are not in a position to give great entertainments, or exercise large hospitalities, will yet allow themselves to have much enjoyment in entertaining, in their own simple way, those whom they love and esteem, or to whom they feel a short sojourn in their house may be helpful. This was quite the custom at the white house in Old Catton, and all who went there cherished the memory of its graceful, heartfelt hospitalities. The door of the little bedroom, carefully prepared, stood open as if to welcome you. The room would have looked almost too white and clean, but for flowers and books placed exactly in the right position, to relieve the effect. An atmosphere of thoughtful love pervaded all, for you could scarcely be conscious of a want without finding, on looking round, that it had been anticipated. Whatever business Mrs. Sewell had on hand was held second to the pleasure of a guest. Her frequent visitors, and the amount of life, social and individual, which claimed her interest at Norwich, hindered the Muse:—

possibly did her fame the service of preventing her writing as much as before in quantity, when declining vigour called for hoarding and accumulation of force, in order to keep up the old standard of quality.

From the time of going to Catton until her son's second marriage in 1870 (an event recorded with great comfort and thankfulness), Mrs. Sewell took up the oversight of her grandchildren with a graver sense of anxious responsibility than she had felt with her own children. They were a joy to her at all times; but as one by one they safely passed the critical period of development from childhood into youth, she seemed to draw breath, and give herself up to enjoy them and admire their exploits, with no conscientious scruples and fears of spoiling them. Charming though she had been as a playfellow, they said, "It was as we grew older, and found out what a delightful *friend* she could be, that we really came to know her." It has been left to another—one of her very dear young friends—to describe this rare sympathy of hers with youth.

"MY DEAR MRS. BAYLY,—You ask me to send you some of my recollections and impressions of dear Mrs. Sewell. To *describe* her would be quite beyond the power of any words of mine, or indeed, I think, beyond the power of words at all. But to have known her so intimately,—to have enjoyed her love and friendship—to have been the subject of her interest and her ready, wise advice, I shall always reckon as among the highest privileges of my life.

"I think one of her greatest charms was her wonderful

power of sympathy. Not only could she throw herself completely into the interests of others, but she seemed actually to retain all the feelings of every age, all through her life; and this it must have been which made her such a perfect companion to the child—the young girl—the middle-aged woman—or to the friend whose years more nearly numbered her own. I often used to say of her, that though she was our oldest friend, she was in reality the youngest. She had never forgotten what it was, and how it felt, to be young. I well remember how delighted I was when, about the time of my leaving school, I first began to know her, and found in her a friend who could view things from my standpoint, and who understood all about me, and standing, as it were, on the same level with me, seemed to take me by the hand, and point me upward, not in any way as if she, at some unattainable distance of perfection, beckoned me to follow her up there. Her whole soul was thrown, for the time, into my youthful interests—my studies, pursuits, and pleasures; and as we roamed together over the moors, I felt what a wonderful *new* friend I had in my mother's *old* friend. It had not even the appearance of condescension; it was reality of interest. The same thing struck me whenever I was with her. Whatever interested me was sure to interest her, and I came at last to consider whether any topic was really worthy of her thought, before I claimed her attention—for it was sure to be carefully weighed and considered over. How often I have been surprised to hear her say, 'I have been thinking about what you were telling me last night;' and then would follow the result of her meditations—perhaps in the form of loving encouragement and approval, or perhaps kindly administered criticism. But it was the thought that she, so much older, so immeasurably superior, should consider anything that I said of sufficient importance to 'think about' afterwards, that gave such a thrill of pleasure and surprise. I recollect that during my last visit to her in the summer of 1882, we were walking together one lovely morning in her pretty garden. I was telling her about my Sunday-school work, and she had been giving me some of her experience as to the best way of conveying religious instruction to the young—advice which I felt was so valuable that I afterwards noted down all I could remember. The next day, after spending some hours in her room, she came downstairs with several sheets of close writing in her hand. She had actually taken the trouble to write out for me her thoughts and experience in religious education. I have the precious papers now, and shall ever value them, not only for the thoughts they contain, but as a proof of that generous love which so gladly spent itself, even in old age and declining strength, for the benefit of the young and inexperienced.

"Closely allied with this wonderful instinct of sympathy, and perhaps springing from it, was her power of entering into detail. Nothing was small or trivial with her. If worth doing or thinking about at all, it was worth her whole thought and application.

"I have heard my mother tell how once when she was staying at Old Catton, before Miss Sewell's death, a favourite servant was going to be married, and was making a patchwork quilt for her new home. The arrangement of the colours in that quilt was a matter to which the closest attention of both Mrs. Sewell and her daughter was given. It was made quite a study. The quilt was brought in and spread upon the floor; the effect of one colour tried, and then another, till, after much consultation, a harmonious arrangement was at last arrived at, and the maiden despatched to work out the design of her mistresses.

"It seemed to me that *Perfection* in everything was what she aimed at—and the arrangement of her flowers, the management of her house, and the composition of her verses all came under the same law, and were but different manifestations of that Order which pervaded and regulated her well-balanced mind and perfectly arranged life.

"With all her wisdom and experience, I never saw any one so entirely humble—so perfectly natural—so artlessly simple. One evening we had been reading together an article which had just appeared in one of the magazines, and which had greatly pleased her, on the condition of the soul just after death; and naturally our talk was of dear ones passed away. She told me she quite believed that heaven was not far off, that we were encompassed by the ministering spirits of those gone before, and that if our eyes were but opened, we should see our friends about us. 'I quite believe that my darling is often near me,' she said —referring to the daughter who had been the light of her eyes and the joy of her heart; 'but,' she added, with characteristic simplicity, 'I should be frightened, you know, if I saw her.'

"I have spoken of Perfection as her aim. And to me she seemed of all people I ever knew to be the most nearly perfect, and yet withal

> 'Not too bright or good
> For human nature's daily food.'

It was pre-eminently in the little things of life, the small everyday troubles and difficulties and pleasures, that the thought would occur, 'Oh! if I could only tell Mrs. Sewell this!' 'How I wish I could ask her about that!' 'I wonder what she would advise?' 'I must remember this next time I see her.' And so she is an everyday loss; and while we feel the world is poorer since she has been taken, we still feel ourselves the richer for having known her and claimed her as a friend.—Ever yours affectionately,

M. J. R."

A few letters can be identified as belonging to this period.

To Mrs. Williamson.

"OLD CATTON.

"I do not think we shall find any one here like you and yours; ... a friendship distinct from the love of relatives—something that you have gained by peculiar affinity, and hold by a tie not touched by instinct. We have a great many calling friends of my brother and sisters, and of my son—not those who have sought us for ourselves, as you did."

"Affinities" very near and close were by-and-by

discovered with neighbours rich and poor, and if the claims of a large circle of acquaintance took up time, they brought new openings for usefulness. In a memorandum of hints for her own guidance, Mrs. Sewell writes :—

"For my own soul, to strive after deeper spirituality—more definite prayer.

"To seek to maintain a more abiding sense of the shortness of my time here, that I may not lose opportunities of giving help in any way that may come before me, especially by way of encouragement.

"To be more in the habit of working during long calls."

To a Friend under Perplexing Trials.
"1868.

"I was quite heavy-hearted about you all yesterday, but I could not find time to write. *I have no time*—no *leisure* time ; engagements are unremitting. . . . When I want to comfort myself about you in this painful business, I try and look forward to the great day of revelation, when all the threads of this intricate plan of our Heavenly Father's shall have worked themselves out into a beautiful and perfect result—when we shall rejoice together and admire over it, and think how much excellence we should have spoiled had we been allowed to have our own will and way unchecked. But oh! dear friend, my heart is a poor sojourner in the region of faith when my friends are in the region of care, sickness, or disappointment. I get down into the dust with them and fret."

These words recall a summer morning at Old Catton, when a young friend, bearing her portion of the ills of life, had forgotten them under the spell of that sunny garden and the sweet company in it, when suddenly dear Mrs. Sewell's hand was laid on her arm, with the words, so plaintively spoken, "I'm such a dunce, I can't reconcile myself to all your troubles. You have to give up so many things!"

To the Same.

"*July* 7, 1868.

"I can only say what you know so well, that there is but one Deliverer,—and He *does* deliver; but He desires to make His deliverances purifications also;—and there is the difficulty. He thinks most of the purification, and *we* think most of the deliverance; and so we are often detained in a lengthened captivity, till our hearts are broken, and our eyes opened. ... I do not expect that you and I will get out of the fining-pot till we have put off our old rags and put on our white robes:—*that* will be a deliverance! Take heart, dear friend, be of good courage, and God will strengthen your heart. He can make a way when we see no way. He can speak peace when the storm rages, and make 'worm Jacob' as a sharp threshing instrument having teeth—what a wondrous change! I often feel like that poor worm, with no ability to go upright, always slipping and seeking to be down upon the earth again. But He is able to make us stand, even fight, and attain the victory. ... What we want is a full realisation of our privileges, to make us strong, and joyful, and holy, and useful, and peaceful."

To Mrs. Williamson.

(Probably *December* 1868.)

"As I look out upon our little patch of snow, I think of the white raiment on the hills round Bath, and the hoar-frost on the trees, and your eyes, my dear friend, resting upon them with ever-new delight. It is very good to have seen beauty; the remembrance is a portion of your riches that in imagination you can look back upon again and again, and thrice blessed for you if you do so without drawing disparaging contrasts. I find myself at it sometimes, but I chide myself for it, and think how much better it is to have the sky and sun blocked out by trees than by a wall, like so many thousands of our fellow-creatures."

To a Friend who had lost a Daughter.
"1869.

". . . I well remember the impression left on me by her last visit to us ;—it was the unusual harmony and sweet balance of her character. . . . There was something especially beautiful in her youthful maturity and wise simplicity, and in the cheerful hopefulness which spoke in her voice and beamed in her face. She could bear patiently to watch and wait by the side of many a frost-bound heart, because she believed that a spring would come when the winter would be over and gone.

"Dear child! how blessed it is to think of a life so spent and so ended! But oh! dear friend, I know that your own heart must be sorely wounded and aching with the great gap she has left: she has taken away so much joy with her, so much help, so much comfort and dependence, and the home must seem very naked without her;—but I know there is One who will not forget you in this time of casting down—it is His old way of refining His children for the unspeakable joy.

"I cannot write more in the way of consolation; that must come from the God of all comfort. We poor pilgrims can but weep with one another, and say, 'Cheer up; be of good courage.' He has housed one of thy lambs with His spotless flock; He has taken one of thy lilies out of thy garden for His own. He is coming shortly to take us all to dwell with Him. Let us forget our sorrow and finish our work, and sing a little praise by the way, and be ready to meet Him.—Your faithful, loving friend,
"MARY SEWELL."

The next letter was probably written in the later part of the summer of 1870, as the "summer parlour" was finished just before Anna's increased illness prevented her availing herself of the sunny shelter so eagerly and hopefully prepared for her.

"Mothers' Meetings have been on my mind for many months. At first I thought I would write fragments which could be used by an unpractised conductor (of which I suppose there are many), for I think I have an intuition of what they should be—or do. But I gave that up, finding my time was too fully occupied to permit of my writing to any purpose; but having now a beautiful little summer parlour in the garden, I decided to invite the women belonging to our Mothers' Meeting, in little parties of about three or four every week, to come and have tea with me there, to walk and enjoy themselves in the garden, and to talk with me freely on subjects not generally admitted into the meetings. Thus you see I am full of interest about mothers, and am prepared to welcome all that you or any one else can do for them."

These little "Garden-Parties" proved a source of great interest to my dear friend. After one of these "receptions," she was later than usual in coming downstairs. When she appeared, we anxiously inquired how she had passed the night. "Well," she said, "there was nothing the matter; but I was rather wakeful, and slept less than usual—the fact is, I was so much interested in what those women talked to me about last evening, I kept on thinking it over and over, and it brought many things to my mind. I have enjoyed my night very much."

Carlyle records in his journal that he dined out one evening, and met twelve or fourteen distinguished people, including members of the Royal family, celebrated literary characters, &c., &c. The only comment he made on the event was—"Horribly dull evening."

The letters that follow are addressed to Mrs. Brightwen, a friend who was accustomed to have little parties of a kindred nature, but for girls instead of mothers.

To Mrs. Brightwen.

"I cannot tell you how much I rejoice that God has given you such a large heart, and such large opportunities —that you have the skill and the will to sow pleasant and good seed into the minds of the present generation, and to give to a little piece of earth some resemblance to the good land that is to be. We are what our forefathers have made us, and those who succeed us will be the heirs of our works, and our example. Does not this thought give a vast importance and dignity to life?

"I wish I could be present at one of your Conversaziones. I should dearly like to be in the place of one of your girls—moulding clay—looking through the microscope, &c., &c. What a world of interest you will give them, and how many open doors you will set before them!"

To the Same.

" . . . Your letter called forth both praise and sympathy. It touched on many subjects it would have been a pleasure to have spoken to you upon; but little duties eat up pleasures, unless the duties become pleasures, which indeed they should be."

The years 1870–1877 are the only ones of which any kind of journal has been preserved. Less than fourteen pages of an old, haggard-looking account-book contain all the events thought worthy of record, noted in Anna's hand:—many deaths: the family tree had come to the stage when leaves fall off. Through 1870 the entries are rather numerous, and give the idea of much activity—care of schools undertaken, visits to friends and to the seaside, and many individual cases carefully watched. A few entries occasionally may give an idea of the family life.

"*January* 1870.—At Old Catton. Father is in his seventy-seventh year, well and active. Mother in her seventy-third year, very well and wonderfully active and competent. I in my fiftieth year, as well as usual.

"*April* 8.—Mother is now engaged in getting signatures to Miss Preusser's Memorial to the Poor Law Board about pauper children.

"*October* 28.—Metz capitulated, 173,000 troops laid down their arms with Marshal Bazaine."

To Mrs. Williamson.

"*August* 8.

"I daresay you find these delightful summer days only too short. I almost grudge every one that goes by, whispering 'Shorter, shorter.' We have had a very happy time. I think we have done little but be happy. It seems just now especially the will of our kind Father that it should be so. He delights to bless with rest and peace as well as with affliction; we are too apt to think the latter His normal state of mind towards us. We have allowed ourselves to enjoy the sunshine all day long, and no harm of any kind has come near us."

"We have done little but be happy." No one who *felt* as my dear friend did could write that of more than a short period of time; but in looking over this slight record of her eighty-seven years, one feels that, as a whole, it is emphatically the story of a happy life. She suffered anguish on behalf of others as well as herself, but when pleasure came, she could enjoy it, as she says of children, "to the tip-top of her nature." Her great delight in simple pleasures made springs of joy abound for her, and she drank to the full, with never a prick of conscience that it could be unlawful to rejoice. She would entirely have agreed with the words of one of her friends at Bath—"As long as I am in this life, I mean to take some interest in it. For what reason is it made interesting to us if we are not to enjoy it? When I have a visitor to whom I try to make things pleasant, I like him to be pleased; and whilst I am upon God's earth—'Day unto day uttering speech'—I shall be a pleased listener: a pleased listener to the pleasant speech of my friends, the fields, the firmament, and also to the footfall of messengers who will some day take me away."

The letter above quoted bears no date of year. It is inserted here because the sunny summer of 1870 was the last happy time when the mother and daughter can have been out in the sunshine together. Towards the end of that same year, the shadow of death began to steal over the white house, and was never wholly lifted again till the last of the household had passed where shadows flee away. First, in November, comes allusion to attacks of faintness and giddiness which the doctor thought might be the precursor of "something serious" to Mr. Sewell. In March 1, 1871, the words, "I have not been well. Dr. R. thinks it is a troublesome case," indicate the beginning of Anna's mortal illness. Henceforward the mother's care and thought were centred in her: the history of the next eight years must be given in a chapter devoted to her; but a few other events which mark that period must be mentioned here.

In June 1871 Mrs. Sewell lost her dear brother, Mr. John Wright. From that time her three sisters lived together, in their pretty house in the park at Buxton.

One consequence of this event to Mrs. Sewell was that she acquired a closer tie with an institution which from the time of its commencement was a great source of interest to her and most of the members of her family—I refer to the Reformatory for Juvenile Offenders established at Buxton in the year 1852.

In September 1852 Mr. John Wright addressed a letter to the magistrates of Norfolk, calling their attention to the great success which had attended efforts made on behalf of youthful culprits elsewhere, and asking if some similar institution could not be established for the county of Norfolk.

This letter led to a meeting being called on the 21st December 1852, when it was agreed—

"That an establishment should be formed for the maintenance and religious and industrial training of forty lads under the age of twenty.

SIR EDWARD BUXTON, *President*.
JOHN H. GURNEY, *Treasurer*.
GEORGE KITT,
JOHN WRIGHT, } *Acting Committee*.

"Resolved—That it was desirable to induce habits of industry, including the cultivation of land. The Committee were requested to look out for suitable buildings in an eligible situation in the county, where a sufficient quantity of land could be hired."

From the time of its commencement the Reformatory was under the wise and fostering care of Mr. John Wright, who in this work was ably assisted by his excellent wife—the sister-in-law so highly appreciated by Mrs. Sewell. This remarkable and gifted lady had an exceeding love for young people, and possessed in perfection the rare talent, essential to success as a teacher, of being able to inspire her pupils with enthusiasm for whatever she brought before their attention. Fortunately, premises were secured within a short distance of Mr. Wright's house at Buxton, so that Mrs. Wright's visits could be very frequent. Her favourite lesson-books were the Bible and Nature—she taught the lads to observe, and how to examine natural objects in all their detail. This opened up to them a new world of interest, and succeeded even beyond her expectations in diverting their thoughts from their old miserable lives, and helping them to realise the goodness of God, and that life, after all, might be worth having, and be turned into something beautiful. Any one acquainted with her books, "The Observing Eye" and "What is a Bird?" will readily imagine what a teacher she must have been.

The institution could not have prospered as it

did without the common-sense and excellent management of her husband, which extended to every detail. His position, too, as county magistrate gave him many advantages; but her nephew writes:—"You could see my Aunt's touch in everything, especially in the early Reformatory documents, which speak so hopefully of the lads to be reformed." This perfect union of management, as might be expected, made the institution a mighty healing power. The "dear sisters at Buxton" often referred to in Mrs. Sewell's letters, took the warmest interest in everything connected with it, and in many ways rendered it valuable assistance. Their nephew writes in 1888:—

"My Aunt Elizabeth, my mother's next sister, now over ninety years of age, took a very active part in the household arrangements, especially looking after the clothing and other things connected with the comfort of the inmates. Her good sense and unfailing Christian spirit were invaluable. Though now blind and bedridden, her interest is unabated, and only yesterday we had a long talk by her bedside over Reformatory matters."

After the death of Mr. John Wright, the care of the Reformatory devolved on Mr. Philip Sewell, in connection with Mr. Wicks of Aylsham, who, however, died within a few years. In a letter I received from Mrs. Sewell, she writes:—

"Philip has taken the management of the Reformatory which was begun by my dear brother. There are between forty and fifty lads there, and they almost all turn out creditably, and many have become real Christian men. The Reformatory is most fortunate in its resident master, described by a cousin of mine as being like 'a Martello-tower in the sunshine'—immense bodily strength and courage, a veritable Christian, with a heart as tender as a mother's. The boys love, fear, and universally respect him. They have forty acres of land, which they cultivate—pigs to tend and fatten, &c. Often a band of them are applied for by the neighbouring farmers, when they cannot get sufficient hands. I think they also learn tailoring and shoemaking, as well as get a good general education. Philip goes over every week, on what is called the 'Court day,' when all the household are gathered together, and everything looked into—the Governors' hands are strengthened, their spirits cheered, and the boys are sure they have a watchful, helpful friend."

This "going over every week" was not always the easiest thing in the world. Buxton is about ten miles from Norwich, and a good part of the road (so called) is through narrow country lanes. Mr. Sewell could not set out for the journey until after his return from the Bank, so that in the shorter days, both going and returning had to be accomplished in the dark.

The story of the Reformatory would be incomplete without the mention of "Bessie," the faithful horse who for long years has not failed to take her master there and back in safety. She is a splendid creature, holding rank with the fastest trotters in the county, with any amount of go, courage, and spirit in her; yet when, in the fading light of the short winter afternoon, she is brought to the door, and the master takes her reins in his hands, then, as if she divined the responsibility of her task, she seems to be made up of caution and care. How in the pitch darkness and narrow lanes, where guiding must be impossible, she manages never to let a wheel get entangled, is only known to Him who asks, "Hast *thou* given the horse his might?"

I think it must have been about two winters before Mrs. Sewell's death that we had a visitation of remarkably cold weather, the snow lying thickly on the ground for some weeks. We were anxious to know how it affected the health of our dear friend, and I wrote to inquire. In reply, she writes:—

" . . . I am quite well, and with the thaw I find the capacity to guide my pen (not to make intelligible writing, as you know to your cost), but to do the best I can. I think the cold must have been as severe here as anywhere —some degrees below zero. Our house is a very cold one, so many windows and doors. If it had not been for 'our shawl,' in which I wrapped myself all the day, I think the low life must have gone out. I have kept in the dining-room, with shutters closed and curtains drawn in two out of the three windows, living in a kind of twilight, and we have now a large screen stretched more than half-way across the room; so you see, beloved, the kind providence of God enables a poor old thing like me to be spared, whilst so many lives more valuable are nipped off. I hope I may make the best of what is spared me.

"Philip has been to Buxton twice — he was much wanted at the Reformatory, and mounted his horse (the one you said seemed to have the spirit of the family)— he knew the road was blocked with snow, so that no wheels could pass, but he determined to get there in some way. He called on me as he passed, to assure me he would not go further than he could. You know well how I charged him, and how I kept praying while he was away. At a little before seven o'clock he called on his return, detailing his adventures in high spirits. In some parts a way had been cut through the snow-drifts just wide enough for him to pass, his knees frequently touching the sides, and the snow higher than the horse's back; when the way failed altogether, he went into the fields on either side, and with his cheerful perseverance, in which his horse entirely participated, he overcame all difficulties. The last time he went was in a sledge—he accomplished ten and a half miles in fifty-two minutes, Betsey delighted and excited by the bells and the lightness of the burden she drew."

As far as I can remember, this "calling on me as he passed" happened on most Monday afternoons—a mutual pleasure.

It was always more difficult on Monday evening to get the mother's undivided attention to anything. Soon after nine o'clock we gave up all attempt at making ourselves interesting, and caught the infection of listening. Shortly before ten o'clock, the welcome sound of distant wheels would be heard, and Bessie's well-known step. As the carriage flew by, a loud "Good-night" penetrated the walls of our room, to which we heartily responded; and when the dear mother had said "Thank God he is back safe again," we returned to our normal condition.

As years went by, and the dear heart of sympathy no longer beat within that house—when all that had made it precious had gone up higher—still, on the same day and hour the same carriage hastens past, bringing back the father of the large family left behind. Bessie must have wondered at first why the loud "Good-night" was left out of the programme, and the kind neighbours who understood it all so well would miss something they had loved to hear. And the bereaved son?—he knows that the sympathy is still his—only it now descends upon him from the home beyond the stars, and the answer to the old greeting would be—

> "Say not Good-night; but in some brighter clime
> Bid me Good-morning."

When all hope of Anna's being able to drive about again was finally renounced, the pony and carriage were sent to the Reformatory for the use of the master and his wife. It was against Mrs. Sewell's mind to keep any good thing which she could not thoroughly use. She could go out but seldom, and when she did, some one from Clare House was always ready to drive her. Mr. Sewell became increasingly feeble, but the house was never dull. "I could not bear for the dear girls to think of grandmother's house as a gloomy place," Mrs. Sewell wrote. To those who know the severe and distressing character of Anna's malady, and the requirements of nursing, the list of hospitalities and outside work recorded in this year's journal is astonishing. Here are a few instances:—

"*August* 9.—Mrs. Riches' class of thirty girls came to tea.

"*Sept.* 1.—We gave a tea and frolic to thirty-four children, Miss H.'s Band of Hope. G. and E. helped.

"*Sept.* 13.—Mother's Sun Lane Infants (50) had tea and play. A. and A. helped famously.

"*Nov.* 6.—Mother's Sun Lane School was inspected by Mr. S. The week previous she went every day, and since then goes one day each week, taking her dinner at Mrs. A——'s. She is trying a new plan of teaching to read without spelling, but making words with loose letters. She is also making clothes for the R——'s. Little Caroline R. comes three days a week. Mother gives her two lessons a day.

"*Nov.* 11.—Mother also began a class for the girls of Miss H.'s Band of Hope on Saturday mornings every other week.

"*Jan.* 1, 1872.—Mother went, with our children, to St. Faith's Union, and gave toys and presents.

"*Jan.* 23.—Jonathan Grubb came.

"*Jan.* 26.—I am quite poorly with pain."

"Quite poorly" seems the strongest expression of suffering that Anna ever allowed herself to use. When the gravity of her illness was first ascertained, the doctors had given her a year and a half to live, but disease did not make the progress anticipated. This year is marked by the death of friends—among them Mr. and Mrs. Ellis, who died within a week of each other. The year closes with "I am poorly;" but in the following autumn there was marked improvement for a time. On October 1st the journal says:—

"Social Science Congress. Mother and aunts went through the whole week. I am very well."

A later entry says, "I keep good nights." In this breathing-space, "Davie Blake" was written.

Every other year there is an entry of clothing given away to from sixty-five to eighty poor widows—every widow in New Catton who was over sixty, and many younger ones. The arrangement of this little charity was very characteristic of the way in which Mrs. Sewell 'considered the poor.' She said she could not afford to give a *good* present to so many every year, and it was better to give something good on alternate years, than to reduce the value of the gift. Each present was to be worth four shillings, and in order to make it as useful as possible, the Bible-woman was sent round to offer each widow her choice whether she would have the money's worth in linsey for a gown, unbleached calico, or flannel : sometimes shawls were offered too. As years went on, the gradual reduction in the price of clothing made this present an increasing pleasure to the giver. A friend who happened to be staying with her when it was being prepared in September 1880, writes :—

"It was quite a pleasure to see her delight, when the patterns came by post, on finding what a quantity of good stuff could be had for four shillings. There were packets of samples from several different makers, and if she had been choosing her wedding-gown she could not have spent more pains than she did over the different linseys and flannels and calicoes.

'Thus to select with anxious care
The very nicest that was there.'"

The Bible-woman was to take the selected sample of each with her, when she went round to learn the women's choice. The clothing was given early in November, since Christmas presents give time for the cold to be felt before they come.

The village of Old Catton being well cared for, with a benevolent squire (S. G. Buxton, Esq.), and other advantages, Mrs. Sewell had from the first turned her energies towards New Catton, an industrial suburb of Norwich lying near her son's house.

The success of "Davie Blake" was one of the interests of this year. Anna writes in June— "'Davie Blake' has had some good reviews. The second edition is going off. It is much liked by sailors' friends."

In October, Mr. Sewell lost his youngest daughter, a most sweet and lovely child, too tender for this rough world. The following lines are by Anna Sewell :—

"Seven young trees grew close together,
All fresh and green in the summer weather.
A little one, beautiful, tender, and tall,
Grew in the middle, the joy of them all;
And lovingly twining their branches together,
They circled it round, in the fine summer weather.
On the Sabbath eve of an autumn day
The beautiful plant was taken away,
And left a lonely and leafless space,
And nothing was found to fill the place—
Nothing of rich, nothing of rare,
Could fill the spot that was left so bare;
Nothing below, nothing above,
Could fill this empty spot but love.
Then closer the young trees grew together,
In the chilly days of that autumn weather;
And every branch put forth a shoot,
And new life quickened at the root.

They grew in the winter, in spring they grew,
Silently nourished by heavenly dew;
And when they came back to the summer weather,
One beautiful group they stood together;
And their greenest leaves hung o'er the place
Where the youngest had stood in its tender grace.
Nothing below, nothing above,
Nothing can heal the hurt but love.

"*18th October.*"

The Brighton Convention, which Mrs. Sewell attended, made the most notable event of 1875. During 1876 Anna was sometimes able to dictate passages of "Black Beauty." The completion of the book, in 1877, belongs to her own story. In June, that year, fresh trouble came to the white house. Up to that time Mr. Sewell's failing powers had been more of a sorrow to those who watched him, and knew what he had been, than to himself; but from this time he became subject to mental impressions of a very distressing character, needing constant effort in those about him to divert his mind. At the age of eighty, with an invalid in the house already who required her close attention, Mrs. Sewell received strength to take up this burden also, and bear it to the end. She had the help of faithful servants, and all that the ingenuity of love could give from the members of her family; but it was always "Mary" that the sufferer wanted —and had. This was the shadow that deepened in the house, while the shadow of death drew near to Anna, and "Black Beauty" went coursing on its way through the world.

To M. J. R.

"I do so heartily sympathise with you in your pleasant prospect of Switzerland that I must just say as much. You will so thoroughly enjoy it, especially if you do not attempt to see (to 'do') too much. Almost every one makes this mistake. They do not give themselves leisure to perceive, and take in, and feast upon anything, but with a greedy rush, try to grasp at everything, and bring away glimpses of things seen by the eye, but not revealed in their depth of beauty and grandeur to the heart. Now, mind what I say—When your father and brother are ambitious of some *great exploit*, do you sit down with your mother, and drink in the glory of the mountains as 'a joy for ever'—behold, meditate, and praise and pray, and fold the exquisite little flowers to your heart. When I have heard these mountain flowers described, I have thought their beauty would kill me with a joy too great to be borne. What a pleasure it will be to me to think of you just receiving through every pore liberty, life, and enlargement amongst the handiwork of our Father in heaven!

"I am glad you have had a little quiet time to think of all we heard and *felt* at Brighton, and *feel* much more deeply *now*. Yes, dear—my Nannie and I are both very happy—hungry and thirsty always, but with no fear of famine. ... Do not be afraid of Dr. Mahan's large book, 'Out of Darkness into Life.' If I had had that book when I first believed in the forgiveness of my sins, oh how blessedly different my experience would have been! It is the book for the sincere convert of any age or stage, *I think*."

To Mrs. Williamson.

"If we could not find poetry ready written, I think we should be obliged to write it for ourselves, it seems so essential to certain states of mind and feeling. In the present exceeding monotony of our household existence, with my husband so feeble, and my darling often in too sensitive a state to bear a word, poetry comes to me like dew and sunshine. . . . Do you think we should have so many very uninteresting Christian people if they oftener gave their minds an airing in the fields of earthly beauty which our Father has so beautifully garnished and illustrated for us?"

To Mrs. R——.

"*March* 1877.

". . . The thing I long to see is the Jews, under any circumstances or influences, going back to the Holy Land. Their hearts will be sifted and converted *there* through manifold troubles, after manifold success and prosperity. I write as if I knew, but *I don't*—yet I think I see a good many things that are beginning to come to pass. *I* cannot see anything distinctly about the *time* of the return of our Lord, but I think this remarkable quickening of the truth, and its rapid spread where it is preached in the power of the Holy Ghost, must be a sign of His approach. He is preparing a people who sigh and cry for His return, and who watch by night. I should be hopeless if I expected the world to be converted *first*. The Gospel is to be preached as a *witness* only, and for the purification of those who receive Him into their hearts, and walk in His light."

To the Same.

(Early part of 1877.)

". . . I have been confined to my room and bed for a fortnight, and creeping from bedroom to dining-room another fortnight, so I am able only just now to take up my pen and go on in my accustomed way. Hard work, late hours, and the relaxment of the foggy weather have brought me down, but thank God I am now all right again, and more able to sympathise with you, dear suffering friend.

". . . It is a habit with Anna and me just now, when we hear of charming things which people are doing, or seeing, or enjoying, and which our present circumstances forbid, to settle ourselves by saying, 'Well, we *have had* that,' and have not to expect its continuance or renewal.

"Dear friend, do you not think that you have done about ten times as much work for the dear Master as most people have done, and that now He is saying to you, 'Come apart and rest awhile'? Supposing you were peacefully to settle yourself to rest on the *Divine Will*, and give Him time to pay you more undisturbed visits, that you might know more of the sweetness of His company, as you sit with folded hands to hear Him speak.

"I have been reading some of the early chapters in Ecclesiasticus (the Apocrypha), and have found them so interesting, fresh, and profitable. There is many a new text. Do read them, pondering every verse for its deep, rich meaning. The descriptions of Wisdom are beautiful, and show the plenteous joy and strength which the dear Master wishes us to possess and rejoice in.

"We both of us sympathise with you so very tenderly in your crippled energies and disheartening pain, terrible to any one, but doubly so to you—you dear Help-everybody friend. Do let people take care of themselves for a little while, or let some one else take care of them, and banish the earnest eagerness out of your heart, and be *content* to be dull and what you call useless: be *content*, not only submissive, but glad, because you are in the Hands of Divine Wisdom, whose object may be to perfect other fruit in you another way; so leave Him to Himself, and wait patiently and expectingly for some *great good*, coming you know not how nor where.

"I am glad to hear that M. is studying, and exercising her other talents; it is not well for the mind generally to attend only to one class of pursuits, even though it be the best; our manifold nature requires manifold exercise of its varied talents.

"I have not yet read Norman Macleod's life. I am reading Kingsley's with intense delight. I will give you four lines—doggerel, but so good:—

> Do the work that's nearest,
> Tho' it's dull the whiles,
> Helping when you meet them
> Lame dogs over stiles.'

There are such a great many lame dogs to help over the stiles; but just observe for your own practice that you are to help them '*when* you *meet* them.' Don't run about after them.

"Kingsley was a wonderful man. I somehow fancy you would not enjoy the book as I do—you would find more wrong; but you could not help admiring him. He worked too hard, and wore out a splendid constitution comparatively early. We want so much to see Dr. Farrar's sermon on intemperance. Is it printed separately? I delight in his 'Life of Christ,' and also in another of his books, 'The Silence and Voices of God.'

"My jewel has been better this winter. The mildness of the weather has suited her well. My husband gradually becomes weaker in body and mind. All well at Clare House, and as busy as bees, studying, and practising good works. I will enclose you an advertisement of a book[1] my sister Maria has recently written; it is *pretty* writing and reading.

"We have just had Joseph Sewell (Madagascar missionary) and his wife staying with us: so good, so happy, so interesting! We have much enjoyed them."

---

[1] "Jennett Cragg, the Quakeress. A Story of the Plague." By Maria Wright. S. Partridge & Co.

CHAPTER VII.

"MY NANNIE."

"The healing of the world
Is in its nameless saints."
—BAYARD TAYLOR.

THIS was the mother's name for her dear daughter. By the world she was known as Anna Sewell, author of "Black Beauty."

The service she rendered to the world by that book, and her own remarkable character, claim that some account should be given of her independently, not only as her mother's companion and helpmeet.

We know from the pages of the autobiography that she was born on March 30, 1820. If I am successful in this chapter in giving anything like a faithful sketch of her life, we shall accept as simple truth the words which follow the mother's announcement of her birth, "An unclouded blessing; for fifty years the perennial joy of my life."

The accident in early life alluded to in the Autobiography weighted her life with a cross hard to bear, and is one of those events so shrouded in mystery that it scarcely admits of comment. That

Your very loving sister
Anna Sewell

one so gifted by nature, so exquisitely trained for the good and the beautiful, so artistic, so intellectual, so charming in every way, should for the larger portion of her life have been handicapped by bodily frailty, is a fact we can only record in silence.

Although her sweet and helpful influences were felt wherever she might be, there is no doubt that a considerable portion of her life was spent mainly in repression. Her very varied capacities enabled her to enter with unfeigned interest into a great variety of subjects. She could see at once how a picture should be composed, a fact or sentiment expressed, a garment cut out; how flowers should be arranged; what a committee should or should not do—but with all these mental resources, the frail body refused to do its part, and days and weeks had often to be spent in enforced idleness. Her hungry nature longed for food of many kinds—political, social, philanthropic—all these departments teemed with interest to her; yet there were periods when to read a short paragraph in a newspaper, or the Report of a Society, was for days together an impossibility.

For long years it was hoped that some remedy would be found. Many infallible cures were tried, and proved most fallible. Much was spent upon physicians, but the poor patient was nothing the better.

During the earlier years of her life, Anna's religious experience was of a very simple character, consisting mainly of a happy trust in God and love to Christ as her Saviour, learned from her mother's bright trust, and her delight in God's works. As a child she used to say, "Mother's Bible was read to make everybody happy and good."

The false teaching at Brighton already mentioned, though Anna escaped from being deluded by it, dimmed and unsettled the old bright faith. The four or five years which followed this "eclipse of faith" were undoubtedly the darkest of her life. She speaks in her Journal of worldly things having an irresistible charm for her, usually followed by an increase of spiritual darkness. The cry of her soul was like Job's, "Oh that I knew where I might find Him!"

"Lord, do break my bondage," she writes, "for I have not strength to do it myself. I have not strength to give up myself to Christ, in the sense of being willing that His perfect Will should be fulfilled in me, lest it should mean an entire crucifixion of self."

Speaking of attending history classes, she says— "They are very interesting, but they do not satisfy the soul. I am very miserable."

The beginning of a happier time is recorded in her Journal under date January 7, 1845:—

"At the beginning of this month we went on Sunday morning to Clarence Chapel. Mr. Warren preached from the text, 'Christ has redeemed us from the curse of the law, being made a curse for us.' It was a powerful sermon, and the Lord mercifully used it as the conveyance of His good Spirit, to bring again life and light to my dark soul. As I listened, I truly felt Christ precious. I believed, and was justified from all things. I was made to sing as in years long past. This is not, I trust, a transient revival. I do now trust in none but Jesus.

"*March* 20*th.*—This is my birthday. Oh, what a happy one compared to any I have had so long! I feel as if I had exchanged a rough, stormy sea for a calm, smooth river.

"Last Sunday was the first time I took my class in the afternoon. I did not get on very well, for in the morning I had given way to sin, and therefore did not get near to Christ, for I sinned wilfully, knowingly resisting the voice of the Spirit in my heart, and so the sting was left behind. The darkness returned for two or three days, then I was able to lay my sin at the feet of my Saviour, and leave it there. To-day (Sunday) I had a very pleasant time with my children, and taught them from Daniel, third chapter."

On May 27 (probably just after the removal to Lancing) she writes:—

"Mother went to Brighton, and I stayed to attend to the planting of seeds in the garden; my feet were very weak, and I prayed that they might be strengthened sufficiently for me to attend to what was necessary. The Lord most graciously heard me, and gave me more strength than I have had for some time, so that I am able to see after the garden properly."

Under the same date:—

"I am very much concerned, in reading the lives of holy people, to find how unlike them I am in my hatred of sin and love of holiness. But I must look to Christ too. O Lord, make me of one mind with Thee. Open Thou my eyes, that I may see things as Thou seest them, and as they really are. My mother very truly says, we cannot love holiness as an abstract thing, but that it must come in proportion as we love Christ."

At a later date :—

"I have felt it very sweet to receive this improvement in my feet (which continues) from the Hand of Jesus. I would not be without this dispensation, and pray Thee, Lord, to do with me what Thou seest best. I thank Thee, for my lameness. I am sure it is sent in love, though it be a trial. I should without it have too much pleasure in the flesh, and have forgotten Thee."

In many respects the lives and interests of Mrs. Sewell and her daughter were so closely associated that the story of one describes the other. It has been shown that the usual relative positions of mother and child were reversed in them. I cannot say that the daughter led, for the impulse to action came usually from the mother, but the daughter pronounced judgment upon it. The enforced sedentary habits of Anna's life were favourable to early maturity of judgment, and Mrs. Sewell was by nature quick to bend to the opinion of one she trusted.

I was once with Anna when her mother read aloud to us something she was preparing for the press. It was beautiful to witness the intense love, admiration, and even pride which beamed in the daughter's face, but this in no wise prevented her being, as I thought, a very severe critic. Nature had bestowed on her a remarkably sweet-toned and persuasive voice. I think I hear her now, saying, "Mother dear, thee must alter that line," or "Thee must put a fuller word there, that will give out more of thy meaning." "Oh, if I can only pass my Nannie, I don't fear the world after that," the mother said.

It was in the autumn of 1862 that I first met

Mrs. Sewell, at the house of her old friend Mrs. Ellis, at Hoddesdon. In the following summer I had the great pleasure of paying her a short visit at Blue Lodge, Wick. She was then engaged in writing the last chapters of her book, "Thy Poor Brother." As we three sat together in the drawing-room, she read me some of the earlier chapters. They were so suggestive, we talked and talked, complaining of nothing but the lapse of time. Anna was lying on the sofa—her mother sitting at her feet, with one hand rubbing the lame foot, with the other holding the manuscript out of which she was reading.

The parting came all too soon. In the afternoon it poured with rain. When the carriage that was to take me to the station came to the door, Anna was standing in the hall, enveloped in a large mackintosh. The future writer of "Black Beauty" was to be my driver. I found that she and her mother were in the habit of driving out on most days, without attendance, the understanding between themselves and their horse being perfect. The persistent rain obliged us to keep up our umbrellas. Anna seemed simply to hold the reins in her hand, trusting to her voice to give all needed directions to her horse. She evidently believed in a horse having a moral nature, if we may judge by her mode of remonstrance. "Now thee shouldn't walk up this hill—don't thee see how it rains?" "Now thee must go a little faster—thee would be sorry for us to be late at the station."

I think it was during this drive that I told Anna of something Horace Bushnell had written about animals. Soon after the publication of "Black Beauty" I had a little note from her, written from her sofa, in which she says:—

"The thoughts you gave me from Horace Bushnell years ago have followed me entirely through the writing of my book, and have, more than anything else, helped me to feel it was worth a great effort to *try*, at least, to bring the thoughts of men more in harmony with the purposes of God on this subject."

I have tried in vain to get the "Essay on Animals" from which I then quoted—it seems to have been long out of print; but I feel sure I remember it with sufficient distinctness to reproduce it. I must not, however, venture to use inverted commas, which would make the author responsible for every word.

Man is constituted with a brain power capable of using and directing a far greater amount of physical force than he himself possesses. Animals, especially horses, were created that he might have a vast amount of strength at his disposal, dependent upon his will, by the aid of which he may accomplish much more than would otherwise be possible. Man is made for God, and just as his happiness depends upon the degree in which, in his life, he lives to do the will of God, so with animals—they instinctively know that their vocation is to do the will of man; and were we as wise and as kind to animals as we might be, and ought to be, their lives, in doing our will, would be supremely happy.

In creation, animals are so associated with man that they must fall or rise with him. If man had never fallen, he would probably have exercised such a benign and excellent influence over the brute creation, that, whilst they would have been perfectly subservient, their own lives would have been full of the highest enjoyment of which they are capable. There is more than meets the eye in that verse in Genesis—"And whatsoever Adam called every living creature, that was the name thereof." To be able to name a creature or thing, implies that it belongs to us. We name our own children, not other people's. Man, in dealing with animals, leaves his own impression upon them —whatever temper he manifests to them, "that is the temper thereof;" and, taking this view of the subject, we see how much these poor creatures have to suffer at the hands of their masters. I never see an animal bearing the marks of man's cruelty, without feeling that in its mute anguish it is saying, "This is my body broken for you;" and perhaps no view of man's sin has impressed me so deeply as the fact, that its consequences have wrung this same cry both from the Highest in the universe and the lowest.

When the Man "without sin" was on earth, He could safely ride an unbroken colt; "one whereon never man had sat." There will be no "breaking in" required when the promised days of universal peace and righteousness dawn upon the earth; then men will know their true place of dignity in God's universe—

> "And all beside be serving him,
> That he may serve his God."

The foregoing pages have shown how earnestly, sometimes almost restlessly, the mother had striven for her daughter's restoration. It was in her nature to be hopeful, and believe that something could be done. But the time came when to her cry, "What wouldst Thou have me to do?" the answer was, "Nothing." Hope was to be no more. For years they had been praying, "If it be possible, let this cup pass from me;" and though they thought that in sincerity and truth they had added, "Nevertheless, not my will, but Thine be done;" yet in their inmost hearts they knew it was for deliverance that they had wrestled and cried.

Who can realise without trembling the awful significance of those words, "He shall *sit* as a refiner and purifier of silver"? The attitude of sitting implies the absence of haste—the intention to remain until the object be accomplished. Whilst we are occupying ourselves in searching for some door of escape, He sits—oh! He *sits*, as if unmindful of our anguish, and goes on with His work as "a refiner and purifier of silver." Unknown to all but Himself are the full issues of the process in hand. Something connected with the establishment of His Kingdom on earth may be depending upon its perfect accomplishment. Anything so momentous in its consequences admits of no risk of incompleteness—so *He* sits. Were an angel to take the Refiner's place, he might be moved by our tears and entreaties, and stop short of perfection. *He* sits, and rises not until He sees His own image reflected in the molten silver.

As the full nature of their ever-deepening trial dawned upon these tried ones, darkening the future with anticipations of increased suffering, they afresh paused to consider. They felt that something more was needed than even patience and hope. They knew they wanted some greater deliverance than they had hitherto either asked or thought, and they threw themselves afresh on the guidance of the Spirit, and asked to be shown how to attain to perfect harmony with His will—how to be *one* with Him in His plans and purposes, and not to be permitted to be so often asking for something which appeared to be crossing His will.

I have often heard them speak of this time, and how by degrees they learned more perfectly the Divine lessons taught by suffering, and consented, with their whole hearts, that their training should be as the Master's, "perfect through suffering." "The way of the Lord is the way of His servants. He enlightened the path they must tread, and showed its end." They no longer looked on every side for escape, but sat down by the side of their great trial, and patiently learned its deep and precious lessons. In the words of one who has gone deeply into this subject, "Responsive love transfigures that which it bears. Pain loses its sting when it is mastered by a stronger passion. The true secret of happiness is not to escape toil and affliction, but to meet them with the faith that through them the destiny of man is fulfilled, that through them we can even now reflect the image of our Lord, and be transformed into His likeness."

The result of this *entire* yielding up the will to God—the consent given on their part that the furnace should be what He chose to make it, was that "He turned for them the shadow of death into the morning." The word is not "exchanged." The wonderful alchemy known in heaven can make morning *out of* the shadow of death. The promise was fulfilled to them—"I will give thee the treasures of darkness."

Years after, when Anna had been brought into still fuller light, she said, "I had always taken my petition and request to Him, but then I knocked from without, somewhat in the spirit of a beggar. Now He has shown me that I have a place in the household, I belong to the family of God, and my very frailty has given me a place among the weak ones in whom His strength is perfected. I know now the meaning of that word, 'Now no longer a servant, but a Son.'"

When a strong man is emptied of self, and goes forth to work for the Lord, he is often astonished at his success, until he learns that the empty vessel is just what Christ is always seeking for, that He may Himself fill it. Spiritual conquest must always be "according to the measure of the gift of Christ." When He FILLS, the reign of failure is left behind. For want of understanding what things mean, there may be apparent failure, but not real. "For all there were so many, yet was not the net broken," is the law of resurrection life.

When this same self-surrender comes to the sufferer, he endures after the manner of Christ. Whilst God's workers wake morning by morning to hear as the instructed ones, and learn how to speak a word in season to him that is weary, His stricken ones remain in the quietness of their chamber, and learn from Him how to "give their back to the smiters"—each alike saying, "For the Lord God will help me, and I know that I shall not be ashamed." The motto for the sufferer is, "Strengthened with all might *according to His glorious power*, unto all patience and long-suffering with joyfulness."

I have seen many patient sufferers who never attained to the "with joyfulness."

The maladies from which Anna suffered were mainly of a very painful and depressing character, and had her face been marred with grief, no one would have been surprised. It was a wonderful evidence of the triumph of the spirit over the body that her face was not only sweet and peaceful, but often radiant; and so evidently did this proceed from the power of the Spirit of God, that in her presence one had a feeling of being on holy ground; her face shone with the far-off light of the morning of the resurrection.

In a letter from Mrs. Sewell, as usual without date, she writes:—

"... At present I dare not myself look fully into the future. I endeavour with all thankfulness to live only in the day, either as to hope or fear about my darling. It is a year and a half since she left the house, except occasionally for a few steps in the garden.... The disease which the doctors expected would have worn her out by this time from extreme suffering, is not manifestly worse, but by little and little the strength keeps wasting, and her capacity for any effort decreases. She is usually in bed till midday, and then dresses, resting between whiles. She lies on the sofa for the remainder of the day, sometimes sitting down to meals with us only for a very short time. She requires almost complete quiet; conversation and reading are usually too fatiguing for her.

"Internally there is perfect peace—the sweetest, most cheerful patient—the most unselfish sufferer I have ever seen—the expression of her dear face combines it all, and sometimes she has such a lovely colour, and looks so animated and beaming, that no one would think she ailed much. I am her constant companion. Since she was confined to the house, I have only been out two days. We have no gloom, except I forget my privilege not to look beyond the day. The doctor attributes the very slow progress of the disease to her tranquillity and her courage, and the exceptional advantages she enjoys in the way of nursing."

Another time she writes:—

"... We have no doctors now. They gave no hope, and did no good, and therefore were exceedingly discouraging, so I gave my darling into the hands of the Great Physician, and He does not discourage. We wait in patience, trusting to see Him work a perfect work for us of the best kind, of which He only is the judge. My sweet one is so cheerful—so charmingly patient, that the days are not wearisome, and just now she is not suffering so much—indeed her general health is better now than it was some months ago. Sometimes she really looks well, and always uses what little power she has; never hopelessly giving up because she can do no more, never wishing or complaining, but cheerfully submissive."

"She could bear pain without showing it in her face or voice," Mrs. Sewell said. "Once I said, 'Do thee *never* break down or fret about it, darling?' She said, 'Sometimes when I am alone in my room, I do say, "Poor Nannie!"'"

Mr. Sewell continued to fail, and his wife was liable to turns of severe but seldom disabling suffering, brought on by the constant strain upon her. Every one who has had experience in such things knows the tendency to depression when two in a household of three are chronic invalids.

Miss Hopkins, in her admirable little book, "Occupation for the Sick," says—"There is a mistake made both in the way we deal with ourselves in sickness, and in the way that others deal with us. We deal with the sick too exclusively spiritually, or as I would rather say, too narrowly, since God is the God of all consolation. We say to them with sinking hearts, and with tears in our eyes, 'It is God's will, and you must bear your burden,' but we forget the ropes and pulleys and levers which might, with a little contrivance on our part, help to lift it—all the helps to bearing it, which may be also in God's will."

Could Miss Hopkins have called at "The White

House that stood in the garden," she would have seen a living specimen of people who never failed to use for the best purposes all the "ropes, pulleys, and levers" which came within their reach, and would also have seen how much they were really helped by so doing.

There was one little pastime of which Anna was very fond; it helped her through many a weary hour. She would get some one to give her a few words, which, notwithstanding their diversity of meaning, she managed to work into a little story in verse. I take the following specimens from a pile by my side:—

"*Prawn, Yawn, Tall, Wall, Missed, Kissed.*

"O Henry dear, don't *yawn* so loud,
 The tea will soon be here;
But Jane has had an accident
 Which might have cost her dear.

"In coming up with that *tall* urn
 She caught a sight of Jem,
She *missed* the step, and *kissed* the *wall*,
 Instead of kissing him.

"*I* do not think the girl is hurt,
 But still she's vexed and fluttered;
So cook will bring the *prawns* and toast,
 And tea-cake, when 'tis buttered."

"*Tomtit, Sooty, Fate, Butter.*

"It happened one day that the birds went to dine,
 By a special invite from the hawk;
The viands were excellent, so was the wine,
 And each guest had a small silver fork.

Robin Redbreast was there, as of course you'd expect,
    And *Tomtit* with a bow and a sputter,
His rev'rence the Rook, with a *sooty* black cloak,
    And canaries as yellow as *butter*.
Ah! little they thought, as they strutted and chirped,
    Of the *fate* that awaited them there;
For the Hawk with his kindred pounced down on his guests,
    Whilst their pitiful cries rent the air."

Another favourite pastime of both mother and daughter was capping verses. As Mrs. Sewell's ballads occasionally seem to praise the olden times in disparagement of the present, it should be mentioned that she thought the poetry studied now-a-days incomparably superior to that of her own time. I think she had not been allowed to read Shakespeare in her youth, and in old age her verbal memory for anything new was gone. "And there, darling Anna would say her beautiful lines of Wordsworth and Tennyson and Shakespeare—such a soul in them!—and I had only my old *Byron*" (with an accent of supreme contempt) "and *Moore* to come in with!" But there were lines of Moore's that she loved much, especially—

"Let Fate do her worst, there are relics of joy,
  Bright dreams of the past that she cannot destroy;
  Which come in the night-time of sorrow and care,
  And bring back the colours which joy used to wear.
  Long, long be my heart with such memories filled,
  Like the vase in which roses have once been distilled:
  You may break, you may ruin, the vase if you will,
  But the scent of the roses will hang o'er it still."

The next letter preserved is a cheerful one :—

"My darling maintains the slight improvement I mentioned to you. It is just about this time two years since she left the house, but she is always my dear cheerful companion, and in our hardest days we have glad surprises, and very often find roses in blossom. We lead by no means a solitary life. We have several young people round us who are earnestly desirous to lead a vital, practical Christian life, and we are deeply interested in them. They are often here to question the old pilgrim, and all this keeps my dear Anna full of external interest, which is so wholesome and happy for her. To my astonishment she never seems to find the time drag heavily, though usually lying unemployed on the sofa."

"Anna has been really better the last few months; it is a comfort and pleasure to see her. My heart is filled with thankfulness, and I think with wonder of all the manifold mercies showered upon us, until I remember the Lord is so very pitiful to all His weak things, made of such poor clay that they cannot take any very high polish."

Any little improvement in Anna's health gave Mrs. Sewell the opportunity she much valued of seeing more of her poor neighbours. When I stayed at Catton, she would occasionally leave me in charge, saying she was going into the village. Before leaving the house, she would return, in her walking dress, to have one more look at her darling, and would be greeted with, "Mother dear, how nice thee look!" or, "Mother dear, don't thee hurry back, I am quite comfortable. Couldn't thee call on Lucy Smith?—it is not her washing-day, and she would be so pleased to see thee."

The year 1874 was a marked one to Anna Sewell.

In that year a friend sent her a little booklet by Mrs. Pearsall Smith, called "A Word to the Wavering Ones." Those who had watched her perfect patience and uprightness before God and man were astonished that she could class herself among these; but through the means of that little book she received something which her soul had longed for all her life. She wrote to a friend that though she had loved her Saviour for so many years, that summer was the first time that she had really known what it was to abide in Christ. It was difficult for us not to feel almost hurt, as though she were doing dishonour to the Grace which had so wonderfully upheld her; but so it was. Her victory had been gained by a constant inward struggle, known only to herself and her Lord. She had accepted His will, and loved it—accepted her lot of suffering without regret, for His sake; but He had better things for her, even a portion of exceeding joy.

From this time forth, she drank of His pleasures as of a river. To use Dora Greenwell's words, "The strain of the inner life had passed over from self to Christ" in a degree she had never known before. The last remnant of the old severity against herself passed away; for the rest of her life, it seemed to outward eyes to be with her, "None of self, and ALL of Thee."

In the following year Mrs. Sewell was able to attend the Brighton Convention for the deepening of holiness. She always referred to those meetings as having been most helpful. She certainly could not speak of her previous spiritual life as "a wearing-out in the wilderness;"—she and her Nannie had together trodden the soil of the Promised Land; but many as yet unexplored regions now came in sight. "There seems," she said, "nothing too good to expect—the riches we have in Christ mean so much, we shall want all eternity to find them out."

On her return home she brought books and papers, which she and Anna read together, and rejoiced as they who had found great spoil. Anna always spoke of this time as one of peculiar joy: she often said, "How good it was of those people to make such an effort to share with many others their own good things! How they poured themselves out to do us good, and kept back nothing, delighting to spread forth all they had seen and handled!"

Mrs. Sewell referred to this Convention and its effect upon Anna in two or three letters written about this time:—

"I cannot tell you how thankful I am for the four days I had at Brighton—you truly divine that Nannie and I have been feeding together on the feast ever since. We are *very happy;* even these cold, wet days cannot make more than skin-deep impression upon us. My darling has more assurance than ever, so full of cheerfulness and sweetness—the drawing-room is always bright, and oh if you would only come!"

To another friend she writes:—

"I look back on my few days at Brighton with unmixed thankfulness. I feel as if I had been into a land of fountains and brooks of water, and seen all the figs and pomegranates and honey, and drunk a little of the wine—oh so sustaining! and as I and my dear Nannie talk about the good land, we keep venturing a step further in, seeing there is no stint, but a free invitation from the glorious Lord of the Country to take full possession, and live in plenty, and in perfect peace. Oh, how great is His goodness, and how wonderful His working!"

To Mrs. Williamson.

". . . He has been showing me lately into some of His treasure-houses, and I have been enamoured with the sights I have seen, and have longed for wings to flee away; but I would not miss any of the discipline of life—I would be made meet for the inheritance with the family of God, and with my dear friends. I do not think that either books or sermons present the joy that is set before us in the Scriptures with anything like, or anything approaching to, the fulness with which it is really revealed to us. Inspiration, as it were, labours to incite hope, desire, and curiosity, and to stimulate the imagination, that we may apprehend, for the strengthening and growth of our own souls, the glorious realities of the future. We are for the most part trotted about in the leading-strings of doctrine in a dry unfruitful round, seldom visiting the garden of spices, or looking for the heights of Lebanon—so the hungry sheep look up and are not fed; and even Christians, when they meet together, have no genuine mother-tongue to speak in, only a few commonplaces. Well, I ought not to find fault, for when do I do better things myself?"

To Mrs. Brightwen.

"OLD CATTON, *August* 20.

"MY DEAR FRIEND,—How lovingly kind it was of you to send me those exquisite leaves, with such careful pains to give me their names! I love and admire trees and flowers with the full capacity of my nature—I never weary of them, and they are always speaking to me in parables, and every one has something good to say to us, if our ears were sufficiently refined and cultivated to understand it perfectly. I often think the gift of a garden, even a small one, is one of the most delicious blessings that the beneficent Giver of all good can bestow, for the cheerful refreshment of travellers passing onward to the other garden, where the seeds of nettles and thorns are not naturally embedded in the soil. As you look at these wondrously variegated leaves, which I suppose have been developed chiefly by human skill, do you not think of the exquisite loveliness which waits to be developed in the Christian character by the infinite skill and tender patience of the great Husbandman?

"Since attending those delightful meetings at Brighton, and reading several of the works connected with the Revival amongst Christians, I have thought how far too little have our efforts been directed to the 'perfecting of holiness,' the putting on of the ornaments held in such rich store for the adornment of Christ's redeemed ones. The prevailing thought seems to be that our Blessed Lord wants to get a great deal of work out of us, and thus we go slaving on upon duty-service, not allowing ourselves time to reflect and understand that His great desire is to make us beautiful vessels that He can fill with Himself—thus converting us into instruments which He can use for His own glory, and for the progress of His Kingdom on earth. I was thinking this morning that one could desire nothing greater for oneself than to be in the hands of the Master as a hollow reed, through which He could speak His loving mind. In this way we could be without carefulness; our only concern need be to remain obedient, trustful, and pliable. But it is so difficult to be emptied of self, to be *so dead* as to leave room for the indwelling of the higher life—the hidden life of Christ, which possessing, we should have 'all things.'

"From time to time, through different channels, I have heard of your great suffering, and am truly grieved that the enjoyment of this little while should be so dashed with bitterness. I know you live above it, as my darling does, and that, like her, you have surrendered your will to His. Some great good—some precious experience for others is to come out of it, which will be known some day, and then you will be more glad than any one."

At the time of my visits to Old Catton, Mr. Sewell was unable to conduct family prayer—or, to speak more correctly, family reading. At half-past nine the servants came in; Mrs. Sewell read a chapter, occasionally making a few remarks as she went on, and then a hymn or piece of poetry. Now and then she read a short extract from a magazine or paper. If any subject of local or national interest was just then occupying attention, she would refer to it in a way that put us into sympathy with the times. Now and then, but rarely, the sweet voice from the sofa was heard, always beginning with "Mother dear, don't thee think" so-and-so. In Friends' houses, vocal prayer is not the rule: a space of silence is given, to make way for it, but it may or may not form part of the service.

When the servants rose, the master rose also, and remained standing until they had closed the door, saying in his courteous way, "Good-night, Emily. Good-night, Jane."

On one of my visits, the evening reading was in Matthew—the Gospel of the Kingdom. When the servants had gone, and the weary master had retired for the night, we sat round Anna's couch and spoke together of the coming Kingdom and its exceeding glory. After one of these evening talks, I went to Anna's room in the morning to inquire how she had passed the night. "Oh," she said, "I have had such a happy night; it was nice to be awake and ready to listen to His teaching about the Kingdom. He not only gives me 'songs in the night,' but 'instructs me in the night season.'"

In a letter addressed to Mrs. Williamson, Mrs. Sewell writes:—

"I have been thinking how your sanctified and well-stored mind must refresh you in your long night watches, and how invaluable, in your present condition, is the possession of a cultivated and refined intellect. My darling says she never feels the nights long; she has so many things and thoughts to hold communion with. It is a great mistake not to cultivate the mind and feed it with a good variety out of the many and varied storehouses within our reach."

Mrs. Sewell usually went for a little walk before breakfast. During the latter years of her daughter's illness, when the fatigue of nursing absorbed nearly all her strength, she contented herself with going for a short walk in her garden, taking with her her chosen companion, "Daily Light." When she joined us at the breakfast-table, it was often with this favourite book in her hand—some special verse had been occupying her mind, and she would pour out to us her many thoughts upon it. When breakfast was over, she went with her morning verse into Anna's room, where I often had the privilege of joining them. They both knew that a trying and suffering day lay before them, and they together hid away some heavenly words in their hearts, that they might not faint by the way. There were no symbols of the body and blood of Christ present, but by faith they fed upon Him in their hearts, and in the strength of that food stood bravely up to meet the conflicts of the day.

One of our happiest talks was over the second verse of the twenty-second chapter of Revelations—"In the midst of the street of it, and on either side of the river, was there the tree of life, which bare twelve manner of fruits, and yielded her fruit every month: and the leaves of the tree were for the healing of the nations." Perhaps the thought most present to their minds, but about which little was said, was that when the time came for them to stand by that tree, the former things would have passed away—there would be no more pain, or sorrow, or crying. Mrs. Sewell spoke of the "*twelve manner* of fruits" as if our love of variety was to follow us into that new life. Then "yielding every month"—we shall not need to store our fruits there; "but," she said, "the happy thought in this verse is that the leaves of the same tree which feeds us with fruit are for the 'healing of the nations.' That will make our enjoyment complete. It will not be selfish. Oh! I do hope my Nannie and I shall be sent out to the nations with these leaves. We would so like to have something to do with the '*healing* of the nations.'"

Her constant study of the Scriptures had given her a profound belief, shared by Anna, in the ultimate healing of the nations. This belief was not based on any lax perception of the stringency of the law of God. That sin, which had broken in upon the harmony of God's universe, and was the sole cause of the intolerable misery which at times almost broke her heart, should ever be spoken of lightly—as a thing that could be passed over—was a thought repugnant to her whole moral nature. Until Christ was accepted as the sin-bearer, the cry of the sinner, both here and hereafter, must be, "My punishment is greater than I can bear;" but whilst holding this belief most firmly, I am not aware that at any period of her life she entirely accepted the teaching called orthodox, on the eternal duration of punishment. She felt it to be out of harmony with other teaching at least equally binding upon us to believe. She would say, "It needs such a power of *un*belief before one can accept it. I should like to have lived in the earliest centuries, before this creed was accepted by the Church."

There are still many saying as of old, "I had fainted unless I had believed to see the goodness of the Lord in the land of the living." In His great mercy, God often in some special way makes His goodness to pass before these troubled ones. He came to this mother and daughter, endowed with the sorrowful gift of an exceeding power of sympathy with the sinful and the sad, and let them see that the thoughts He had towards His redeemed world were "thoughts of peace and not of evil:" they knew Him as "a mighty Man of wealth," with all the riches of the universe at His command,—able to do all He had promised, even to "destroying the works of the devil."

"The shepherd in the parable seeks the lost sheep until he finds it; shall we add to the parable and say 'or till he cannot find it'? If we do so, it is in view of the fact that the will of man made in the image of God is a mystery only less deep than the mystery of God Himself."

I think that to Mrs. Sewell's mind the parable stood complete without addition. Doubtless many would rejoice to go as far as she did, who yet feel compelled to pause and say with Dr. Maclaren, "Reverently accepting Christ's words as those of perfect and infallible love, the writer feels so strongly the difficulty of bringing all the New Testament declarations on this dread subject into a harmonious whole, that he abjures for himself dogmatic certainty."

"The Destiny of the Human Race," by Henry Dunn, was read by Mrs. Sewell and Anna with the deepest interest. It led them to make a further minute examination of the Scriptures on this special subject, with the result of confirming their bright hopes of the extent of Christ's final triumph.

I should leave a wrong impression, however, if I made it appear that they were satisfied that they had surmounted all the difficulties connected with this most solemn subject. To the end, they ever felt that there were deep mysteries connected with God's government of the world, for the explanation of which we must wait His own time; but they rejoiced in finding abundant encouragement to look forward with hope.

For the rest—God had spoken to them as Boaz did to Ruth when she came to him full of earnest thought as to how the lapsed inheritance could be restored. He did not tell her then that it was all to come back through himself, but bade her "lie down until the morning."

Ruth, always obedient, lay down until the morning. The night was not painful or wearisome, for she lay at the feet of the master she entirely loved and trusted; and in the morning, what glad surprises awaited her!

The night of waiting, even in its outward aspect, was by no means all suffering to these patient, trustful ones. The echoes of the tide of life that went on at Clare House came pleasantly to the ears of the quieter party in "Grandmother's" house. "Philip's" frequent visits brought with them something fresh from the outward world, and Sunday afternoon, when he came to tea, was reckoned the bright spot of the week. I remember, after Anna had been reading to us a letter from a friend, full of condolence, she said, "I don't think I can appropriate all this pity. No one need be pitied who has mother and Philip."

For the last seven years of Anna's life, the work

which formed for her an unfailing interest was the writing of "Black Beauty."

The first mention of it occurs in the Journal, under date November 6, 1871:—

"I am writing the life of a horse, and getting dolls and boxes ready for Christmas."

No other entry on the subject occurs till December 6, 1876:—

"I am getting on with my little book, 'Black Beauty.'"

The next is dated August 21, 1877:—

"My first proofs of 'Black Beauty' are come—very nice type."

It is touching to remember that this "beautiful equine drama," as it has been called, was thought out almost entirely from the sofa where so much weakness and pain were daily endured. When a time came during which she was capable of enduring the fatigue of writing, it was done in pencil—the mother, sitting by, received the paper from the weary hand, and made a fair copy of it. That a book accomplished in such a fragmentary way should "show no joins" says much for the skill of the writer; but oh what discipline must have been endured in having perpetually to "leave off in the most interesting place!"

I have found a paper which seems to be separated from something else to which it belonged; whether it be a part of a letter written to a friend, or intended as a kind of journal, I have no means of knowing. It is among the very, very few papers I have in Anna's handwriting:—

"I have for six years been confined to the house and to my sofa, and have from time to time, as I was able, been writing what I think will turn out a little book, its special aim being to induce kindness, sympathy, and an understanding treatment of horses. In thinking of Cab-horses, I have been led to think of Cabmen, and I am anxious, if I can, to present their true condition, and their great difficulties, in a correct and telling manner.

"Some weeks ago I had a conversation at my open window with an intelligent Cabman who was waiting at our door, which has deeply impressed me. He led the conversation to the Sunday question, after telling me that he never plied on the Sabbath. I found there was a sore, even a bitter feeling against the religious people, who, by their use of cabs on Sunday, practically deny the Sabbath to the drivers. 'Even ministers do it, Ma'am,' he said, 'and I say it's a shame upon religion.' Then he told me of one of the London drivers who had driven a lady to church—as she stepped from the cab, she handed the driver a tract on the observance of the Sabbath. This naturally thoroughly disgusted the man. 'Now, Ma'am,' said my friend, 'I call that hypocrisy—don't you?' I suppose most of us agree with him, and yet it might not have been done hypocritically—so few Christians apparently realise the responsibility of taking a cab on Sunday."

"Black Beauty" was published near the end of the year 1877, and Anna lived just long enough to hear of its remarkable success.[1] But can she ever know what a mighty power for good it has

---

[1] Up to this time 91,000 copies of this book have been sold.

been, and is, in this country? We have frequent opportunities of conversing with the London City Missionaries to Cabmen. Their testimony is, that many agencies have been at work of late years which have greatly helped to ameliorate the condition both of the men and horses, such as Cabmen's shelters, systematic religious and temperance teaching, the watchful vigilance of the Society for Prevention of Cruelty to Animals, &c. ; but they say nothing has told so strongly for good among the men themselves, or induced such humane treatment of horses, as the influence and teaching they have gained from "Black Beauty." Both men and boys read it with the greatest avidity, and many declare it to be "the best book in the world." Many of our public organs, foremost among them the *Times*, have for some years past borne the strongest testimony to the remarkable improvement which has taken place in everything connected with Cabs and Cabmen. Perhaps few who chronicle these changes and improvements know how much of what they commend is due to the genius and prayers of one fragile woman.

"She never went forth to sow."

"But there rose from her lowly couch of pain
The fervent, pleading prayer:"—

the prayer for happier men, happier horses, and happier homes, and that we might know how to use and not abuse God's munificent gifts to us; and God has heard her prayers, and permitted

s

her to be a fellow-worker with Himself in bringing about these beneficent changes.

I have a packet of letters by my side, all referring to "Black Beauty;" some written by friends and relatives, others by strangers; also many reviews, laudatory enough to satisfy the vainest author. From all of these a very few quotations will suffice.

The *Nonconformist* for January 1878 writes :—

"Had the Society for the Prevention of Cruelty to Animals published this, we should say it had published its best work. As it is, it would be difficult to conceive of one more admirably suited to its purpose."

From a Cousin :—

"I am so delighted, so proud of my cousin, that I can never thank you enough for my Christmas present. Read it!—I should think I did. Do you remember, when you and Philip were children, how you used to have Christmas Day for your '*very own*'—choose your own amusements, your own pudding? Just such a Christmas Day did I promise myself, with your capital book for my special delectation. I could not quite carry out my wishes, for J. A. had to be invited to dinner—but directly he was gone, I petted Black Beauty, and enjoyed myself.

"I do like the book exceedingly, it is *so good;* and, forgive me, so unladylike that but for 'Anna Sewell' on the title-page, and a certain gentle kindliness all through the story, no one, I think, would believe it to be written by a lady. Where you have obtained your stable-mindedness I can't imagine, but that you fully understand your business is a *fact*. I like your grooms, only I am afraid you had the pick of some most exceptional ones. Manly, James, and even little Joe Green are just the jockeys for me. Would they could be counted by thousands!

"The story of poor Black Beauty and Ginger is most

touching, and the different characters of the horses admirably carried out. The only fault I find in the translation is making Ginger exclaim, 'Thank heaven!' that being, as I suppose, a place not dreamt of in Equine philosophy; but were I to tell you of all I admire, I should not get this letter posted to-night. The best bit of writing, according to my ideas, is the drive through the City—that is really wonderful. Are you sure you have never stood on the steps of an omnibus to collect passengers and watch the traffic?"

"TORQUAY, *January* 18, 1878.

"... As an imaginary entrance into and mastery of horse nature, it is extremely clever,—as a story it is thoroughly well planned and told; and last, not least, it must do good among all, high and low, who have the care of these noble creatures. ... It has made me cry more than twice or thrice. Poor Ginger! Then the fall on Ludgate Hill! My dear Anna, you have been doing angels' work in writing this book, bringing messages of peace and good-will from the Lord of all to these His poor dumb creatures, of whom man too often proves himself so unworthy a guardian."

"NORWICH, *December* 24, 1877.

"You will be shocked to hear that a work intended to benefit mankind has been the cause of my neglecting all my duties—I *could not* leave Black Beauty till I left him safe in Joe's care. I cannot think how you could ever write such an Equestrian story. One would think you had been a horse-dealer, or a groom, or a jockey all your life."

"... You have so filled my mind with the thought of what these poor animals suffer from the bearing-rein, that I feel quite breathless as I look at some of them, and only my sex, and fear of the police, prevent my cutting the leathers and setting them free."

"... To induce fashionable ladies to forego the style of the bearing-rein is simply to wait for an altered fashion;

nothing short of that arbitrary foe will have any very evident effect, I fear; but the book is a thoroughly good step in the right direction. May it circulate widely, and may many a neglected Black Beauty find a resting-place in the kind consideration of some happy home."

The following letter from Mrs. Toynbee refers to Mr. Flower,[1] the well-known friend of animals, who by his writings, his personal advocacy, indeed by every means in his power, has striven to ameliorate the sufferings of the brute creation—more especially of the horse. The letter is addressed to Mrs. Sewell :—

"*January* 29, 1878.

"Captain Toynbee and I went yesterday afternoon to see our friends the Flowers, in Hyde Park Gardens, and found Mr. Flower in a complete state of enthusiasm over 'Black Beauty.' 'It is written by a veterinary surgeon,' he exclaimed; 'by a coachman, by a groom; there is not a mistake in the whole of it; not one thing I wish altered, except that the cabman *should* have taken that half-crown. I shall show Mr. Bright that passage about horses in war. I *must* make the lady's acquaintance; she must come to London sometimes—she is my Araminta' (Do you remember Miss Edgeworth's 'Araminta, or the Unknown Friend'?). He particularly wished me to say that he would like to write himself, but writing is troublesome to him, from the weakness of his hand. Are we right in supposing that the book is written (translated, by-the-bye) by your daughter? Is it being actively circulated? That was a point Mr. Flower was very anxious about. . . . Will you forgive so many questions, but Mr. Flower could talk of nothing else. Now and then, when the conversation strayed away to the war, or anything else, he would exclaim 'How

---

[1] Mr. Flower has published two pamphlets, one on "The Bearing-Rein," the other, "Horses and Harness." The two pamphlets are now published in one by Cassell & Co.

could a lady know so much about horses! I should like to have a talk with her; do persuade her to come to London.' I need not add anything—my *ignorant* admiration for 'Black Beauty' would be so poor after Mr. Flower's thorough appreciation."

The following letter was written by Mrs. Sewell in reply to Mrs. Toynbee's :—

"I should have thanked you for your most welcome letter the day it came, but an infirm household and an invalid friend staying with us, obliged my pen to be quiet.

"Your letter was indeed a great encouragement both to me and Anna. It was the first of the kind that had come to hand, and was accordingly treasured. Many letters followed, but when I took yours to Anna, I said I was come to put her crown on. I assure you it was a triumphant moment. She had ventured to send a copy of her book to Mr. Flower, but had thought, if he noticed it at all, it would be chiefly to point out inaccuracies; but when his entire approbation came, it brought indeed a full measure of gladness and confidence. If he would add to his kindness by writing a few lines expressive of his commendation, he would be giving it a standing beyond what any one else could do.

"We are expecting every day the proofs of the School Edition; we have both a great desire that it should become a reading-book in Boys' Schools. This also was the sanguine hope of the publisher, but his sudden death, just before its publication, has deprived it of his energetic aid.

"After all this about the book, I fancy you would be interested to know a little about the author. There is no doubt most persons will have imagined her a robust young woman, mostly in the saddle with the reins in her hand. Instead of this, for the last seven years she has been confined either to her bed or couch, and has not in all that time passed beyond the garden-gate. At the beginning of this time, the subject of the book took root in her mind, and from time to time a few portions were dictated—reading or writing being equally impossible to her. Years went on, and no progress was made, except in her mind, where many pictures were clearly drawn and stored away in her memory.

"The year before last, she was so far improved in strength as to be able to write in pencil her clearly arranged thoughts, I immediately making a fair copy. Her thoughts and pictures were the fruit of previous experience. When a child, she severely sprained both ankles, which ever after prevented her taking much walking exercise, and made riding and driving a necessity; and so it came to pass, between her and her own horse, and horses in general, a mutual confidence and friendship sprang up, and she learned all their secrets. She learned much through her ear, in this way quickly detecting if anything is wrong with a horse's foot, and through her eye she knows at once if anything annoys them."

Mr. Weylland, of the London City Mission, wrote to offer

"Congratulations warm and sincere at your entry into the great republic of letters, which your mother has so long adorned with a power and dignity peculiar to herself."

A relative writes :—

"I am so glad the precious mother's mantle will find a suitable resting-place. The graceful folds and sweet embroidery of natural flowers can, I truly believe, fit *no* other shoulders; but its warmth, its truth, its honesty of purpose will be your own rich covering.

"Dearest Anna, how I envy you the power of that dedication! God bless her—she well deserves every word of it."

The words of the dedication referred to are :—

"To my dear and honoured mother, whose life, no less than her pen, has been devoted to the welfare of others, this little book is affectionately dedicated."

The motto chosen for the book is an extract from the "Life of Charles Kingsley:"—

"He was a perfect horseman, and never lost his temper with his horse, talking to and reasoning with it if it shied or bolted, as if it had been a rational being; knowing that from the fine organisation of the animal, a horse, like a child, will get confused by panic fear, which is only increased by punishment."

It is our life friend—the horse, who performs for us the last service we need on earth—he carries us to our graves. For our sakes these spirited animals allow themselves to be trained to the measured step, the crawling pace, the drooping head, indicative of grief. When the hearse which was to bear Anna to the grave drew up at the door, Mrs Sewell saw from the drawing-room window that the horses had bearing-reins. Her much-loved friend and neighbour, Mrs. Buxton, was present, and caught her exclamation of distress, "Oh this will never do!" she said, and hastening downstairs, spoke to the men, and had the bearing-reins removed from all the horses in the train.

To one so frail, and dependent upon quiet, the excitement of this torrent of praise and congratulation must have been physically trying, in spite of the calmness of the chastened spirit. It seemed as if the feeble flame of life had leaped up brightly for a last effort, and now flickered down again. In July of this year, the Journal records, "I began milk diet two weeks ago, and hope for benefit." The hope was so far fulfilled that a marked diminution of suffering ensued; but the patient was never able to take the full quantity prescribed, and she wasted away. In the course of the following winter, cold settled on her lungs, and the feeble, worn-out frame had no power of resistance: rapid decline set in. The letters that follow tell the story:—

To Mrs. Williamson.

"The darling has not been so well for the last few weeks, quite unable to work or do anything but be an angel of patience and sweetness in the house."

To a Friend.

". . . I wish to keep the day's work up with the day, as a different one is, I think, not far off. Step by step, day by day, the dear life seems to be slipping away, gently just now, comparatively little pain, quiet and praiseful, taking medicine, food;—but the life goes. She can scarcely be moved without faintness. The water-bed is a great comfort. She has not been moved to the couch for three days —it is all too much—but the Comforter is here. We do not talk of the future—the parting; it might unnerve us both, and we each know what the other thinks and feels. She has done the day's work in the day, and no arrears press on her tranquil spirit, which is resting in the arms of Eternal love. She never loses an opportunity of sending her love to her friends; all are affectionately remembered—thee most especially."

To Mrs. Williamson.

"I have been wishing to send thee a line, but nursing brings many interruptions. I wanted to tell thee myself of the goodness of the Lord—not in restoring bodily strength—but little more of this remains to be taken away— but in restoring the soul. We are both of us kept in such wondrous peace and trust. He is taking us down on the sunny side of the valley, where the dew lies still, and every sharp stone as we touch it is taken away—we *touch* it, and feel it is there, and then recognise the Hand that removes it. There is now no acute pain internally, but the poor bones, barely covered with skin, have passed through at the lower part of the back. . . . The difficulty of raising the mucous phlegm is the most trying, but her sweet patience accepts all from the Hand of love. The majestic grandeur of her countenance is never disturbed, excepting in sleep; then we see what she suffers, and how she restrains herself from showing it. Her thought is about me—we know each other's thoughts and feelings so perfectly, that words would be an intrusion, and might overcome us both. How long it may last I know not, but think it cannot be long—she now never rises from her water-bed. I have moved her into the drawing-room. The nurse always sleeps there, and I go to my own bed. My health and strength and appetite continue good. The Blessed Lord sustains me. The prayers of my loving friends seem to keep me ever before Him."

"*April* 1878.

"You are longing, I know, to hear of my Jewel, but what shall I say? A little weaker, and a little weaker—two or three words at a time is all she can say, and all she can bear to hear. I dare not say a word that would touch her tender feelings. 'My dearest Jewel,' I say, and her response is, 'My dearest Mother'—we neither of us venture further. She has been sorely tried with her poor back—no ease. . . . Her sweet patience is past description, and her thankfulness for any little change that promises ease, if only momentary, is truly touching. The dear Lord is putting on the last ornamental touches, and beautifying her exceedingly. But oh! it is too touching—with all the sweet springing of the flowers, the joyous songs of the birds, and the sunshine, and she, fading away, never to look at them again with me.

"Oh! you know, you so well know how the poor struggling heart scarcely knows how to bear it; but I have freely given her to the Lord; and there are days when I find myself carried along, like a child in arms, without effort and without pain.

"I stole out for a short walk before breakfast this morning, to be alone with the Comforter. The grass was glittering all over with dewdrops, myriads upon myriads everywhere, with all the fair colours that the glorious sun could produce; and then I saw my darling drawn up to pass into the pure light of the Sun of Righteousness, and the Comforter Himself comforted me, and I returned strengthened for the day; and so the days come and go."

I give one extract from the letters of "loving friends:"—

". . . For our invalid, now slowly recovering, we are rejoicing that it is the Spring, not the Autumn. For your loved one, dear friend, I think the Spring is to be on the other side, by the Tree of Life, where no Autumn or Winter will ever follow, where she

'Will see and hear and know
All she desired and wished below.'

And oh how much that means!—the desires and wishes of *such minds* as hers are not easily grasped, but she will be satisfied, and so will her mother. 'Such high love' as you two have had for one another 'is not of things to perish.' I am sure the Lord must be keeping some of His 'choicest cordials' for this 'deepest fainting' of your life."

The next letter from Mrs. Sewell refers to Mrs. ——'s name for mental inspiration. When poetry came into her mind, she used to say that her "friend" had spoken to her. Anna had been inquiring why nothing had been heard of this "friend," and the reply was, "It is so long since my 'friend' has spoken to me, I am afraid it must be dead."

To Mrs. F. ———.

"*April* 23, 1878.

"Your tenderly sympathising letter, my beloved friend, has been a real comfort to me. I read parts of it to my darling, and whilst they are fresh in my remembrance, I want to tell you the words she said, at broken intervals. 'How we have loved her, mother, and how we have admired her! I have so often wished to write to her since I had her last letter. I have been waiting till I was stronger, and that has never come. Say to her from me' (alluding to a portion of your letter to her), 'Do not mourn your "dead friend." If God takes it away, it is because He has some other work *now* more wanted, and therefore more worthy of being done; the other is only laid aside for the present time. I have many "dead friends" in which I delighted—they were taken away from me one by one. They might have carried my heart away. I think they would, but I think they were taken away to be restored. I shall find them when the new life begins, and rise and enjoy them without danger. Meantime God has given me a few "humble friends" to employ my small talents, and keep my thoughts from myself—little works for children and poor people, that have made me glad and busy, and thankful *now*. Give my most dear love to F. and F.'

"This was about the substance of what she said. I am not apt at rendering the exact words, but I do entirely understand her feelings and thoughts.

"Day by day the precious life is longing for its home. 'Here in the body pent,' weary and breathless; suffering night and day. *That* is one side of the picture—there is another—resting in the Will of God, without the shadow of a cloud between her soul and her Saviour. She is longing for the hour of her liberation, and I do not hold her; I give her up freely to her blessed portion—the remainder of my days sweetened by the thought of her certain gain."

The last little note before the end :—

"BELOVED FRIEND,—We are going through the valley in tender sunshine. Every rough stone is taken away before it appears in sight. We are both together under His feathers. He knows our frame. He remembers we are but dust. Blessed be His name for His tender mercies. —Most lovingly yours, MARY SEWELL."

About three or four days after this, I received a card in the well-known writing, and read—

"For ever with the Lord"
"All tears wiped away."

At the end of a week came the following letter :—

"I will try to write you a few lines. It is a week to-day since my bright jewel was taken from me and put safe into the heavenly casket, out of my sight. You know well the kind of days I have been passing since. I can only say I have been carried along by a strong supporting arm, and by a tenderness which does not refuse me the relief of tears, which I had been unable to shed for weeks.

". . . In the morning of the day, I went into her room about four o'clock in the morning, having heard her incessantly coughing for a long time. 'Oh,' she said, in her bright sunny way, 'thee art not so good as thee said thee would be. Go to bed, darling; I really have had some nice sleep.' I returned again at six, with something very soft to place under her shoulders; every part of her back was so tender that no position afforded comfort. She said she would have it the next time the nurse moved her. In about an hour the nurse called me hastily, saying Anna was faint. I found her breathing with difficulty, but as soon as she could speak, she said, with one of her inexpressible smiles, 'I am not going yet, I am so strong.'

She then asked the nurse if that was dying. For four and a half hours this painful breathing continued, becoming more and more difficult, and she was perfectly conscious till the last few minutes. She, as it were, girded herself to endure the pains of death, that she might spare the feelings of those around her. Her lips were often seen moving, and her clear, beautiful eyes raised upwards; then her face would become overspread with an almost luminous smile as she evidently received the answer. She did not move the whole time, but her sweet eyes were ever seeking me with inexpressible tenderness, as if with her whole soul she would comfort me. About a quarter of an hour before she passed away, she said, 'Pray,' and my Philip commended her into her Redeemer's hands, giving thanks for her full salvation, for all He had revealed to her, and for her perfect peace. She said, 'Amen; it is all quite, quite true.' Then in a clear voice she said, 'I am quite ready.' Her eyes sought me again. I laid my cheek on hers; a few more long-drawn breaths and she had left me behind. The angel had gone out of the house, and left a void never to be filled till we meet again.

"On Tuesday she was laid in the little, quiet burying-ground where her ancestors for many generations sleep undisturbed. It is in the village next to Buxton, where my sisters live, and belongs to the Friends, who were numerous in those parts. It is a sequestered spot, surrounded by trees and a high hawthorn hedge, where the birds are never disturbed.

'O my dear friend, I do pray that the little remainder of my life may be spent wholly in my Saviour's service. The Lord has been wonderfully good to us, giving us everything, softening the trial in every possible way. Blessed be His name."

I had a treasure—so dear—so dear—
  So strong for comfort, so fair to see;
A whisper came from the heavenly shore,
  "Wilt thou give the light of thine eyes to me?"

My jewel! my jewel! But I only cried,
  "He must not take thee by force away."
I gave thee, I gave thee, with joy and pride
  Such a gem at His feet to lay.

And I thought of the glow that would light His eyes,
  As He turned from angels to welcome thee.
But ah! my Lord, if with Thee I joy,
  Thou wilt not forget to weep with me.

CHAPTER VIII.

CLOSING YEARS.

"Old age is a blessed time. It gives us leisure to put off our earthly garments one by one and dress ourselves for heaven."
—"The Experience of Life."

Six months went by, heavy with the shadow of death—the "bright jewel" gone, the husband failing more and more, dependent on "little, constant, cheerful attentions" to divert the current of his thoughts. Very pathetic was it, in those sorrowful days, to witness the cheerfulness of these attentions. Mrs. Sewell would have no one but her sisters to stay in the house at that time, but my daughter was able to spend a few hours with her one day in September, and saw with astonishment the degree of elasticity in mind and body which grief and age had left untouched. The spring of life was gone indeed. "Now, when I wake in the morning—it's a burden," she said. "It was never so before." Never, through all her weary nursing! but, far from wishing to lay the burden down, she spoke with surprise of some persons having offered as a comfort to her the thought that her own remnant of life must be very short. "I *cannot* want to go till I have seen my goodman laid to rest," she said; and besides, as my daughter wrote, "The world was going on: she was intensely interested in it, and wanted to live, and see what would happen next."

She talked of trying to make little corners of time in which to write lessons for children, founded on simple proverbs and illustrations from nature, and laughed over one she mentioned. "I am a lady, and you are a lady, and who is to drive out the pig?" Another she liked was, "God sees the black ant on the black stone in the dark night." But no time came until her long watch was gently ended. Mr. Sewell died on November 7 in that same year.

To a Friend.

" I want to tell thee our dear weary wayfarer has entered into rest: at last that dimly expressed longing is fulfilled, 'to get Home.' After all the long waiting-time, the final stages of the journey were so rapidly completed that it seems to me still like a dream of the night, and I listen for the heavy foot, and the ever-repeated question, 'Mary, are thee there?' and tears come with thanksgiving, that our Heavenly Father has taken him to Himself. . . .

" God is very gracious. The last evening but one before he left us, I was standing by him at the bedside; suddenly his spirit was caught away from everything but joy and praise and thanksgiving, and for half an hour or more, as I stood amazed, he poured forth, in the most fervent and exalted language, a strain of praise to God—of perfect rest in Christ, and such an overwhelming sense of happiness that he said, ' I could shout for joy.' His passing away was as gentle as that of a child falling asleep in its mother's arms—the repose on the still face afterwards was perfect. Have I not cause for trust and thankfulness, and an assured hope that in God's good time I shall be permitted to be where my dear ones are?"

A few weeks later she writes:—

"I am not alone; my dear granddaughter is come to live with me. I am feeling much like a day-labourer on the Saturday night, when all his work is done, and he looks forward peacefully and thankfully to the Sabbath. God is ever very good to me."

Folded up with a number of reviews of "Davie Blake," all most commendatory, I have found this little prayer:—

"O my Lord Jesus, may the one effort, the continuous desire of my heart, be to serve Thee fully, either by doing or suffering Thy will.

"Choose all the future for me, and help me constantly to regard whatever comes as Thy place and will for me, and thankfully regard and cheerfully accept it, whatever it may be—diligently striving to abstract the blessing which, coming from Thee, it must contain.

"Thou hast my treasures safe in Thy keeping—my service for them is over, and Thou hast left me more at liberty. O Lord, that every step may now be forward to the end. The past has closed in. I begin my new life. The past is rolled up and put aside till the time for unrolling comes."

In this spirit my dear friend turned to begin her life again at eighty-one.

The granddaughter whose privilege it now became to cheer her declining years, was in every way adapted for the task—fully in sympathy with her philanthropic ardour, very executive, and among other charming gifts, possessing one inestimable to those who live out of the stream of life themselves—she was a first-class reporter, able to make her listeners partake in all she saw and did. But the first months of the new life could not be otherwise than sorrowful.

Throughout the long and chequered years of Mrs. Sewell's life, one joy had never failed her. Each year, as the time came round, the Spring was ever longed for, waited for, watched for—she was never so absorbed in either the joys or sorrows of life as to forget to listen for the "Voice" which failed not to say:—

> "I come, I come! ye have called me long,—
> I come o'er the mountains with light and song;
> Ye may trace my step o'er the wakening earth
> By the winds which tell of the violet's birth,
> By the primrose-stars in the shadowy grass,
> By the green leaves opening as I pass."

In the year following "the darling's" death, the Spring was again welcomed, but it was with a chastened joy—the Voice was the Voice of Spring, but the words were not the same:—

> "But ye!—ye are changed since ye met me last;
> A shade of earth has been round you cast!
> There is that come over your brow and eye
> Which speaks of a world where the flowers must die!
> You smile—but your smile has a dimness yet—
> Oh what have ye looked on since last we met?
>
> "Ye are changed, ye are changed! and I see not here
> All whom I saw in the vanished year!
>
> .   .   .   .
>
> Are they gone? Is their voice from the green hills passed?
> Ye have looked on Death since ye met me last."

In a letter dated March 10, the bereaved mother writes :—

"... Still I am sad. The primroses coming, and no darling to carry them to—the birds beginning to sing to each other, and my bird is flown away, and will sing to me no more here; and I am deaf, and cannot hear her singing in that enclosed garden full of perfumes, though I am sure she is there; and I rejoice for that, but cannot help saying 'How long!'"

The dear mother often spoke with pleasure of the fact that her own birthday and Anna's both occurred early in the Spring; she always rejoiced in finding affinities with the bright and hopeful, all her life continuing on the side of youth and hope. Their birthdays into "The Better Land" waited for no Autumn, only for advanced and perfected Spring — the daughter dying in May, and the mother early in June. In their death they could still follow "The Voice of Spring," and say :—

"For me, I depart to a brighter shore;
 Ye are marked by care, ye are mine no more;
 I go where the loved, who have left you, dwell,
 And the flowers are not Death's: fare ye well, farewell!"

To Mrs. Williamson.

(*When the house had been cleaned and painted.*)

"You have been building and beautifying for others, and have had the charm of unselfish labour; the great drawback in mine has been that I had no one to do it for but myself, and it has been such a dry, heartless service, that I almost dislike the look of my clean walls and well-painted stairs. I have been wanting my Nannie; but, oh, how sorry she would be to be recalled to this poor lean world! I think she would say with Samuel, 'Why hast thou called me up?' or rather, 'Why hast thou called me *down?*' How near heaven becomes when your darlings are there! Wherever it may be, or whatever it is, we know it will satisfy all our desires."

To the Same.

(*After the death of a young helper very dear to Mrs. Williamson.*)

". . . These severing strokes from our dear companions have brought us into our last dispensation—our completeness is gone. That generous, flattering love that could see no fault in us, which unconsciously placed us on good terms with ourselves, and beguiled us away from discouraging influences with the sense that we were everything to some one, and that no one else could ever be the same—that is for ever gone.

"Our path is not so flowery now—there are none of those little love-songs we used to sing together when no one else heard—no one else could know the tunes. . . . Yes, everything is changed. These are the last days with us—the time of perfecting and finishing up, and doing the things that remain. Our expectation is only from Him, who alone knows what the 'lone heart' means. Oh for the reunion! Can it ever be? Only the spiritual body could bear such joy. Many a time in the day, when it looks all fair weather, I comfort myself with the sweet joy of folding my beloved again to my heart."

(*After returning from Church.*)

"This morning in the Church, when the Organ was beautifully playing 'Wherefore with Angels and Archangels, and with all the company of heaven'—I could fancy I heard my Nannie's sweet voice among them, and I strained my hoarse little pipe to join in with her. Oh!

beloved, what will that meeting be, and the age after age, and the more and more!"

"In my own experience I do not know what is meant by getting over a deep heart-loss, though I am well aware that circumstances arise which incline us to thank God that He has taken away our treasures, and hidden them away for a while, in His grand Storehouse.

"What wonderful and beautiful things must grow out of sorrow and bereavement, that now, with only our dim anticipations, we are able quietly to endure the tremendous griefs of life! When there existed no hope of a resurrection, there could have been but the choice between stoicism and insanity. Christianity has no doubt increased our power of feeling, but it has also provided us with an anodyne."

But her note was not always sad, even in addressing the very few whom she trusted with her sadness. The young and ardent about her saw little of it at any time, and the following letter to Mrs. Williamson strikes a cheerful chord:—

"*November* 2, 1879.

"I want to know, dear friend, how it fares with thee—how the tenement is keeping in repair, and whether this early cold is warning thee to take more care.

"Your photograph stands in a little frame upon my chimney-piece. I frequently go up to it and say, 'How do thee fare, precious friend?' It answers always in the same words, or I do not understand variations, 'What I see clearly ought to be done, I have faith to undertake. Do thou likewise;' and I answer, 'O friend, give me thy faith. Thou hast received abundantly according to it. I cannot do like thee.'

"How gorgeous will the autumn tints be, from the pleasant windows at Fairstowe! It will truly be a fairstowe, and it will charm your eye and taste, and will feel to you like a great cathedral full of praise.

"During this summer, up to the present time, I have usually taken my early morning service between seven and eight o'clock, in a quiet walk on the edge of Mr. Buxton's pretty park. I cannot express the refreshment, help, and enjoyment this has been to me. It is goodly to praise with all the praising creatures, and they are so cheerful that one can but feel our Father means us all to be truly happy, and has provided for our being so. Sorrowful yet always rejoicing, not stopping short at the first word. Well, I think we do not, we *could not;* every day comes laden with mercy, and the greatest mercy of all is that we feel it to be so."

The previous habits of our lives tell strongly on our later years. Those, then, have a great advantage who have habituated themselves to a kind and loving consideration for others. The infirmities of age pass over such comparatively lightly—they escape the danger of dwelling too much on their own ailments when their hearts are so full of other things. The power for active service may be lessened, but if life has been rightly used, a reserve of experience has been accumulating, which, laid out to the best advantage, may prove to be the highest offering of the life. When both the head and the heart can still do so much, it becomes of little consequence that the hands and feet can do little.

Dora Greenwell writes :—" It is wonderful what the heart can go through, when it has some one thing that it really delights in, to turn to as a green spot. A beloved being is best of all, but even a favourite, congenial occupation, will do a great deal."

Mrs. Sewell was still rich in "beloved beings"

and congenial occupations. Many of her morning hours were spent in converse with those who needed just the counsel and sympathy she knew so well how to give. It was interesting to observe how fearlessly these inquirers trusted her with their ignorance, without a thought of being despised for it. The consciousness of it only made them feel the more sure of her help and sympathy.

The following letter reveals the secret of her patience :—

"When one sees one's friends tossed and troubled, and then turns within one's own heart, and feels so filled *full* with blessing—when that love and trust are granted to us so richly which others sigh for,—how can we wish, having this, to ask or desire anything more than this peace of God shed abroad in the heart? How could we bear life, or our fellow-creatures, without it? From it comes the saintly gift of patience—the love that covers the many sins with its own atmosphere of tender colour and tone. It is this that makes bearable the waywardness and wilfulness of both young and old—causing it to appear only as the ruggedness which casts needful shadows, the full meaning of which will be one day understood in God's own clear light."

Another letter touches on the responsibilities of human intercourse :—

"How often we have been conscious that a light word spoken, a suggestion thrown out, has changed the whole current and atmosphere of conversation, raising its tone, or it may be depressing it to a very low level! Possessing, as we certainly do, these latent forces within ourselves— these stimulating agencies to develop either the better or the worse,—how careful we should be that we call forth only the latent angel."

In summer-time, especially if any visitor were staying with her, Mrs. Sewell liked to take her callers into the "summer-parlour" in the garden, where she was more secure from interruption than anywhere in the house. There many a sorrow has been poured out, comforted, or, if it chanced to be of home manufacture, rebuked. The Bible-woman, who came every Saturday morning to tell her long story of the week's work, was often received there, and there Mrs. Sewell would take letters which came asking her advice and sympathy in difficult matters, to think and pray over them before writing in reply. I give two specimens of her answers :—

"As far as I have heard and read, the really great things in the world have not been done by great companies or great men, but by one man here, and another woman there, whom the Lord chose because He could trust them. He may choose you, my dear, to be a light in a dark place. You can't tell what sort of people you may be set down among, but whatever they are, you are put there to do them good, and get good yourself."

" . . . You ask me questions I cannot answer. With regard to the great enemy of mankind, I leave that without any speculation or desire, excepting that he should be shut up."

To a Friend who had been visiting Old Catton, and had a great appreciation of " Warren's Pot"—an innovation which Mrs. Sewell's cook had resented.

"Your letter this morning was like balm and honey. I was waiting till it came, for I was sure it would come—

we could not leave off quite all of a sudden to speak to one another, even though the world is dashing along at such a rate. I wanted to tell you again how full of love and pleasantness you left my heart—so comforted and refreshed. I like the word refreshed: it sounds like new life and strength together. This is a fine talent, this talent of refreshing, which some persons especially possess. Don't you think it might be classed among the Gifts to be exercised for the Great Refresher? There are many, many, with heavy hands and sinking hearts, waiting for these sweet messengers.

"My dear Philip spent last evening with me. After tea we sat in the greenhouse, and I read to him 'The Man at the Gate,' which he much appreciated. We had a sweet and comfortable talk together, till the moon was walking in her brightness, and we found that time had been travelling even faster than our thoughts.

"I am so glad you are better for your little visit here. Was it not a little one? I trust, in the Autumn, when my garden is full of flowers and fables, that we shall see your dear face here again. My maids were quite 'took up with you,' as they expressed it. The 'Pot cloud' has been lifted from Cook's face, and she is quite bright again. 'Bear ye one another's burdens,' though it may be only a pot.

"I found this morning, in the inkstand of your room, a knife with an ivory handle; it looks as if it had been a faithful pocket companion to some one for some years, and might have had a suffering time of it. Is it yours?

"I remember with much humiliation what a penance my letters are to read, and I have to inflict it upon another friend before the post leaves, so no more."

The "flowers and fables" of that pretty garden linger fondly in the memory of all who rested there. To the right of the house, under an archway where convolvulus and canariensis climbed up to meet the Gloire de Dijon rose, one passed the dividing hedge, and came in sight of the pansy bed—a daily delight to its mistress, on account of the variety of expression in the flowers' faces. "Do look at that pert little thing," she would say. "Did you ever see anything so saucy?" When told that the Germans called them "stepmothers" because they had such cross faces, she was up in arms on behalf of both stepmothers and pansies. The old country name, "Jump-up-and-kiss-me," she thought much more suitable for some of them, and others were "pansies for thoughts," grave and pensive. Then there were the favourite white anemone-japonicas, "like happy schoolgirls with such open faces," opposite the summer-parlour; and coming back along the straight walk at the top, one went down to the house again by the path skirting the bed of wild-flowers. The latest improvement there was to sink two large earthen pans, painted dark green, and fill them with water for the lilies and forget-me-nots to look into.

"I have two ferns here that are mad for new fashions," Mrs. Sewell said one morning; "all the frills and furbelows that you could think of."

They were hedgerow ferns which, planted in the richer soil of her garden, had thrown out a crop of green curls above their natural fronds.

"It's a perfect caricature of fashion," she said; "and this other one—how lady-like it looks beside them! Now all these ferns, when we see them crowded up in the hedge, are limited and small; they can't put out their powers. Plant them here, and we see how they develop, with the help of human science. They are just like mankind, struggling for perfection—struggling blindly, so that these"—pointing to the curly ferns—"when they get well fed, with plenty of space, instead of developing in a nice, orderly way, run off into all these frolics."

On the other side of the lattice-screen behind the ferns, very dear neighbours had lived, but they left several years before Mrs. Sewell's death, oft remembered and lamented. From a thick clump of beech-trees beyond—

"The deep, mellow cush of the wood-pigeon's note
 Made music that sweetened the calm."

Mrs. Sewell interpreted it to say, "You *be-e* so pretty! You *be-e* so pretty!" and a low sound used to come, like an answer from the mate, "Yes, yes."

There was a little bark house for bees on the top walk. One autumn, Mrs. Sewell writes:—

"We had a tremendous storm last Thursday. The leaves were sent off quite without warning, and the garden, which was quite pretty last week, lost all its glory."

This storm was probably responsible for the following:—

"Now I must end with a tragedy. Having observed no bees going in and out since the great rain, I felt anxious, thinking it must be too early for them to go to sleep, and when G—— was here, I got him to lift off the top of their house,—and they were all dead corpses. As I turned sorrowfully away, a gracious pigeon said, 'That *be* a pity!'"

A visitor once had the misfortune to call the bees' house "an apiary." Mrs. Sewell turned upon him and said, "It's a *bee-hut!*"

Another case of fine language she took very patiently, the speaker being below herself in position. A person usefully employed in London, having occasion to come to Norwich, asked, as a great honour, for permission to call on the illustrious authoress. On arriving, she dramatically kissed the hand held out to her, and began a speech—an outpour of admiration, which the hostess benevolently allowed her to finish, as it would have been a great disappointment for anything so elaborately got up to fail in reaching its object. As soon as it was over, the admired lady began, in her usual quiet way, to speak of the work in which Miss R—— was engaged; but whatever was said only became the occasion for a fresh display of complimentary eloquence. When at last the visitor took her departure, as Mrs. Sewell closed the door after her, she said, "Miss R—— is a good body, but afflicted in her manners."

I told her of Mr. Smithies' remark, when he had been presented with a testimonial accompanied by most flattering speeches—"If we must be rewarded, or rather punished in this way, I think we might stipulate to have our praise administered in homœopathic doses, not in shovelfuls."

When confined to the house by a cold, she wrote :—

"In one way or the other, I find plenty to do and think

about. I know nothing about long weary days. I often think how wonderful it is that every day finds its own little occupation and excitement, sufficient to keep the wheels going, even though we may not have what is called an important vocation."

I once told her of a Hospital Missionary, who, at the close of his long service, said to me, "For thirty years I have spent my time in going up and down, in and out, among the same rows of white beds." "That sounds rather monotonous," I said; but he answered, "No; His compassions were *new* every morning."

"That just describes my life," she said. "People think I must be dull! Why, I wake every morning with quiet joy, expecting the new mercies the day is sure to bring, and He never disappoints me. If in the evening He were to ask, 'Lackest thou anything?' I could only reply, 'Nothing, Lord.'"

Perhaps one of the pleasantest things that happened any day was to hear the sound of carriage-wheels, and "Bessie's" well-known step. "Grandmother" would be at the door to welcome "my girls," who had no end of things to tell. In some unaccountable way Bessie must have learned manners, for she was deeply impressed with the conviction that a call should not extend beyond a quarter of an hour. As soon as that had expired, she began to paw and fret to be off, and the father's voice would be heard calling, "Come, girls, come; Bessie wants to be going." Then a number of heads would be thrust out of an open window, calling out, "Oh, Bessie dear, do be quiet; we haven't half done yet. Do stand still, there's a dear; do." This procured perhaps another five minutes—then again came the summons, "Come, girls, come; I can't hold Bessie any longer." Then out rushed the merry girls, clambering up the carriage as best they could, as people must when horses cannot be made to stand still—the dear Grandmother looking on at the fun all the time,—the proudest and happiest of Grandmothers. It was a pretty sight to see her standing at the gate, watching her precious ones until they were out of sight—then stopping to speak to any poor neighbour who might be passing by, inviting them to step inside the gate and have a look at her flowers. If it were late in the afternoon, men were often returning from work, and she would gather a handful of flowers for them to take home to "missus" and the children.

To a Friend suffering the trials of house-cleaning.

"... 'A fellow-feeling makes us wondrous kind' (or sympathetic). I am in deep sympathy with you now—in the turmoil of house-cleaning, *ill supported*, the sweep and whitewashers contrary—Cook gone home to see if she can mend up sufficiently to take her place again—Emily, and a good, Christian, know-nothing woman, to help attire the house in her Spring clothes, and give her a sweet, cheerful face. Amie and I help and arrange, and cook a little, and clean a little, and put up with a great deal. We do not make long faces, but often have a hearty laugh over these passing troubles, which are just the size and weight you make them. All work is interesting if you throw your energies into it, and *if* it is worth doing.

"I have stopped a moment, enchanted with the blue, blue sky, the fine white clouds sailing over it, and the delicate green of the beech-trees. Oh, if you could but see it with me, and gaze and wonder and praise!

"Did you ever read a tiny little book, 'The Practice of the Presence of God'?—the experience of Brother Lawrence. If not, I will send it to you. If we could attain to his experience, we should know nothing about picking and choosing, but only accepting."

"She taught me one lesson which I shall never forget," writes a friend. "I was smarting under a trouble for which there seemed no redress, and no human help;—and to her, my best earthly comforter and adviser, I had confided it, sure of her ready sympathy and attention. In two words her help and her comfort were given. '*Accept it*,' she said. 'There is nothing else for you, and nothing better.' And so I found it."

From this time, letters are abundant, and the story of the years that remain can be told almost entirely in Mrs. Sewell's own words.

To a Friend, advising her to defer a promised visit until the extreme cold had passed away.

". . . I am hardy, and do not suffer as some do. The darling needing so very much care happily kept me from self-indulgent habits, for which I thank her, as I do for many other things—my jewel! And yet, oh how I do wish you could see my dear robins, sparrows, thrushes, and blackbirds, instead of only your poor little citizens!

Then there is the exquisitely dazzling snow in the sunshine — the bare branches of the trees covered with diamonds, the brilliant shining stars at night!

"Shall we ever believe that we are ourselves when we get into our *new* bodies, and find ourselves able to converse with delight upon that which now lies to us almost in a haze, or only occasionally emerges out of the mist, to sparkle for a moment?

"I like to try to make myself at home in that which is to be, and though I see but through a glass very darkly, yet this little helps to quicken desire, and release our feet from the mud."

"I don't know where Heaven is; therefore I am more than satisfied to spend a portion of Eternity here, and see some of the evil transmuted into good."

Speaking of some excellent people in high places :—

"It is so encouraging to see the capabilities and excellences that exist in so many of our fellow-creatures. They seem to say to us, 'Up and gird yourselves.'

"If we could but begin again, retaining what we have learned, I wonder if we should do better. Perhaps not— in this limited body that coughs, and catches cold, and gets so frozen. We'll have to wait. As I sit here, with my stiff hands making all kinds of erratic dashes, I can even rejoice that my darling is all safe and warm in the sunshine of His presence."

On her birthday, April 6 :—

"I knew I should hear from you this morning; you always send me loving thoughts on my birthday. I think it is my periodical setting-up day. I find afresh every year that I have *so many* dear friends, and that they keep on loving me from year to year. Birthdays would be excellent institutions were it only for the pleasant little inflation they bring."

To a Friend.

"It was this day fortnight, one of the days which Southey somewhere says send into the heart a summer feeling, when all the insect tribes leave their dark nooks and coverts, and issue forth for one more day of joyful existence. I took my Sunday morning service in the garden, and felt my heart unspeakably full of joy and peace and gladness—it was to me such a privilege to give myself and every one I had to the Lord, and so *safe!* It was a temple service that morning to be remembered."

To the Same.

"I have at last got rid of a cold and cough that kept me in the house till lately, speaking unkind things of the east wind, which has been unusually spiteful, even for a Norfolk east wind—never remorseful. The flowers turned up their faces pitifully, or hung down their heads despairingly. But oh how quick they are to 'take heart again!' Yesterday's sweet, mild, gentle rain has quite inspired them, and they and the birds are rejoicing together, and I could not keep back my note of praise even had I desired to do so. I took my walk in the old way early this morning, and saw the trees standing in their new garments, in the first still hush of this resurrection morning. I think the Great Assembly will be silent before they break out in the great general acclamation of joy and praise."

In the spring of 1880, "The Martyr's Tree" was completed. Two lines, written of the martyr, are expressive of the writer's spirit at this time :—

"As through the mist, he saw the radiant clime
That borders on the way-worn waste of time."

She lived in prospect of the "glory shining far," though in no haste to depart to it.

(Probably May 1880.)

"Norwich has been *mad* to-day with the elections. My sisters came in this morning: they had been invited to come and see a Liberal demonstration. I cannot forget the fervour of my patriotic devotion to the Blue colour. My father was a staunch Whig, and as I always thought my father right in everything, I have never changed sides."

Speaking of those early days, the fear of invasion, precautions taken, &c. :—

"All these emotions filled us with indescribable fire and enthusiasm: though I was a little Quaker girl, and my father was a good Quaker, nothing availed to temper us down. When I open my eyes in the 'beautiful country,' the bliss unspeakable to me would be to see my father standing with my Nannie beside him—his 'little maid,' as he used to call her."

To Mrs. Brightwen.

"How I should like to be associated with you in all your interesting work!—but my lot is

'To keep the forward road in view,
Delighted to sit still,
And evermore, if not to do,
To bear God's holy will.'

And what a blessing it is to be permitted to rejoice in the sweet and precious work of another; united in full sympathy and companionship, to thank God for every member of the body that is efficiently and hopefully working in its place, for the benefit of the whole! Oh that the rising generation that are learning to read might be taught to read God's Works and not trashy novels!— the juvenile race of sceptics would then learn another language. You see I am almost frantic for the children, and that good Mother Nature should not be left to stand only upon her scientific foot."

To the Same.

"My very dear Friend,—How pleasant it is to write 'very dear,' even when there has been little personal acquaintance! This needlessness of the body gives me very many delightful thoughts as to the resurrection power that will be given to us to recognise all those great and good ones of all times, into whose spirit we have drunk here.

"As I have to-day only a few minutes to spare, I must at once attend to your questions, and say how sorry I am I can give you no help on the subject which so painfully interests both you and me, and many more.

"I know the general opinion is that a woman once habitually a drunkard is unreclaimable. *I* would not say so, because I know one of this class entirely reclaimed—the worst and most shameful case I have ever known; but I can scarcely tell you how it came about. I believe it was the fruit of persevering, ingenious, hopeful love, in some who would not cease to hope, and would take no denial, and who were fruitful in schemes, fertile in encouragements, prudent in help. I believe it is the tenderest essence of Christian love that is required for this work: warning and argument seem to avail nothing. 'He laid His hands upon them and healed them'—it is just that close, tender, uncalculating self-denial which is so specially difficult to exercise towards these poor revolting creatures. I do most earnestly hope that you may have so much of the spirit of wisdom and love in your Committee on Friday, that you may be able to find a way to these hopeless, helpless ones. I should be so glad to hear of anything practical. There is no possible class for these—if they are gathered, it will be one by one."

To the Same.

"To develop and not to satisfy were but to intensify human sorrow by the increase of human wants.

"Does, therefore, universal culture tend to universal happiness?"

To the Same.

"... I have delightful accounts of your charming place. I should like to have my weary eyes rejoiced with it, but to-day I had almost as much joy as I could carry in a ferny corner of my own little garden, where the most brilliant American creeper was glorifying the ferns. How good God is, in giving us intense perceptions of natural beauty!

"I am delighted with the book you have sent me (Patience Strong).[1] I think I find as much pleasure and *surprise* in it as you expected I should. The writer has a most happy and unique talent in throwing away the old clothing of our thoughts, and giving us a fresh dress with many lovely and tasteful decorations. I have not read very far yet, but at the earlier part, Patience and her mother made me think much of my Nannie when we were together—when we fought the battle of life with one heart and one soul. I often think now that even heaven itself could scarcely exceed the full content of that united, vigorous fellowship in thought and action, for I do not centre the bliss of heaven in *Rest*, but in restful work. In reading, this afternoon, I came upon a passage which struck me very much, relative to pain. It says—'Pain is a thing of the spirit, and it may be that only those who can make of it a sacrament are baptized into the full intimacy of suffering with Christ: with such, it works towards a far more exceeding and eternal weight of glory.' ... Ah, dear friend, how happy I should be to hear that the frail temple in which your spirit dwells was permitted to be a little stronger! My constant thought with comfort is this—that we have each one of us a definite *place* and work preparing for us in the next stage of the great For Ever, and that we are as definitely being prepared for it now, and as tenderly, as the wisdom and love of Him who delights in His people can arrange it. He sees the end from the beginning, and surely it is an animating satisfaction that He has chosen us to suffer for Him, and for purposes connected with His great redemptive work."

---

[1] "Patience Strong's Outing."

The same thought is further carried out in the following letter to a friend in deep affliction :—

" . . . My dear friend, how little did I suppose the suffering you have again been passing through ! I have been gladdening myself with the thought that the trial was passing over. What a place you are fitting for ! This thought keeps continually pressing itself upon me. I could not bear to look upon this keen trial without regarding it in its honour and recompense, and this I must do. I have been thinking many times lately of the condescension of our Lord in leaving it to His faithful servants to fill up the measure of His sufferings, to set an example in those things which the shortness of His earthly life prevented His doing Himself. He has given you, oh how many times, His thorny crown to wear ! and I do not love you enough to put a thorn into you; I should pick them all out. Oh how well that you are in His loving Hands, and under His loving care, where the ignorant affection of friends cannot interfere to harm you ! "

To Mrs. Williamson.

" Buxton, *April* 5, 1881.

" To-morrow is my eighty-fourth birthday, and I must send you the line so long delayed. I have often wondered if you have been brought down as low as I have been by cold, and the dark stormy weather. I have often thought that the little shred of life might unexpectedly give way and make no ado about it; but I have so far weathered the storms, and am now on a visit to my dear sisters, thinking a little change might stimulate life, and set me going again. I have not been ill, only the warm blood was chilled, and could not find its way about the old house. This morning I have been out for a walk before breakfast, and hope to continue to do so. This long habit has become essential to both body and mind. I scarcely feel I have had my breakfast unless I take in the air first.

" *6th*.—This letter was laid aside yesterday, and now the clock has struck eighty-four. I think it will not strike again.

During the last few months I have perceptibly felt wearing down, not because the works were much out of order, but because they have completed the circle for which they were wound up. So let it be—whatever my God wills. I now only want to finish my course in the near presence of Him who brought me into existence; who has redeemed me; has borne with my manners in the wilderness, and given me the blessed hope of spending a joyful eternity in His presence and service. Time can only be called short in comparison with eternity—looking back to my childhood, life does not at all represent itself to me as 'the weaver's shuttle.'

" . . . We have not a leaf on tree or hedge yet, but the primroses and daffodils are forced to keep their season—the law of their nature is so strong upon them."

To the Same.

" My days might be occupied in counting my mercies on all sides.

. . . .

" Thank God that He has placed us in this hard school, with such a holiday at the end."

" I filled my Nannie's own little glass vase with single white hyacinths and double white daisies, so fragrant and lovely. If the garden will afford a flower, I always put it in this vase by the side of her likeness in my bedroom, and then we talk together; at least, I talk as if she heard."

Speaking of the anniversaries of her husband's death and Anna's :—

" I have not got over my double loss, but I have become satisfied to live with it."

During the severe weather of the winter of 1880-81, when much confined to the house, Mrs.

Sewell began "a new industry," which became a great enjoyment and solace to her. "Broidery upon satin," she wrote, "and have accomplished two beautiful pieces, quite to my own surprise and everybody else's." I believe the correct name for her material was "Roman sheeting." She worked all her flowers with single threads of filozel, and even in the leaves, rarely condescended to take a double thread, unless they were very large. She planned her own patterns, with a little help from her granddaughters in drawing them out, and put in her colours from the living flower whenever she could get it—in winter, from copies. This work was her pastime, not to be pursued when she had anything more important to do; nevertheless, by September she had six or eight "beautiful pieces" completed, life-like as paintings. There was a Village Industrial Exhibition that month, in the museum-rooms which Mr. Buxton had built in his grounds, and she had great pleasure in sending two pieces—blackberries and white clematis—which occupied places of honour. By this time she thought very ill of her first performances, and was bent on accomplishing a number of pieces in her best style, one for her son and his wife, one for her sisters, and one each for her grandchildren and two or three chief friends. Having now done a great deal towards this, one evening, when the four girls came to tea, she brought out her whole stock for them to appraise, lay aside the best for their elders, and make choice for themselves. It was very touching to hear her say afterwards, "I *should* like to live to finish some for the dear boys too." The "dear boys," being the youngest, came last in turn. Each piece was large enough to serve for a very large cushion, or a mounted screen. The difficulty is to bring one's mind to expose anything so precious to the risks of use. Her beautiful study of honeysuckles is my treasured possession. It gave her a great deal of trouble, for she said the leaves were "so *very* unsentimental," it was hard to make them effective.

Her sight, though wonderful for her age, was not the sight of youth, and with fingers so often stiff, it is surprising that she could work as she did.

The years since Anna's death had brought many losses. Mrs. Buxton's death quickly followed. This was an irreparable loss; and other dear friends left the neighbourhood. During this year, another family very dear to Mrs. Sewell removed from Catton. The circle of life narrowed around her; the "pleasant speech" of friends came less frequently; her ears were next to hear the footfall of the Messenger who would call her away.

CHAPTER IX.

THE LAST STEP.

"In Thy presence is fulness of joy; at Thy right hand there are pleasures for evermore."

On November 30, 1881, Mrs. Sewell wrote:—

"I keep the even tenor of my way at a great rate—not intellectually engaged, but remaking both sets of curtains for dining and drawing rooms, after dyeing; and considering that there are twelve curtains in all, you may fancy that hasty diligence and speed have been requisite; but they are just done, and look well. My upholstery-woman could not come, and A.'s time was filled in other ways, so I put on my youth again, and found it quite fresh."

After this, we were unprepared for the following:—

"I am not very well. When I last wrote, I felt so remarkably well that I dared to talk about 'youth.' Since then I have had a severe attack of the heart, which I had supposed to be quite sound. For a week I had pain quite strange to me. . . . I asked the doctor whether I might calculate on any certain time. He did not think I could. I might live a year, or it might be very soon, and as I have fully run out the term of the family lease, and this has come on so rapidly, I think the latter most probable. My dear friend, I feel shaken in having to meet the prospect of death so suddenly, but quite unshaken from a perfect peace and faith in Him who has so long been all my trust.

I should be glad to live a little longer, if it pleases God. There are a few things I should like to finish a little more perfectly; but the only perfect thing is perfectly to yield oneself to the Will of God."

To another Friend (after speaking of her approaching end).

". . . What an unspeakable mercy that the great account is signed and settled and sure, and that there is no fear of failure or default with the ever-blessed creditor—no change of purpose! I am often surprised, with all my daily faults and infirmities and shortcomings of all kinds, that I can feel so composed in the spirit of my mind. How glad we shall be to meet each other on the other side, when we shall wake up in His likeness and be satisfied, and yet know each other, and look forward and backward without a fear! Blessed be God our Father."

"Yes, the shadows are increasing. I live on the 'Everlasting arms'—still there is something very affecting and pathetic in this dim struggling, when the fogs of time *will* becloud the heights."

To a Friend.

"Well, dear friend, since writing to you last, another messenger has been sent distinctly to me, saying, 'Set thy house in order, for I may come quickly.' . . . I keep going about the house as usual, but softly. I am not left alone, lest an attack should come on suddenly. My blessed Lord and Master possesses me in perfect peace. I cheerfully leave all that is to be in His wise and merciful hands. The suddenness of it has shaken me a little, but not disturbed me. It is difficult to realise at once that I am so soon to leave all my dear children and friends—so very dear—but this will come step by step, as all life has done, and the last step will be into the glorious land of promise."

The "last step," however, was not as near as it

had seemed. The severe symptoms passed away, and she was able to be released from the necessity —very irksome to her independent nature—of having some one always with her. The letters of the following spring say little of her ailment; it was put into the background, and the "stirring world" resumed its old place in her keen interest, only watched in a more chastened spirit. The following letter to Mrs. Brightwen seems to have been written during the winter :—

"I was so pleased to read in your letter that you had been teaching some of the teachers and pupil-teachers how to handle with loving, reverent, and admiring hands some of the wonderful works of God. I believe Natural History Lectures, delivered by holy, reverent men, who understood, and could explain without preaching, would be invaluable in the present state of our population, when children's minds so early take a bias, and young people are so ready to question if there be any *good* God who loves His creatures. I would there were a school for this very purpose. The usual College Professors and Natural History Lecturers do not exactly serve the purpose I mean. They usually treat the subjects as bare science, thus edifying the mind without touching the heart. I have no doubt a number of young men might be found, and trained to treat these subjects more in harmony with the mind of the Great Teacher. After a time I think they would find ample employment and encouragement in the country; but they must be God's servants, or they would do no good. Cannot you stimulate some to turn their attention to this? There are a multitude of poor fellows who have given up the pleasures of the Public-house, and are wanting something to fill their minds. Our Blue-Ribbon Armies are wanting something to fill their evenings and occupy their thoughts. We succeeded in uniting a Club of working men in New

Catton this winter. They hailed the prospect of being taught something. The great difficulty is to get the teachers—it is *so* difficult to find any one *competent*, who is not overdone with engagements. The Club is now separated for the summer, but we are looking anxiously to the gathering again in the autumn, and casting about how to secure the best help. It is, I suppose, this anxiety which has made me run off on this subject."

This Club was a subject of great interest to Mrs. Sewell, often referred to in her letters. The next is to a young friend who was fretting over printers' errors discovered in her first book—rather a long, unwieldy one for a beginning :—

"Old Catton, *March* 23, 1882.

"I have seen 'The Child,' and now I want to encourage you not to fret at the little crumples you may find in her clothes. I *felt* how you feel, from old experience—but they will all wear out in a day or two. You supplied her with such a very heavy wardrobe for the size of the box, that it is inevitable that some little defects may be found, which neither the mother nor the dresser need take to heart. I have been ready to gnash my teeth over trifles which probably no one else would notice. . . . I am so glad to hear the doctor speak so well of ———. This poor old world wants you both, never more, I think; not because there are not good people and good works, but because of the wonderfully strong counter-current. The most useful work now appears to me not to reform the *bad*, but to reform the *good*, that they may be strong to love and to shine.

I have greatly enjoyed this delightful weather, notwithstanding that I have had a slight return of my—shall I say friend or enemy?—but I am getting round again, and find that my great *labour* will be to do little or nothing. Three long calls from three kind friends one after another, took the life-power out of me."

To Mrs. Williamson.
"*April* 3, 1882.

" . . . I think I have grown much older in these few months. On Thursday will be my birthday—eighty-five! I like the idea of time being no longer—having no longer the calculation to make by these little driblets of space, but going on and on with the grand 'For Ever,' always joyful, never weary, though probably tasked to the full extent of our powers—there may be *ambition* then—a glorious, unselfish ambition. When we think of these things, how strong is the assurance within us that we are not now what we shall be—what we are made to be! We are made to be *fully satisfied;* now we are empty, except for hope and anticipation.

"I often wonder at myself that I have such a zest and zeal in carrying out improvements that probably I shall never see; but I suppose it is the natural instinct of progress, implanted in man that the whole of the Divine plan may be worked out."

To a Friend.
"*April* 11, 1882.

"Now that the sun is shining again and the birds seem to be out of their senses with glorious prospects, I get courage to take my pen again.

"I have been out all the morning, superintending garden operations. I have turned out the Aloes which came from the Moorlands, and removed the Pampas grass, and doted over my Daffodils, quite appreciating Wordsworth's feeling of his heart dancing with the Daffodils. What pleasures our Father gives us!

" . . . 'Thy sun shall no more go down, nor thy moon withdraw itself'—and this spiritually is true *now;* we have not to wait for the great realisation to know what is meant.

"I have again been stopped in writing; my Cook has just brought me in a beautiful Thrush's nest, which last night's wind has blown out of the tree close by the kitchen window, and all the eggs are broken; but they will gather heart, and after a few days' silent submission, will build another nest."

To the Same.

"*January* 1883.

"DEAREST AND BEST FRIEND,—Comforter in so many days of suffering and sorrow, you have been brought with such a flow of tender affection to my mind this morning, that I felt as if I must take up my pen and see what it would write. It was in this wise—the first Sabbath in the New Year—dear G—— just off to her devoted work in the Sunday-school for the whole day, which would seem rather long to me till Philip came in the afternoon, especially as the fog and wet shut up the garden; so I began my frequent perambulations up and down the room, saying to myself in a somewhat doleful voice, 'Is there nothing that either branch or rush can do?' feeling myself very much like a broken rush in a swamp; and then, how it was I can't say, my dear friend came into my mind, now laid aside, after the vigorous life and energy of years.

"These verses came into my mind, 'And the disciples gathered themselves unto Jesus, and told Him what they had done, and what they had taught. And He said, Come ye yourselves apart into a desert place.' A desert place! *We* never send our friends, when they are weary and worn, into a desert place to be refreshed and strengthened —we choose for them the pleasantest places we can find, where they may be delighted and diverted, and so come back (rather dissipated) to labour again. The Blessed Lord thought not so; in the desert He prepared them to feed the multitudes, not from their own resources, but from the bread He had created and blest; and I thought to myself, so He is preparing my dear friend, in weakness, trial, and prostration; and I tried to be glad, and thank God that He was dealing with you as He dealt with His dearest friends on earth; but oh how difficult it is to enter into the Lord's mind when suffering is in the case—and yet I believe we should never love each other so much if we were in the heyday of prosperity all the year round. By-

and-by the spirit of heaviness will melt away before the brightness of the garment of praise; but not quite yet, till He comes to receive the Kingdom. When will that be?"

Sunday morning was always a time of solitude to Mrs. Sewell: unless she were quite ill, she would not hear of any one remaining away from church and Sunday-school on her account. Nor would she have chosen to be without solitary hours: talking fatigued her, listening being an effort now that slight deafness had come upon her, and she was too sympathetic to be long silent when with a companion. Yet as she grew weaker, she became less independent of society.

To a Friend deeply tried.

"What a blessed arrangement it is that love and knowledge are not the same thing!—for here I am, loving and loving and loving, and yet in the most profound ignorance of where you are, and how you are; but I really cannot endure this any longer. The wood-pigeons have begun their compliments, and always remind me of you; and all the sweet Spring sounds of the last few days keep you ever in my mind, and yet always shrouded in mist, and painful thoughts will arise. . . .

"Your last dear letter touched the very core of my heart—that you had been appointed to suffer the heaviest of sufferings—for a dear child of the Father to walk in darkness and have no light. I marvelled at the honour done you, and the trust reposed in you. One dimly understands these mysteries by thinking of the multitude of trained servants of every class that will be needed in the many mansions. What a firm and pitiful patience the angels must possess, to be able to carry on their training in us and for us!—as I suppose they do. Are they not all ministering spirits? But oh how thankful I am, my dear friend, that the ordeal is past—I trust it is—and that you are now abiding sweetly and peacefully in one of 'the chambers that look to the east;' but do let me hear; a scrap, a card, anything will satisfy me, only I must know whether to praise, pray, or sympathise.

"I have struggled through, so far, by dint of selfishness. Wearing a quantity of clothes, making grand fires, feeding myself with wholesome and pleasant food, I am strong and comfortable; and here I am this day (eighty-six on Friday), without ache or pain or stiff joint, able to enjoy my friends' company here, while earnestly looking forward to the meeting above the clouds and out of the storms.

"I expected to have met those who 'have passed on before,' before this. I can hardly believe that it is five years since my jewel left me; she is as fresh as ever in my heart and in my thoughts.

"I will not say any more now, as in my ignorance I may fail to say what I want to say—something helpful, if I could but think of it; but my true love cannot be a mistake."

To Mrs. F. ——

"OLD CATTON, *May* 30, 1883.

"Your delightful letter could not have been more opportune. I laid it down, and thanked God for it and for you again and again: especially for those small details which you called the 'barefaced' part. That was the cream of it to me. I am sure it is often very good to be quite free and open with our *friends* for mutual cheer and courage, and not to be dumb when we trust there is a little working of the true life granted to our efforts. It is the *dry* work which is so painful and so discouraging, and so common, that the thoughts and hopes of the generality of workers rarely rise much beyond duty and system. It is almost an unexpected surprise and pleasure when a soul springs up new-born—yet surely we should not rest satisfied short of this. . . .

"There appear to be times in God's providence when

the Spirit goes forth with more effectual power; when the ear is more ready to hear, and the heart to believe, and the stammering tongue to speak eloquently. I have thought that such a season is now being granted to our country—perhaps before sterner times arrive.

"During the last winter, an attempt was made at New Catton by a few (a very few) to gather the working-men together in the evening for social and educational purposes. There had been nothing of the kind. The population, though exceeding 3000, are almost entirely of the working class, scarcely any gentlefolks. About three working-men rose to the occasion, with the help of a clergyman and a friend. A large meeting was held, resulting in the formation of a Society and a Club. The men themselves say this has quite improved the spirit of the neighbourhood. Sceptical talk in the streets is not now paraded as it was before, and one of the leading members said if one of the gentlemen would give a Bible-Class in the week, he believed all the men would attend it. All opposition was taken away, and a good, neighbourly spirit much increased. They have now separated, to meet again in the Autumn.

"It has struck me that God's gracious intentions are larger and richer than our expectations, and that when we think of *amusement*, He thinks of *improvement*—that we think of the body when He thinks of the soul. I can well believe what you say about simple vocal prayer, and its uniting effect when the impulse is given. . . .

"I have been reading two books which I think would interest you. Pulsford is the author."

These books ("The Supremacy of Man" and "Christ in His Seed") were a source of deep interest and pleasure to Mrs. Sewell. Though she could not resist occasionally making fun of Pulsford's flow of exalted language, she delighted in his thoughts. "Only, when he goes so *very* far back in the counsels of the Almighty," she said,

x

"one is a *little* inclined to question how far he has been informed himself."

To Mrs. Williamson.

"I knew I should have a long, lonely Sabbath till my dearest Philip's afternoon visit, so after reading The Book, I decided to take your book, 'Wayside Wisdom,' with me into the greenhouse, where it was delightfully warm and genial, and fragrant with sweet flowers. All the windows of my heart are thrown open to the day, and the light comes in, and peace and joy and heartfelt praise. *His Works* open to me as wonderful and beautiful exceedingly, and my heart is fed as with the bread of heaven and the water of life."

To Mrs. F. ——

"OLD CATTON, *November* 26, 1883.

"I have been so very sorry to leave your welcome and delightful letter so long unanswered, but for the last few weeks my right hand has been crippled by the old enemy, who, you may remember, was wont to afflict me. I have been fain to leave undone much that I should have been glad to do. After so many years of steady friendship, I was not afraid that silence would drive you away. It has been quite as much a heart-pain to me not to write, as it would have been a hand-pain to do it; but now that I sit here in ease, pen in hand, I feel the want of a greater relief than it can give; so much of painful interest surrounds us that one cannot be still about. This Bitter Cry of London is sounding in my ears all the day long, and the feeling that England must awake to it, or take the fearful consequences, keeps pressing upon me with the home question, What must *I* do? It has long been a strong belief of mine, that the union of a kingdom *in all its classes* is essential to its safety and prosperity, and our present dismemberment, and independence of each other, appear to my short sight very ominous; but I will not go on writing on this subject now, for ever since receiving your last letter, my interest in your writing has much increased from knowing the subject which engages your attention. . . . I can well believe what you say, that you have found intense pleasure in writing—to use our faculties with any sense of power is a healthful delight, and to do justice to one's subject, and do good at the same time, is one of the greatest pleasures we can have.

"I well remember how much enjoyment I had in reading your MS., and being allowed to criticise it, and how often your wise, caustic, and friendly criticisms have saved my little matters from disgrace. Oh! what a long time it is since we were all so animated together at Blue Lodge!—when she was there who had *not* written a book, but helped those who did write. Now I would fain hope she sees her own book doing for her dear Lord His work of mercy. I was much interested in hearing the other day that a gentleman who holds an official position in China, but is now staying in Norwich, accidentally met with 'Black Beauty,' sat down and read it through, then went to Jarrold and ordered a hundred copies to give away. Besides this, he offered to give readings from it to an evening class of working men, which he is now doing.

"And now about your own men's class. My observation, in reply to your question, would incline me to say, *one* lady who has a real influence is better than more. Even country lads are capable of an enthusiasm which does them good, and is stronger when undivided. Do you not think that in their dull, often heavy life, amongst clods animate and inanimate, to feel an admiration for something or some one great and noble, would be to them both a delight and a benefit? Enthusiasm is sadly snubbed now—we shall die without it.

"The Working Men's Club at New Catton which I told you of, and which was begun last year, has opened most prosperously, and some of the very best results have arisen from it. The men's characters and powers have in many instances developed surprisingly. They have found their places, and their hitherto unknown talents have found space and scope. The self-denying energy with which some of them have worked for the benefit of the classes has surprised and charmed me, and, I think, themselves also. They *look* differently, they *speak* differently, and *stand* differently, with more self-dependence. The laws they have made themselves, they keep. A remarkably friendly spirit has sprung up among them. The clergyman, Philip, and a schoolmaster are their friends for counsel, but take no authority, and as a consequence are very much valued.

"Do you not think that President Garfield's Life would be a very improving one to read to boys? But I must change my subject if I am ever to leave off.

"I am pretty well in health: quite as well as such an old woman can expect to be, and so thankful that I have the use of my faculties, and oh! so many mercies! My dear people are all in fair health, and none of them selfish or idle.

"I expect in a very short time all my poetical works will be brought out in two vols.[1] They have hitherto been so scattered; I have had to look them all through for correction. The prose works are to come afterwards. The 'Mother's Last Words' are, I believe, to have an Apotheosis, having reached a million.

". . . Jarrold is printing a very small selection of my ballads just now, the profits to go to the aid of a mite of the distress in London. I will send you one, although I dare say you may remember them. . . . How many mercies belong to a Christian life!—and the more Christian, the more mercies. God is very good."

Mrs. Sewell never wrote anything more characteristic of herself—few things more touching, than "A Sad Story," included in the last little reprint of her verses which she lived to see go forth,—"The Suffering Poor." "That element of tragedy which lies in the very fact of frequency" had deeply inwrought itself into her emotions. She writes the

---

[1] "Poems and Ballads," by Mrs. Sewell, in 2 vols., 7s. 6d. : Jarrold & Son.

slow and undramatic tragedy of a poor woman's life in a home not worthy of the name.

"Oh, what a little thing would make
    A toil-worn woman glad!
But all the round of day and night
    Is only sad, and sad;
Shut out of light and air and room,
    And pay and victuals bad.

"I've been a fool, I know, sometimes,
    For really I could stop
And cry my heart away before
    An ironmonger's shop,
And wish a little cooking-stove
    Would from the heavens drop.

"One might begin to see a chance
    Of management once more,
Which seems to me a banished thing
    From many people's door;
We have not things to manage with,
    And so—we've lost the power.

"I've sometimes thought, and sometimes dreamt,
    About a little range,
And through me ran a thrill of joy,
    A happy sort of change;—
I saw the home-baked loaves come out,
    All smelling sweet and strange.

"I thought of puddings made of rice
    To fill the children well,
Just sweetened up with treacle too,
    To make it taste and smell;
And baked potatoes! nice and hot!
    Almost too good to tell.

"Yes, then I'd manage with a hope,
    And prize my little pelf"—

That was the essence of all her plans for helping

the poor—to make it possible for them to "manage with a hope." About this time, the eldest daughter of a family she knew well got married in a very imprudent and reprehensible way—not quite "wi' naether blankets nor sheets," but with very little beside. Mrs. Sewell was grieved and disappointed, but the thing was done, and she had a regard for the young people's families, who were doing their best to mend the matter. "So I sent the Bible-woman," she said, "just to get her the things a girl can't keep a decent home without—brushes, and tubs, and pots, and so on; and when her father went to see her, she had her room as neat as it could be—all her few little things bright and tidy—and he burst into tears to think that the girl had a chance! If she wanted to keep a nice home, she could."

Another letter touches on the same subject:—

"I have been wanting to know how you are, and what you feel about this terrible 'Bitter Cry of Outcast London.' The picture drawn haunts me day and night, and the apparent impossibility of doing anything effectual to lessen the evil. In a certain sense it is a comfort to see the whole country roused to its foundations for a little while, but the times look big with omens of evil. It begins to be time to look up, or else to faint, and that would never do. My holdfast is, The Lord Reigneth."

Mrs. Sewell's last little published book was "Sixpenny Charity,"—one more appeal to help the poor to "manage with a hope;" and in her graphic way she describes the difference that even sixpence a week can make in a very needy home.

Emigration was another subject that occupied her thoughts in her last winter on earth. She said "an old woman was not the messenger to stir up the world about it," but what she could, she did.

To Mrs. F. ——

"OLD CATTON, *February* 5, 1884.

"It is only about three weeks since I regained the use of my hand, and then fell ill, so that breathing often became a business, not an insensible pleasure. I think I have now started afresh, and there is so much to do, even for the aged, that I really grudge to be idle; and life and thought and action are so intense and interesting, and so various, that going to sleep (that is, die, if there be such a thing, which I do not believe) feels postponable, whilst there is any capacity left to help or comfort any one. I believe this does not *sound right* at my age, when I ought to be longing to depart. Oh! if it was *only* by departing that we could be with Jesus, one might indeed desire to do it. In your sweet, quiet home, I think the pressure of life cannot come as it does in the sound and stir of the great city; and yet I know you may there bring it more profoundly near to the inmost centres of thought and feeling, as you do, and ponder if there be any way out of this great dismay.

"I do not think I ever felt our Blessed Lord's words on the duty of personal self-denial so imperative before as I do now, in seeing and knowing the utter destitution of my fellow-creatures living almost within call. In most of their essential features, the slums of Norwich may be said to rival those of London in the want of *all* things, and the inevitable consequences. An appalling want of work prevails almost everywhere, especially in the shoemaking (the Norwich trade)—this has been at almost stagnation point since a little before Christmas. A——'s attention was drawn to a squalid mass of children whom the officer appointed to hunt them up had drawn into the great St. Augustine Schools. They looked so utterly forlorn, that she and another lady decided to find out their homes, and the revelations would make another 'exceeding bitter cry,' which must in some way be responded to. I think misery must have made the people dumb or despairing, as not one out of the multitude of families they visited asked for anything, and evidently expected nothing. The patient, sometimes even cheerful, endurance they manifested was most pathetic. . . . I think I never sympathised with and admired the poor so much, and never was so indignant and astonished at my own hard-heartedness. What manner of men and women ought we to be, with so many enjoyments, advantages, and opportunities,—'Our good things'?

"I had this morning a visit from my old friend Jonathan Grubb, whom you will know by name, if not personally. Never did a man so little answer to his name. As he kept talking, I wondered if I might claim to belong to the same race of beings as himself, not because of any sublime flights or heights of spiritual attainment, but for the intense, practical, self-denying sympathy with his fellow-creatures in the lowest abjectness of character and morals. He gave a lecture last night to the members of the Friends' First Day School, numbering 1000, on 'Outcast London, by one who has seen it.' He would more than confirm G. Sims' account in every particular. Filled with his Master's Spirit, he has never grown in the least hard-hearted in the midst of his most revolting work; but he seemed as if he could have wept tears of blood over it all.

"I have not read Mr. Drummond's work yet. I have only seen Reviews in *The Friend*. I had a letter from a lady—a deep thinker—she says, 'I cannot think Drummond's work can be entirely adopted.' I thought there were very profitable truths in some of the quotations I saw, but in the multitude of thoughts now presented to us, we must feel free to reject or accept.

"I have now a charming collection of sermons by

Phillips Brooke, an American. The title is, 'The Candle of the Lord;' that is the subject of one of the sermons:— they are very elevating and invigorating.

"I have also another book, quite different, by George the American, who, I suppose, thinks he will do our country good by exasperating the feelings of our working people. I have his second work, 'Social Problems.' I am so very anxious about the state of our country,—one cannot help believing there is much amiss, much that needs alteration—much that I should like to look at through the eyes of an impartial, straightforward man. It has been quite a relief for me to find that George has not obtained very enthusiastic audiences. I am told by a farmer that he sees our malady very clearly, but not at all the remedy.

"Do you know any interesting, easy books that would be likely to create a desire to emigrate? 'Letters from Successful Emigrants,' with something of the 'Robinson Crusoe' aspect in it, might be inspiring. It would seem as if England were intended to replenish the earth by the rapid increase of her population—but so much ignorance prevails on this subject, the spirit for it is not yet awakened. The word 'emigrant' scarcely brings other ideas than leaving all your friends, getting into a ship, and taking your chance you know not where. The boys who are now training up in our Board Schools and Sunday-schools, Temperance Societies, &c., ought to make good colonists, and the education they get would all grow into use more profitably than it might in the old country, where people are treading on each other's toes.

"Oh! dear friend, do excuse my running on about all these things, but I feel so confident that you feel into my heart as I into yours, and that we both love our country, and would both rather bestir ourselves to give her the least mite of help than only sit down to weep over her."

The fairer country—the hope she never failed to dwell on, in all she wrote of the sorrows of the "toiling folk," was drawing near. Her last birthday found her still able to delight in its lovetokens. One of the letters she received I will insert here :—

"*April* 5, 1884.

"I woke early this morning, and lay thinking how much joy would have been subtracted from my life if you had never been born, and then I thought I was only one out of very many who would not only thank God to-day that you had ever lived, but that, in His great love and kindness, it has pleased Him unusually to prolong your life; and still more that until quite lately you have enjoyed an unusual degree of health and peace, and freedom from those aches and pains which often make old age to be rather dreaded than desired. We have decided that this must be a day of praise—whatever clouds may come, we will keep the sunshine in our hearts for God's great mercy to us in permitting our beloved friend to enter in peace on her eighty-seventh year. It always seems to me so especially appropriate that you should be born in this month of hope and brightness, when fresh flowers are daily, hourly, coming from the great Giver, and the birds are too full of joy to be very particular about interrupting one another.

" . . . We have just been talking about the wonderful arrangement in Nature for releasing the trees from their leaves—so gently—so noiselessly. What machinery we should need if we had it to do! What ropes and pulleys and ladders—what bustle and confusion there would be! Now, only as many leaves come down at a time as can be easily got rid of, instead of our being blocked up, as we should be if they all came down in a night; and our eyes have time to get used to their absence.

"It is sweet to think that it is the same loving and kind Hand which is taking *us* down, and He is doing it with the same object in view,—that we may hide our decay for a while, until the same Voice which in the Spring wakes up everything to loveliness and beauty shall wake us up to put on our beautiful garments, and wear the glorified body, which will never grow old.

"Dear friend, I daily pray that you may just yield yourself to Him—perfectly and entirely 'lie passive in His Hands,' and He will walk with you step by step through these Autumn days; and the leaf of your life, which has been sweet to Him, and to which He has granted a long Summer, will fall, guided by His Hand, and will be precious in His sight."

To Mrs. F. ——

"Old Catton, *May* 1884.

"Just one line of dear love and thanks. I am recovering from an acute attack in my heart, not much expected a few days since. All is well with me, dearest friend, either way, and I do not choose. Mercy and goodness are heaped up around me. May the best of blessings rest on thee and thine. I must not write more than my enduring love."

Gently and gradually her strength gave way; yet still a word of sorrow from one she loved drew out a quick response.

To Mrs. F. ——

"Old Catton, 26*th May*.

"Most loving and true Friend,—I have just read your touching letter in my bed, and thank you so much for it. Only a very few lines in return. I do earnestly hope and pray that dear Mr. —— may now make continuous progress out of this fiery trial, and that your health, beloved friend, may still be upheld to bear the unwonted strain upon it. 'God is able.'

"I am in the 'Border Land,' not knowing whether the next step may lead back into the old country, or whether into that fair land where we all hope to meet together and dwell for ever. I have not been well since Christmas, but the last few weeks have sent me rapidly downward. The props of the old house are naturally giving way, after eighty-seven years of work, and especially my breathing, and general strength. I am very happy, F——dear, and no dark shadows lie before me; and I have all the comfort that the dear love of those around me can give. The doctor thinks I *may* get better: if so I will write and tell you. My affectionate love to you both, dear friends.—Now and for ever yours,   MARY SEWELL.

"I do not keep to my bed, only a sleepless night kept me later than usual, and I wanted to write to you myself, and feared you might have left home, and I not been able."

The pen which had written so many loving words, and cheered and helped so many human hearts, had finished its work at last. Just fifteen days after this letter was written, the writer left the "old country." There is little to tell of those last days. The failure of the breathing organs made everything an effort, and words were few; yet she would brighten up for a few minutes with all her old zest for hearing of fresh things doing in the world. Within four or five days of her death she listened eagerly to what a friend had to say about emigration—the subject which had so much occupied her mind during the previous winter.

Her son writes:—"Almost my dear mother's latest expression was, 'I do not feel as if I were dying—only going into another room in the same house.'

"To her the Father's presence made wherever she was His House, and all the plants, and birds, and trees, and flowers, and sunshine, part of its furniture that He had put there."

On the morning of her last day on earth—the 10th of June—she begged to be lifted from her bed to the couch beside the window. It was a glorious summer day—the birds sang; the fair earth was adorned in its best furniture. She seemed to take one look around, but no one could tell whether she saw anything, or heard the singing of the birds. Consciousness ceased. It was as though some Strong One had taken her in His arms and closed her eyes in deep sleep that she might not feel the touch of the cold river of death; and when she awoke on the other side, He whom she had so loved and trusted in her earthly home would be there— " a living, bright reality." The time for the fulness of joy had come.

The following lines were found among her papers, in her handwriting :—

> " She died, yet is not dead !
> Ye saw a daisy on her tomb :
> It bloomed to die, she died to bloom.
> Her summer hath not sped.
> She died, yet is not dead !
> Through pearly gates, on golden street,
> She went her way with shining feet."

It was on a cloudless November day that I drove from Buxton with "Elizabeth" (the sister so often mentioned in the Autobiography) to the Friends' Burying-Ground, about a mile distant, and found myself standing before three graves—the sleeping-places of the father, mother, and daughter.

The air was wonderfully soft and genial for

November. The robins were singing as if there was no such thing in the world as death. The sunshine and song in which these sleeping ones had delighted on earth seemed to have followed them to their last resting-place. Yet not the last—

> " O base, ungrateful thought,
> To call the grave the last long home of man.
> 'Tis but a lodging, held from week to week,
> Till Christ shall come."

THE END.

RECENT BIOGRAPHY.

ALEXANDER BALFOUR. A Memoir by the Rev. R. LUNDIE, M.A., Liverpool. With Portrait, and View of Mount Alyn. Third Edition. Large post 8vo, 6s.

"Mr. Lundie succeeds in conveying to the reader a distinct and living impression of the overpowering and irresistible earnestness which was the basis of Mr. Balfour's character."—*Liverpool Daily Post.*

PROFESSOR WILLIAM GRAHAM, D.D. ESSAYS—HISTORICAL AND BIOGRAPHICAL. Edited by his Brother. With Personal Reminiscences. By the Rev. W. M. TAYLOR, D.D., LL.D., New York. With Portrait. Crown 8vo, 5s.

"Will be interesting to many even outside of the Church in which he held a high position, as a memorial of a pious, learned, and genial man."—*Scots Observer.*

THE HOME OF A NATURALIST. By the Rev. BIOT EDMONSTON, and his Sister, JESSIE M. E. SAXBY. With Illustrations. Crown 8vo, 6s.

"We would fain linger long over the scenes which this excellent volume brings up before us. The authors have put together a very refreshing set of memories."—*Saturday Review.*

"Mrs. Saxby is at her best in her Shetland folk-lore. Mr. Edmonston's stories and simple style of telling them will charm every reader."—*Manchester Guardian.*

"Mr. Edmonston's chapters on Shetland sport and fauna—the notes on the habits of the strange menagerie of pets that were gathered about the naturalist's home, and of excursions after wild fowl and seal in this remotest nook of the British Islands—are specially pleasing and well-written, and should give the book a permanent interest and value in the eyes of naturalists.."—*Scots Observer.*

W. LINDSAY ALEXANDER, D.D.: His LIFE AND WORK. By the Rev. JAMES ROSS. With Portrait. Extra crown 8vo, 7s. 6d.

"Mr. Ross has executed a difficult task with excellent taste and skill. The book reveals the characteristics of Dr. Alexander with force and coherence, and is altogether readable and interesting."—*Saturday Review.*

"A very good account of an interesting and scholarly man. Mr. Ross gives, in passing, glimpses of many of the principal figures in Scotland during the last half century, and of some of the phases of the religious life of the country."—*Contemporary Review.*

"The memoir of such a man was well worth writing, and Mr. Ross has done the work judiciously."—*Scotsman.*

Dedicated to the Archbishop of Canterbury.

TOLD FOR A MEMORIAL: The Story of MARY ANN. With a Preface by Canon MASON. A Portrait and other Illustrations. Second Edition. Small crown 8vo, 1s. 6d.

"This little book is unusually edifying—quite above the line of those pious records we know so well."—*Literary Churchman.*

"A very interesting biography."—*Church Quarterly Review.*

"Considering her environments Mary Ann was certainly a remarkable example, and her history well worthy of record."—*Church Times.*

"A simple but charming story of a Cornish widow. The present Primate took a warm interest in Mary Ann Davie, and valued her intercessions for himself."—*Church Bells.*

ST. AUGUSTIN, MELANCHTHON, NEANDER: Three Biographies. By PHILIP SCHAFF, D.D., Author of "Through Bible Lands," "Christ and Christianity," &c. Crown 8vo, 4s. 6d.

"Dr. Schaff writes here, as usually, in good, honest, straightforward English, with no attempt at rhetoric, but with a style so laden with information that the perusal of his pages is a pleasure. He has given what must be owned to be three very graphic and informing sketches of three of the greatest men the Church has produced."—*Scottish Review.*

MISCELLANEOUS LETTERS OF FRANCES RIDLEY HAVERGAL.
Edited by her Sister, MARIA V. G. HAVERGAL. Fifth Edition. Crown 8vo, 5s.

"It is a boon to the public to be permitted to enter into the inner life of this true poetess. Many who turn over this volume will get a message pregnant with light, and go on their way instructed and rejoicing. Its naturalness and fulness of sympathy give a wonderful insight into the daily life of one who was specially gifted, both to stimulate and refresh."—*Academy*.

"Rightly to estimate the character of this truly Christian woman, it is necessary to read the correspondence which is now laid before the public."—*Public Opinion*.

"Here, more completely than in any former publication, Miss Havergal is depicted, by her own pen, in all the moods of her highly-gifted nature."—*Literary Churchman*.

MEMORIALS OF THE LATE FRANCES RIDLEY HAVERGAL.
With Portrait and other Illustrations. Crown 8vo, 6s. Cheaper Edition, paper covers, 6d. In cloth, with Portrait, 1s. 6d.

AUTOBIOGRAPHY OF MARIA V. G. HAVERGAL.
With Journals and Letters. With Portrait. Crown 8vo, 6s.

OUTLINES OF A GENTLE LIFE: Memorials of ELLEN P. SHAW.
By her Sister, MARIA V. G. HAVERGAL. With Frontispiece. Crown 8vo, cloth, 1s. 6d.; paper cover, 1s.

SAMUEL GOBAT, BISHOP OF JERUSALEM: His Life and Work.
A Biographical Sketch. Edited by Mrs. PEREIRA. With Portraits and Illustrations. Crown 8vo, 7s. 6d.

"A pattern memoir; short, compact, and full. It throws much light on Scripture by its vivid description of places, persons, customs, &c., and is otherwise very valuable for its amount of interesting and useful information. A standard work on Missions to the Holy Land."—*Christian World*.

"Those who wish to read a record of vigorous missionary work prosecuted under many difficulties, will find much to interest them in this book."—*Court Circular*.

THE FIRST EARL CAIRNS: Brief Memories of HUGH M'CALMONT, First Earl Cairns.
By Miss MARSH. Seventh Thousand. Crown 8vo, 1s.

"Miss Marsh is enabled to draw for us some delightful pictures of Lord Cairns home and family life."—*Record*.

"A simple, yet heartfelt tribute to the memory of a great and good man."—*Morning Post*.

"This little book is, of course, only a mere outline of the career of such a man; but we believe it will do far more good than will ever be accomplished by those huge masses of rubbish which are so often piled upon good men's graves."—Mr. SPURGEON in the *Sword and Trowel*.

LIFE OF THE REV. JAMES HAMILTON, D.D., F.L.S.
By the Rev. WILLIAM ARNOT. With Portrait. Post 8vo, 7s. 6d.

"It is rare that so fine a subject, endeared to the literary and religious English-speaking world, finds so capital a biographer."—*Princeton Review*.

MEMOIR OF THE LATE REV. WILLIAM C. BURNS,
M.A., Missionary to China. With Portrait. Small crown 8vo, 3s. 6d.

"William Burns is one of the few men of modern times who have carried the Christian idea into such active revelation in the life, as would compel, even from the most sceptical, a reluctant consent to the Divine origin of the truths he taught and lived by."—*Contemporary Review*.

LONDON: JAMES NISBET & CO., 21 BERNERS STREET.

www.ingramcontent.com/pod-product-compliance
Lightning Source LLC
Chambersburg PA
CBHW030259240426
43673CB00040B/1000